COPS UNDER FIRE!

Twelve gripping stories of real-life police shootouts (and what to make of them)

BRIAN MCKENNA

OXFORD SOUTHERN
an imprint of Sunbury Press, Inc.
Mechanicsburg, PA USA

OXFORD SOUTHERN

an imprint of Sunbury Press, Inc.
Mechanicsburg, PA USA

For information about special discounts for bulk purchases, please contact Sunbury Press Orders Dept. at (855) 338-8359 or orders@sunburypress.com.

To request one of our authors for speaking engagements or book signings, please contact Sunbury Press Publicity Dept. at publicity@sunburypress.com.

FIRST OXFORD SOUTHERN EDITION: June 2021

Set in Adobe Garamond | Interior design by Crystal Devine | Cover by Lawrence Knorr | Edited by Lawrence Knorr.

Publisher's Cataloging-in-Publication Data
Names: McKenna, Brian, author.
Title: Cops under fire : twelve gripping stories of real-life shootouts (and what to make of them) / Brian McKenna.
Description: First trade paperback edition. | Mechanicsburg, PA : Oxford Southern, 2021.
Summary: Police officers who have courageously faced death at the hands of armed criminals can teach us a lot about what it's like to fight for one's life, how to prevail over danger, prepare for life's many challenges, and much more. This gripping account of twelve real-life police shootouts offers readers the many lessons to be learned from these events.
Identifiers: ISBN : 978-1-62006-486-3 (softcover).
Subjects: SOCIAL SCIENCE / Criminology | TRUE CRIME / General | LAW / Practical Guides.

Product of the United States of America
0 1 1 2 3 5 8 13 21 34 55

Continue the Enlightenment!

To those whose stories fill the pages of this book, to all those officers who have paid the ultimate sacrifice, and to all officers everywhere who, with full knowledge of the risks involved, hit the streets every day so their fellow citizens may live in greater safety.

～ ～ ～

For every predator who has been righteously deprived of his freedom for the crimes he has committed, there are now all his potential victims who have the freedom to live their lives without becoming his prey. The average citizen does not think about this much and rarely appreciates or understands this gift that law enforcement gives him.

—ALEXIS ARTWOHL, PH.D., FROM
"ENJOY YOUR FREEDOM? THANK A COP"

Contents

Author's Notes and Disclaimer

The incidents in this book are true, but the names were changed in chapters 2, 6, 7, and 10 to ensure the privacy of those personally involved. Though every effort was made to ensure the accuracy of the events recounted here, it was occasionally necessary to alter some of the facts slightly to preserve confidentiality and clarity. However, in no case did these changes affect the case's essential elements or the analysis of the officer's actions.

I have had the opportunity to meet and work with many dedicated and highly proficient female police officers during my 32-year police career. Whereas I have the highest regard for women who choose to serve in this dangerous and challenging profession, I have used the masculine pronouns *he, him,* and *his* in this book for the sake of clarity and ease of reading. This is in no way meant to imply any lack of respect for my female counterparts in law enforcement, and it is my sincere hope that it will not offend anyone. If so, please accept my apologies.

The author makes no warranty, expressed or implied, regarding the applicability of any of the suggestions or opinions expressed in this work, nor does he assume any legal liability for the utility, effectiveness, or legality of the information presented. The information in this work is intended only to present a general discussion of the incidents recounted and stimulate thought. The opinions and advice given are not legal opinions or legal advice. Readers are encouraged to seek counsel from legal professionals regarding any legal issues pertaining to the incidents recounted here or the author's analyses of them.

Foreword

What can be learned from our brothers and sisters in law enforcement who have experienced victory against overwhelming odds? Well, plenty; and in this excellent book by my friend and colleague Brian McKenna, those who take time to read and study these stories of officer-involved shootings will come away with a wealth of well-analyzed and considered "Do's and Don'ts" tips on personal safety and survival.

In my nearly twenty-five years as a street officer, undercover officer, and detective, I used all levels of force including deadly force. In my forty-two years as a law enforcement use of force and police practices instructor and a court-qualified expert, I have trained thousands of law enforcement officers and military assets, and have investigated, analyzed and opined in court on hundreds of officer- and civilian-involved shootings, and other serious and tragic uses of deadly force. I can honestly tell you that if the officers and civilians in my cases had read this book, by far, the vast majority of those incidents would either not have occurred, or would have ended quite differently and in a manner that would have benefited the involved officers and civilians.

Upon opening this book, the reader will immediately engage in a compendium of critical incidents involving officer-involved shootings, encounters with the violent mentally ill subjects with psycho-medical emergencies including agitated-chaotic events, drug influence, and those so behaviorally enraged and goal-oriented towards killing officers that they were oblivious to pain from multiple torso hits from .45 caliber rounds, multiple baton strikes, pepper spray and being struck by moving vehicles. These are the circumstances that visit officers in the middle of sweaty nights as they lay awake staring at the ceiling and wondering, *"Why did I do that?"* or *"Could I have engaged quicker, stronger, or better?"* Those of us who have worked the mean streets and been involved in similar events have similarly experienced such lonely, scary, heart-thumping nights. It's how we processed the lessons learned from these events that separates victors from those who were unable to learn and move forward. This book allows the reader to move forward.

One experienced generation of law enforcement heroes and warriors passes the sword of duty and experience along to the next, and this is exactly what author Brian McKenna does here. Each case is well-analyzed from the prism of an experienced field officer. This, when combined with the time and experience of the officers in this book, provides the reader with the benefit of several generations of law enforcement field craft and experience. The reader is offered an abundance of tips on training, personal safety, pre-contact threat assessment, situational awareness, use of force options, weaponry, human factors related to performance under stress, and perhaps most important, understanding the perspective of our police officers. Contrary to what many believe, with rare exceptions our officers do not see themselves as being at war against their communities. Rather, they follow the "to serve" warrior ethos, which entails duty, loyalty, devotion, justice, and most importantly the courage and compassion to run toward the sounds of gunfire. There are so many take-aways from this book that I don't have time to discuss them in this foreword. However, I strongly encourage both civilians and police officers to invest in this valuable resource text.

Always remember:: *"Without truth, there is no justice."*

May God speed and protect all our law enforcement officers, and those they serve.

Dr. Ron Martinelli, Ph.D
Forensic criminologist, retired police detective,
and Amazon best-selling author

Acknowledgments

I would like to express my deep gratitude to the people who have supported me in this project and in my continuing efforts to make the streets safer for our gallant police officers and fellow citizens. First, I would like to thank my loving wife Lynn and lovely daughters, Elizabeth, Rebecca, and Katherine, who have supported me in so many ways. They have always stood beside me, rarely complaining and always caring, as I spent countless hours researching and writing my "Officer Down" column for *The Police Marksman and Law Officer Magazine*, from which many of the stories in this book initially came. And this is especially true for Lynn, who has had to put up with my many long hours away from home and my annoying habit of focusing so much of my time and energy on this book. More even than my girls, Lynn understood that, although my work often kept me from spending as much time with my family as I would have liked, it was worth it because it helped my fellow officers stay safe, and now with this book, because it does the same for my fellow citizens.

My brother Dale, a fine writer and one of the best police officers I have ever known, also deserves my gratitude. He has always supported me in my writing and spent a great deal of his own time editing this book, as well as many of my articles over the years. But more than that, he has been someone I can turn to for ideas. He is an experienced and knowledgeable police officer with brilliant instincts for officer safety and dealing with the public. Many of the ideas in this book and other works came from the time we have spent together exhaustively discussing law enforcement issues. I owe much of whatever success I have achieved to Dale.

I would also like to thank my parents, William and Rejeana, who instilled me with a love for learning, concern for others, and all the encouragement and support for which a son could ask. Although he was never published, my father especially loved to read and knew how to write a good story. He taught me a love for the English language, a passion for writing, and an even greater love of reading. As one of those quiet veterans of World War II who humbly did his part without fanfare, he made it clear that it is an honor to put yourself in harm's way to serve others. He also taught me to care deeply for my fellow citizens, love my country, and respect others, especially those in uniform, whether military or police. These values led me into a law enforcement career and inspired me to become a writer.

I owe a special debt of gratitude to all the people who were kind enough to help review this book for me: Jan Zacharias, a dear friend and passionate supporter of law enforcement; Lisa Poppelvig, an English as a second language instructor for the Denmark national police; my brother Dale, my daughters Elizabeth, Rebecca and Katherine; my brother-in-law and lifelong friend, John Milner; my neighbor and friend, Debbie Orcutt, and retired USAF pilot, Lt. Col. Mike Wood, the author of the finest, most detailed analysis of a police gunfight I have ever read, his exceptional book, *Newhall Shooting: A Tactical Analysis*. I would also like to thank Captain Eric Dickinson of the Vinton (IA) Police Department, EMT, police trainer, and author, for his invaluable assistance with this book.

Finally, my deepest gratitude and most profound respect go out to the heroic officers whose experiences fill the pages of this book. They were, without exception, more than willing to bare their souls in discussing these events. Many paid dearly in blood and tears for these lessons, and their willingness to share them only adds to their heroism. We all owe them far more than we can ever repay.

Introduction

When I told a friend what I wanted to accomplish with this book, she asked, "In other words, you want your readers to *feel* what it's like to be a cop in a fight for your life?" It was an insightful comment that expressed my feelings in the most concise manner possible, and it also got me thinking. Since the infamous Ferguson shooting, I have the realization that much of the criticism against the police is rooted in the fact that most people have no idea what it is like to be a cop and know even less about the realities of officer-involved shootings. The harsh truth is that armed encounters are terrifying, chaotic, and ever-changing, with everything happening so fast that there is hardly time to think. To survive, the officer must be skilled, quick-thinking, and highly adaptable to ever-changing dangers under enormous stress.

Contrary to what is portrayed on television, cops are not immune to fear, nor are they particularly well trained. They are certainly not trained to a level comparable to elite military units, professional athletes, or anything even remotely close to either one, as many citizens seem to believe. This misconception is often promoted by police leaders who assert that American police officers are the best trained officers in the world, but this is untrue and misleading. In truth, while some of our officers are exceptionally well trained, most are trained to minimal standards that are barely adequate for the job, and none are trained up to the superhuman standards that many Americans expect of them. This misconception is especially concerning because it can lead the public to believe that our officers are so well trained that any questionable use of police force is motivated by malice or racism, rather than inadequate training or the confusion, fear, and dangerous surprises so common to violent confrontations.

Another popular misconception often propagated in the media is that many police officers are brutes who regularly default to deadly force when threatened. After over 32 years as a police officer, more than 30 years of researching police shootings, and well over 20 years of instructing police officers in tactics, officer safety, mindset, and lawful use of force, I can say without reservation that nothing can be further from the truth.

This is not meant to imply that our police officers never use excessive force. The sad truth is that police officers are fallible human beings. They are not immune to overreacting under stress or even out of fear or anger, and a minuscule few are brutes who disgrace the badge. However, it is absurd to say that any but the tiniest minority would even consider maliciously shooting another human being without adequate justification. With rare exception, they have the highest regard for human life, as is so often proven by their selfless willingness to put their lives on the line to help others.

Furthermore, officers are trained to use great restraint in the use of deadly force, reinforced by frequent reminders of the severe legal, career, financial, and emotional consequences of using excessive force of any sort. Many officers fear making such mistakes more than they do a violent death. To lump all of our courageously dedicated officers into the popular stereotype of trigger-happy thugs is no less damaging and unjust than grouping any other group of people into such negative stereotypes.

No conflict between human beings can hope to end well until all parties begin to understand one another's perspective on the issues involved. I am convinced that police work is one of the most misunderstood professions in America today. The growing rift between the police and the public is ripe with distrust fueled mainly by this misunderstanding about the police, police training, and the dynamics of armed police encounters. I hope that by helping build a greater understanding of these and many other elements related to violent police-citizen confrontations, this book will help heal that rift, improve police-community relations, and reduce violence between the police and their citizens.

This is not my only goal in writing this book, however. I also want to show the heroism of our police officers. They are human, of course, and—sadly—some may not be entirely up to the task, but the great majority are highly committed to protecting their citizens. For many of them, the most rewarding part of the job is knowing that they are one of the chosen few whose duty is to protect their fellow citizens, even at the risk of death. They are the ones who run to the sound of the guns, and they feel honored to do it. Heroism requires more than just doing something dangerous. People who face danger because it pays well, or just for the thrill of it, are brave and should be recognized as such. But they aren't heroes. Heroism requires a selfless willingness to make sacrifices for others. The cops in this book are true heroes, and it is important to know who they are and what they have done. I also trust their stories will make it clear that there are many more like them, courageously ferreting out and confronting those who threaten our property, security, and even our lives and the lives of our loved ones.

Finally, I hope to pass on the gift these courageous officers gave me—lessons learned from the challenging experiences they endured and overcame. These officers have many essential traits in common, many of which came naturally to them. But they had to develop others deliberately, and anyone can similarly learn them. By learning them and ingraining them into your habits, they will be there for you if you ever need them. While the bulk of these traits are most applicable to violent confrontations with human adversaries, they can be applied to various other severe trials as well, including accidents, serious illnesses, financial setbacks, personal/family problems, etc. Life is sometimes hard and even cruel, but the mental toughness, courage, and tenacity of the officers in this book can inspire us to persist against all odds during these trying times. We owe it to them to honor their sacrifices by learning as much as we can from them.

Similarly, as you read through the book, you will also see various tips I have gleaned from these brave officers' stories, my law enforcement career, and my police training that you can use to help keep you and your loved ones safe. I added these items as they occurred to me to add value to this rather unusual self-help book.

HOW TO USE THIS BOOK

This book is loosely based on an earlier book I wrote exclusively for law enforcement. In that book, I recounted stories about officers involved in deadly encounters, followed by analyses of their actions for learning points related to officer safety. The book was well-received in the law enforcement community and often used in training, but its distribution was limited to police officers because it revealed many vulnerabilities that threaten the safety of our officers.

In this book, I have endeavored to do the same thing for my fellow citizens by following the same format of stories about police officers, followed by analyses of what we can learn from them. However, instead of focusing my analyses on lessons related to officer's safety, I offer lessons appropriate for any citizen interested in gaining a better understanding of the dangers our officers face every day, the dynamics of armed police encounters, how to stay safe, and how to deal with the various challenges of life. To gain maximum value from these stories, I recommend that you read them deeply with the intent of learning as much as you can. Read each story carefully and pause at key points to predict what might happen next, how you would approach the situation confronting the officer, and how various options might affect the outcome. Then read the analyses in the same careful manner. Analyze each suggestion critically and try to determine how it can apply to your life. Ask yourself if there is a better way to achieve the same purpose, and try to anticipate what suggestions I might offer next. This will help you learn how to think more critically about safety and improve your threat assessment capabilities. It will also help you develop one of the most essential yet most difficult-to-learn mental skills related to safety–mental flexibility.

You will probably notice that many of the concepts are repeated in other chapters. This was done for three reasons. 1) Repetition helps us retain what we have learned. 2) Many of the learning points apply to more than one chapter. This is not surprising because human beings, police officers included, tend to make common mistakes. For example, we all become complacent as we gain experience doing dangerous activities without suffering any negative consequences (e.g., less cautious when driving, less attentive when working in dangerous environments, etc.), and most of us tend to ignore our instincts when they warn of us danger (e.g., dismissing an uneasy feeling about someone or something as undue nervousness, etc.). Likewise, there is a great deal of commonality in the positive attributes of officers who, like the officers in this book, perform courageously under stress, and these bare repeating. Therefore, learning points related to complacency, trusting one's instincts, and maintaining a positive mindset are repeated to emphasize their frequency and importance in a crisis. 3) Like all violent encounters, no two incidents in this book are the same. Thus, no matter how frequently a particular learning point may be raised throughout the book, it fits into each case's context differently. For example, the ability to recognize and properly respond to danger signs was critical in almost every case, yet the details of how it came into play and was used by the officer were different in each incident. By seeing how this and other learning points apply to various circumstances, we enhance our all-important mental flexibility.

Finally, if you want to garner maximum value from this book, I would like to suggest that you read it one chapter at a time, with a day or more between each one. We learn and retain information better when we learn it in short chunks rather than in just a few long sessions. Also, this allows you to give deeper thought to each chapter before moving on to the next, which aids in long-term learning and helps you learn how to apply what you learn to your particular circumstances.

Stay safe, be strong, and God bless you and yours.

CHAPTER 1

A Warrior's Sacrifice:
The Keith Borders Case

"Greater love has no one than this:
to lay down one's life for one's friends."
—JOHN 15:13 (NIV)

INCIDENT DESCRIPTION

The gun felt ominously light in Keith Borders' hand as he wiped the blood from his eyes and headed to the back of his patrol car. He knew the Glock 21 well from long hours on the range and was thoroughly familiar with its feel as its hefty .45s emptied from its magazine.[1] It was nearly empty now, but the slide was still forward,[2] letting him know that it still held at least one round.

Don Mettinger, the gentle family man now turned beast, was getting to his feet again, still firing the deadly shotgun and seemingly oblivious to the blood flowing freely from a torso riddled with bullet holes. This was Borders' last

---

1. Magazines, often incorrectly referred to as "clips," are the objects that hold a firearm's ammunition. A small number of them are internal to the weapon, but most are detachable so they can be quickly replaced with another full one after they go empty. In pistols, they are long and rectangular in shape to fit into the weapon's handle, and generally hold 6-19 cartridges. In rifles, they are usually long and rectangular like pistol magazines, but are sometimes curved like a banana (frequently referred to as "banana clips"), and usually extend from the bottom of the gun, just in front of the trigger. Rifle magazines usually hold 10-30 cartridges, but some hold considerably more.

2. The slide (i.e., upper portion of a semiautomatic handgun) slides back after each round is fired, and then forward to its original position again to ready the weapon for its next shot. This occurs with each shot until the final round is fired, at which time the slide stays to the rear, thereby indicating the gun is empty. Thus, the fact that the slide on Officer Borders' gun was still forward indicated that the gun still held at least one more round.

magazine, and he would have to make this shot count. He took a deep breath and released it slowly as he stopped next to his cruiser's right rear fender. Raising the Glock into firing position, he inhaled deeply again, let its sights settle squarely between Mettinger's eyes, and pressed the trigger.

The bloody ordeal had started about a half-hour before with a call that Borders, a 34-year-old, three-year veteran of the large metropolitan police department, would never have handled alone under normal circumstances. It was a domestic disturbance that had been holding for over 15 minutes, and he had tried to wait for another car to break free before taking it, but most of the department was tied up working a major biker run several miles away, leaving the rest of the city shorthanded. When more calls started coming in from neighbors, Borders grew increasingly concerned that someone would get hurt. Unable to ignore the possible danger to one of his citizens, he reluctantly took the call alone.

As Borders approached the residence, a luxurious two-story, he spotted two women, a large middle-aged man, and a little girl in the garage. He remembered the man, a salesman named Don Mettinger, from an auto accident he had worked in front of the same house two weeks earlier. In that case, Mettinger had come outside to help and then struck up a conversation with Borders, leaving him with the impression that he was an obliging, good-natured man.

But now, Mettinger was in a heated argument with the two women that grew hotter as Borders came up the driveway. Before Borders could reach them, Mettinger shoved the older of the two women, causing her to stumble violently backward. Borders stepped between them, facing Mettinger

"You need to calm down and talk to me," he said.

Mettinger's eyes bore fiercely into Borders'. "You're not gonna arrest me!" he growled.

"I'm not here to arrest you," Borders answered. "We just need to talk."

"I'm not goin' to jail!"

Then, before Borders could do anything to stop him, Mettinger turned, ran into the house, and slammed the door. Borders was close behind, but the deadbolt engaged before he could reach the door.

He turned to the older woman and asked, "Is that your husband?"

"Yes," she answered, "I'm Debbie Mettinger, and this is our daughter Jenny and our granddaughter."

"What's going on?" Borders asked.

"I don't know. He just lost it today. I don't know what's gotten into him."

Borders hadn't liked what he saw in Mettinger's eyes. "Are there any guns in the house?" he asked.

Debbie gasped out a sob. "I'm afraid so. Lots of 'em. He collects guns."

"We gotta leave," Borders commanded, "Let's go!"

Without argument, Jennifer grabbed her daughter and headed down the driveway, followed by her mother with Borders bringing up the rear. Borders herded everyone across the street to the relative safety of his cruiser, ordered them to the opposite side of the car, and called in a barricaded subject.

"It isn't safe here," he told them. "You're gonna have to leave while I stay here and try to calm him down."

Both women refused, but Jennifer capitulated once she realized her daughter might be in danger. There was a pickup in the garage and a Honda in the driveway, but it was too dangerous to allow anyone to get that close to the house. Borders told her to leave on foot, find the nearest officer, and ask him for help.

After Jennifer and her daughter left, Borders turned to Debbie again and urged her to follow, but she was determined to stay. As he continued to plead with her, he was interrupted by a barely audible sound from the right side of the house—a door closing. He looked in that direction and noticed movement just above the top edge of a six-foot stucco fence that surrounded the yard to the right of the garage. Shining his flashlight in that direction, he spotted Mettinger peering at them over the fence.

"Come out here so we can talk," Borders commanded.

Mettinger refused, and Borders repeated the order twice more with the same results. Then on Borders' next attempt, Mettinger answered with an ominous demand. "No!" he yelled, "You come to me, and I'll give you my gun."

Borders drew his Glock, squatted down for cover, and shinned the flashlight directly into the man's eyes. "Put the gun down and come out through the garage with your hands where I can see 'em!" he commanded.

"Get that f__kin' light outa my eyes!" Mettinger screamed.

Borders repeated the order, got the same response, and repeated it again. This time Mettinger answered with a gunshot. Though just a wild shot fired in Borders' direction from a revolver poked over the top of the fence, Mettinger had just upped the ante. Borders grabbed his shotgun.

Meanwhile, Mrs. Mettinger began crying uncontrollably as her husband ran back inside through the side door and then closed the garage door with its remote control. Again, Borders urged her to leave, but she refused. Even worse, she repeatedly tried to stand up. Borders already had his hands full trying to watch for Mettinger while coordinating the responding units on the radio. The added burden of trying to keep Debbie down made the shotgun dangerous to handle. He threw the cumbersome weapon back into his car and drew his Glock again.

Moments later, the situation worsened once more. As the first assist officer approached the residence, gunfire erupted from an upstairs window, peppering the patrol car with lead. Braking hard, the officer slammed the transmission into reverse and accelerated backward to safety. Borders knew he couldn't leave, and it was too late now to safely remove Debbie from the scene, but there was no sense in putting anyone else in danger. He keyed his mic and requested that all his assist units stay back.

An eerie lull followed, and Borders, now hunkered down next to his car, used the pause to try to calm Debbie down. Suddenly, the lull was shattered by two booming gunshots from inside the garage, punctuated by the appearance of two bulges in the overhead door, both of them peppered with jagged points of light from the garage's well-lit interior. The door began to rise, and Borders watched as Mettinger's bare legs came into view near the back of the garage. Mettinger's baggy shorts appeared next, topped by the man's hefty belly. Stuffed into his waistband were a .357 magnum revolver and a 9mm pistol, but even more worrisome was the 12-gauge pump shotgun he was holding.

Borders crouched low next to his right front fender, kept his gun trained on Mettinger, and ordered him to put the gun down. Instead, Mettinger took cover along the left side of the pickup truck parked in the garage and then moved outside to the Honda in the driveway and advanced toward the street. He stayed low and kept the vehicles between him and Borders as he moved, leaving the officer with little at which to shoot from his present position. Borders started moving toward the rear of his car for a better shot, but Debbie was also there, sobbing as she begged her husband to stop.

Borders knew he was just seconds away from a gunfight, and he didn't want Debbie caught in the middle. Grasping at one last chance to avoid gunfire, he calmly said to the gunman, "Look, Don, put the gun down and come here so we can talk."

"It's gone way past that," Mettinger answered as he swung the shotgun up toward his wife.

Horrified, Borders snapped off two quick shots at Mettinger and ran toward the man's wife. To let this innocent woman die was unthinkable. Driven by the selflessness that burns deep in the heart of every warrior, he threw his body across the imperiled woman just as Mettinger's shotgun roared.

Border's body was twisting with his feet still in the air when the blast hit him in the forehead like a baseball bat, snapping him backward onto the ground. Bursting lights inside his head accentuated the gruesome sensation that his forehead had just been blown away. He forced himself up onto all fours and grabbed his forehead, fully expecting to touch his exposed brain. It was a bloody mess, but there was no gaping hole. He looked at Debbie, noting that she appeared unharmed. "Is my head all there?" he asked.

She nodded. "I think you're OK."

Borders was alert, breathing without difficulty, and able to feel his extremities. He knew he could still fight but assumed some of the pellets had penetrated his skull, inflicting a mortal wound. There was only one thing to do—stop Mettinger before he killed his wife. Only then would his death mean something.

Borders looked across the street. Mettinger was still standing there, apparently stunned into inaction by Borders' apparent resurrection from the dead. As Borders rose, gun in hand, Mettinger backed away and retreated up the driveway, firing as he went. Borders opened fire almost the same instant and, using the patrol car for cover, kept up a steady fire as Mettinger moved back inside the garage (Figure 1).

Meanwhile, Debbie, now shocked out of her stubbornness by the violence around her, crawled to a spot near the patrol car's right rear fender and stayed there. Now free from worry about the woman's wellbeing, Borders was able to focus entirely on stopping his adversary.

Mettinger was making himself a hard target by moving and keeping up a heavy fire with both handguns as well as the shotgun, but Borders was returning fire with equal vigor. As the fight went on, Borders soon realized there was something in the left rear corner of the garage that Mettinger wanted badly. Time and again, the man headed in that direction, only to be met by a hail of lead from Borders' .45. It worked—Mettinger was driven back on each attempt—but at a heavy cost in Border's supply of ammo. Borders emptied his first magazine, reloaded, kept firing, and had to reload again.

Borders could tell he was getting hits because Mettinger's bare torso was growing slick with blood, but the man seemed not to notice. It was disconcerting to see the powerful .45 having so little effect on his opponent, and Borders also had his own wound with which to contend. The blood flowing into his

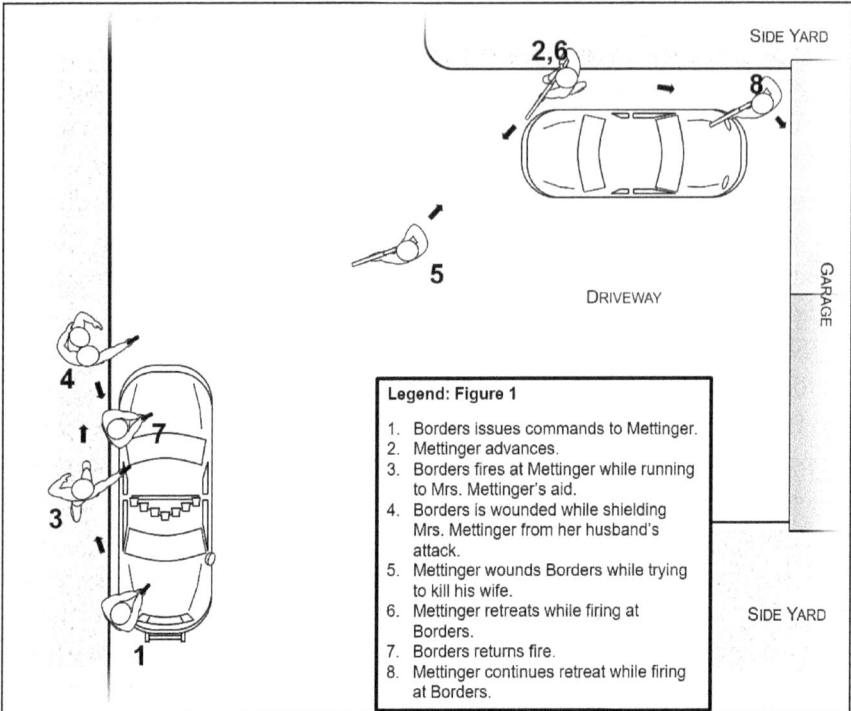

Legend: Figure 1
1. Borders issues commands to Mettinger.
2. Mettinger advances.
3. Borders fires at Mettinger while running to Mrs. Mettinger's aid.
4. Borders is wounded while shielding Mrs. Mettinger from her husband's attack.
5. Mettinger wounds Borders while trying to kill his wife.
6. Mettinger retreats while firing at Borders.
7. Borders returns fire.
8. Mettinger continues retreat while firing at Borders.

FIGURE 1: Mettinger advances, wounds Borders while attempting to kill Mrs. Mettinger, and then retreats.

eyes blurred his vision, forcing him to stop repeatedly to wipe it away so he could see to shoot.

The wound also served as a reminder that he was probably dying. But as a man of faith, Borders wasn't especially bothered by the idea. Instead, it only drove him to fight that much harder. If he were going to die, he would save Mrs. Mettinger first.

Dissuaded from entering the garage by Borders' gunfire, Mettinger made his way along the left side of the Honda to its left rear fender, where he knelt and opened fire with the 9mm while reloading the shotgun again. Borders returned fire and saw the man drop down out of view. Lowering his eyes to the pavement below, he immediately spotted Mettinger lying down, partly concealed behind the car's rear wheels and firing the shotgun from under the car.

Borders had been taught to skip shots off the pavement in situations like this one, and he had practiced the technique often enough to be confident with it. Mettinger's side was partially exposed, so Borders aimed at a spot on the driveway a few feet in front of it and squeezed off three rounds. All three found their mark, causing blood to spread over Mettinger's side.

Nevertheless, Mettinger was on the move again. Unsteadily, he rose to his feet, raised the shotgun, and opened fire. The Honda provided Mettinger with good cover, and Borders wanted to make sure he could get a clear shot at him. Staying low, he headed back to the rear of the squad car for a better angle, wiping the blood from his eyes again as he moved. The Glock had grown light in his hand, and he had already emptied his first two magazines. Now brutally aware that he was almost out of ammunition, he started deep breathing[3] in preparation for what could well be his last shot.

He stopped next to his cruiser's back fender, squatted there briefly as he took another deep breath, and then brought the gun up to fire. His vision narrowed until he could see nothing but Mettinger's anger-laden face and his sights resting on the bridge of his nose. He fired, striking Mettinger in the left eye, instantly dropping him to the ground (Figure 2).

Borders had been right. The Glock's slide was still forward, but its chamber had closed over his last round. Realizing that Mrs. Mettinger would remain at risk as long as her husband was still capable of fighting, Borders wiped the blood from his eyes, stepped around the back of the squad car, and moved cautiously forward to check on his downed adversary. He had barely covered half the distance when he was met by several officers coming to his aid. While two of them confirmed that Mettinger was dead, another went to check on the man's wife. Though hysterical with fear and grief, she was otherwise unscathed by her husband's savage attack.

Borders was escorted to a waiting ambulance and conveyed to the hospital, where it was determined that he had been hit not with buckshot but with #4 shot[4] instead and that only four pellets had struck him. After x-raying his skull and with little more than a cursory checkup, the emergency room physicians bandaged the pellet holes and sent Borders home.

---

3. Deep breathing is a method of breathing that calms the nerves and improves performance under stress. It requires four steps: 1) Breath in through your nose to a slow count of four, 2) hold your breath to a slow count of four, 3) breath out through your mouth to a slow count of four, and 4) hold your breath to a slow count of four. Ideally, the process should be repeated 3-5 times, but even one or two times can help a great deal.

4. Shotgun shells are filled with various sized pellets depending upon the kind and size of the game being hunted. *Buckshot* pellets are meant for large game, and are much larger and heavier than *shot* pellets. As a result, they inflict far more destructive injuries. Fortunately, Officer Borders was struck by the much smaller and lighter *shot* pellets, which is probably the reason why he survived.

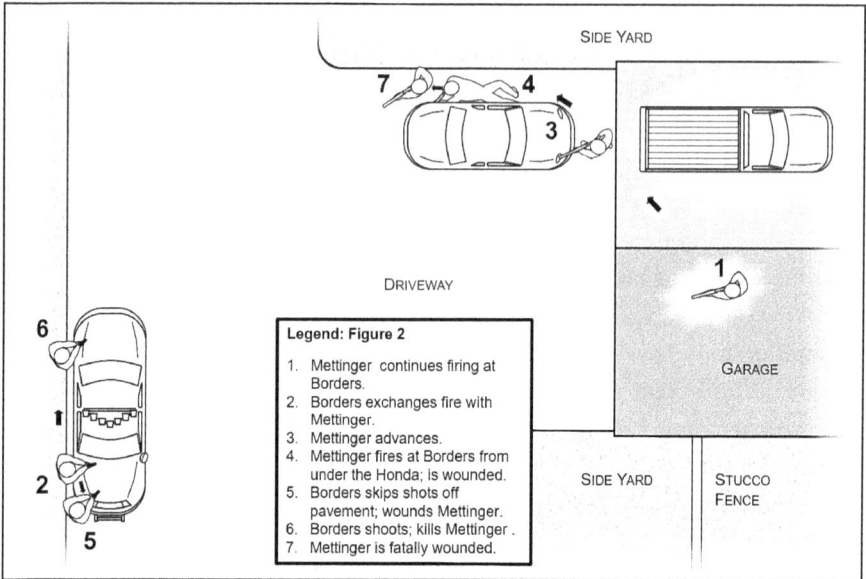

FIGURE 2: As the gunfight continues, Officer Borders fatally wounds Mettinger with a gunshot to the head.

THE AFTERMATH

Besides the bullet to his brain, Mettinger had taken six hits in the torso, one in the thigh, and two in the right ankle, all of which were with hard-hitting .45-caliber ammunition. Sadly, he had also been a law-abiding family man until earlier that evening but had inexplicably become enraged with his wife and daughter not long before the call came in. He had been drinking heavily that night, but a definitive explanation for his bizarre behavior has never been determined.

Subsequent investigation revealed why Mettinger had been so intent on reaching the back of the garage. A full box of 12-gauge 00 buckshot[5] was found on a shelf there.

Mrs. Mettinger, though grieving over the tragedy, recognized the necessity for Officer Borders' courageous actions in her defense. She never blamed him for what he had to do.

---

5. *12-gauge 00* buckshot is among the deadliest loads that can be fired from any shotgun, especially when discharged at closer ranges, like the distance between Mettinger and Officer Borders when the gunman tried to shoot his wife. If Mettinger had been able to load his shotgun with the ammunition stored in his garage, there can be little doubt that he would have killed Officer Borders, and most likely his wife as well.

To add to this tragedy, it was later discovered that two of the shotgun pellets had penetrated Borders' brain. Furthermore, he had suffered two fractured vertebrae in his neck and back and an additional brain injury from the whiplash effect of the blow to his head and subsequent impact with the ground. When combined with generally poor care from some of his doctors, these injuries caused Borders' condition to worsen with time. Despite a valiant effort to remain on the job, he eventually learned that his condition was irreversible. And although it wasn't evident to those who worked with him, he realized his decision-making and response time were not what they used to be. Now mindful that his condition could put others at risk, he decided to retire on a medical pension. Since he is unable to work without losing his pension benefits, he remains unemployed.

Nevertheless, Borders has never regretted what happened that night. Despite the cost, he still firmly believes it was worth it to rescue Mrs. Mettinger from her husband's homicidal fury.

ANALYSIS

Situational Awareness

Keith Borders was a sharp, safety-conscious officer who made a point of always being ready for the possibility of violence. Because of this, he immediately focused on Mettinger's unusually intense reaction to his intervention in the dispute. But more importantly, he didn't hesitate to act on his observations. Rather than ignore the danger signs or delay acting on them, he trusted his instincts and wasted no time in getting the two women and child out of the garage. His decision to trust his instincts likely saved the lives of Mrs. Mettinger, perhaps her daughter and grandchild, and even Officer Borders himself. And if Mrs. Mettinger had left the area with her daughter and grandchild as he advised her to do, Borders could have retreated to a safer location and kept the house under observation until help arrived. With his wife out of the picture, time to cool down, a greater police presence, and a negotiator's help, it is possible that Mettinger could have been talked into surrendering without violence.

There are two critical lessons to learn here. First, it demonstrates why police officers are trained and expected to be situationally aware at all times and to act on their suspicions. Some police critics hypothesize that this makes officers paranoid and even trigger happy, but nothing is further from the truth. In fact, the practice of continuous situational awareness makes officers better at accurately assessing danger and more confident in their ability to protect themselves and others, which in turn reduces stress, enhances clear thinking, and improves decision making. And in some cases, it can allow them to take defensive action before the confrontation escalates to into lethal violence, or, as in this case, even enable them to retreat to a safer location, where they can have a better chance of stabilizing the situation

The other critical lesson is a simple one. Since no one can ever know where or when danger will materialize, we should make a habit of practicing situational awareness at all times. This is not to say we should be overly cautious to the point of becoming paranoid, but we should always have our eyes and other senses open to the things going on around us.

Equally crucial, we need to learn to trust our instincts and be willing to act on them as Officer Borders did. Our danger instincts are not a mysterious sixth sense that we can afford to ignore. Instead, they are hardwired into our DNA to help keep us safe, and they work like this: Even though we are not consciously aware of it, our subconscious mind is continually taking in incredible amounts of data from our environment and quickly assessing it for what it means to us, especially concerning our safety. When it sees, hears, feels, or even smells or tastes something that it deems to be potentially dangerous, it sends an immediate warning signal to our conscious brain that something is wrong. This all happens at the subconscious level, and since the subconscious mind assesses data far faster than our conscious mind, it happens almost instantly. Unlike our conscious brain, it doesn't communicate with words but solely with emotions, like uneasiness or fear. We may feel uneasy when the presence of danger is not particularly clear, but that doesn't mean we should ignore it. We still need to do something to make things safer for us. Often this is nothing more than paying more attention and looking for more danger signs, slowing down, speeding up, backing away, or even giving a suspicious person a look that tells him you know what's going on and are ready to defend yourself.

When the danger is more apparent, the subconscious brain will signal danger with a feeling of fear or even alarm. This, too, requires immediate action. Sometimes this can be a low-profile response like those mentioned above. Still, at other times it must be something more obvious, like running away, taking cover, taking a fighting stance, or when appropriate, drawing a weapon. The key point here is to listen to and trust our instincts and act on them when they warn us of danger.

Reluctance to Shoot

From a purely tactical perspective, Officer Borders could probably have prevented Mettinger's attack if he had shot him sooner, either immediately after the garage door opened or when Mettinger left the cover of the Honda to approach the street. He had more than an adequate legal and moral justification for doing so because Mettinger—who had already fired at him once, shot up a patrol car, and fired through the garage door—was initiating a confrontation while armed with no less than three firearms. Moreover, he continued to advance while staying behind cover even after Borders ordered him to put the gun down, making it clear that he was determined to initiate an attack. Nevertheless, Officer Borders tried again to avoid bloodshed by calmly asking the man to put the gun down.

Contrary to the opinion of many police critics, most police officers are exceptionally reluctant to shoot, as evidenced by the countless body and dash cam videos that show them repeatedly ordering armed individuals to put their guns down, sometimes even after the offender has pointed a gun at them. This is far more dangerous than generally believed because an action is faster than a reaction, which means an armed offender can raise his gun and shoot before the officers can return fire. However, despite the danger and the fact that such warnings are generally not required by law,[6] most officers will, like Officer Borders, go to extremes to avoid shooting another human being.

There are various reasons for this, not the least of which is the natural reluctance of ordinary human beings to kill one another. Even though police officers are trained and expected to shoot when necessary to defend themselves or others against lethal attacks, this instinctive reluctance to kill can cause them to hesitate. Also, officers are regularly reminded during their training and in the media that their legal, professional, financial, and even emotional well-being will probably be severely jeopardized after a shooting, making them even more hesitant. On the other hand, officers are sometimes legally and—more importantly—morally obliged to use deadly force. If they shoot too soon or without adequate cause, they violate their duty to protect their citizens' rights and may go to prison, and if they wait too long, it may cost them or innocent citizens their lives.

---

6. There are two exceptions to this. The most common is the US Supreme Court requirement that officers should give a verbal warning before shooting a fleeing felon, but this is only required when it is practical for them to do so (Tennessee v. Garner, 471 U.S. 1 [1985]). The other is the argument put forth in some appellate courts that officers should also give warnings in cases when the offender is directly threatening them, but this argument has generally been dismissed by the US Supreme Court.

Fortunately, considering the vast number of dangerous encounters officers face every day, they make remarkably few mistakes. This is exceptionally extraordinary when we consider the conditions under which most lethal encounters occur. The average police gunfight lasts approximately 3.5 seconds, from start to finish, which leaves the officer a dangerously short period to spot his assailant's threatening move, recognize it for what it is, decide how to defend himself, and, finally, execute his response. This doesn't take long because of how the human brain works, but even a few milliseconds can make the difference between life and death in a gunfight. There are remarkably few occupations that require such life-and-death decisions under such incredible stress. Emergency room doctors, EMTs, and other medical personnel must also work under stress, of course, but none of them must make such rapid decisions with their own lives hanging in the balance.

Moreover, unlike people in virtually every other profession, police officers rarely have the time to consult with peers, supervisors, or anyone else before making a crucial decision. They must act alone under extreme stress, under field conditions that often work against them, and with inadequate information or time to make a well-considered decision. It is indeed remarkable that officers don't make more crucial mistakes than they do.

Nevertheless, even one fatal mistake is one mistake too many. Unfortunately, since police officers are only human, some mistakes are bound to happen, especially considering their training. Contrary to what many believe, police training in this country is grossly inadequate for what is expected of our officers. We expect perfection from them when it comes to the use of force, particularly lethal force, and we expect such perfection to occur under the difficult conditions mentioned above. While it is currently impossible to train our officers well enough to meet these expectations every time flawlessly without fail, it is possible to come much closer than we do now. But it won't be easy, and it won't be cheap. Training officers to think and perform beyond reproach under the severe pressure and time constraints of real-life armed confrontations requires training under simulated conditions that come as close as possible to real life.

Moreover, many of these skills are highly perishable, which means this training must be repeated at frequent intervals. Since all this takes a lot of time—time that the officers could otherwise use to patrol and respond to calls for service—more officers will have to be hired to maintain current manpower levels, or officers will have to train on overtime. Also, this kind of training requires a much larger number of trainers per trainee than other kinds of training, and the cost of training equipment, ammunition, etc., is much higher as well. We can have much better-trained officers who will do a better job of meeting the public's expectations, but the cost will be high.

Why Officers Must Sometimes Shoot Offenders Multiple Times

Mettinger absorbed nine rounds from Borders' of .45—six of which hit him in the torso and two more of which severed his right foot—without any significant effect on his fighting ability. This would have been remarkable even if Officer Borders had been firing marginally effective rounds, but he was using .45 caliber Gold Dot ammunition, which is considered by many to be one of the most effective anti-personnel rounds on the market.

Unfortunately, such resistance to gunfire is not particularly unusual, as evidenced by several other shootings recounted in this book. The human body can stand up to an incredible amount of punishment, especially when fueled by alcohol, drugs, mental illness, anger, or other strong emotions. In this case, Mettinger's near-superhuman ability to take rounds appeared to have been bolstered by alcohol-induced rage, but sometimes the only identifiable explanation for such resistance to gunfire is sheer willpower. Regardless of why, it is alarming and distracting to face an armed assailant who seems impervious to gunfire.

There are two things we can learn from this. First, it explains why police officers sometimes shoot assailants a seemingly excessive number of times. Since reality makes it clear that some people are amazingly impervious to gunshot wounds for various reasons, officers are trained to keep shooting until their assailant is no longer a threat. Even a mortally wounded attacker can do a lot of damage in an incredibly short period, making it imperative to keep shooting if he doesn't collapse immediately.

There is another valid but little-known reason why officers sometime fire so many shots. Once we humans start a series of actions, like repeatedly pulling a trigger, it is virtually impossible to stop those actions instantly, especially under stress. This is because it takes time for us to shift gears mentally and then more time for our decision to reach the involved muscles and stop them from moving. Since combatants in a gunfight often remain mobile after being shot one or more times, officers often fire more than once, which puts their already highly stressed minds into a repetitive pattern that requires conscious effort to stop. Moreover, since our survival instinct drives us to work at maximum speed when in danger, and the average time it takes for a human to pull a trigger is three times per second, it is not unusual for officers to continue firing several more shots after they realize the offender is no longer a threat. It is hard not to be shocked when we hear of such shootings. However, the harsh truth is that they are often physiologically unavoidable.

Our Own Resistance to Gunshot Wound and
Other Severe Injuries

The other lesson we can learn from Mr. Mettinger's ability to withstand so much physical trauma is that we must never assume that we will die if shot or otherwise severely injured. Since far less than ten percent of all gunshot wounds inflict mortal injuries, and most of those kill instantly, the odds are excellent that you will survive if you are still alive after being hit. This is true even for head wounds, as evidenced by the fact that Officer Borders not only survived his but was able to win the gunfight despite it.[7]

Similarly, many other significant injuries can be equally survivable. Modern medicine has made great strides in treating traumatic injuries, and the human body can take far more punishment than most of us realize, especially when we possess a strong will to live. Regardless of how badly you may be hurt, focus on your bodies' ability to withstand tremendous damage and keep going no matter what.

Winning Mindset

Officer Borders understands the police officer's role as a warrior at the deepest, most personal level. It cost him his career and much of his health. Nevertheless, when asked if he regrets the sacrifice he made, he quickly points out that we only regret the things we wish we could change and then goes on to say that he wouldn't change anything if he could do it all over again. It's not that he isn't unhappy over the way Don Mettinger's rampage changed his life, but he deems Debbie Mettinger's life as more important than his wellbeing. This kind of selfless devotion to others separates warriors from those they protect and makes them view the risks they take as a privilege, not a burden.

Besides proving himself a warrior by his willing sacrifice, Officer Borders displayed many of the other key traits of a winner, all of which can be applied to other challenges we may face in our lives. Like so many others who persevere against incredible obstacles, he stayed focused on the only thing that mattered—overcoming his adversary. Disregarding his seemingly mortal head wound, the

---

7. Granted, Mettinger was killed instantly by a head shot, but that was a bullet through an eye socket. For the most part, the hard, curved bones of the face and skull are more resistant to bullets than most of the other bones in the body, and the most vulnerable parts of the head are especially small targets.

blood flowing into his eyes, and his attacker's apparent invulnerability to his bullets, he refused to give up. He kept shooting, kept moving to maintain cover while jockeying for a clear shot, kept wiping the blood from his eyes, and most importantly, kept thinking (a crucial quality to possess in any crisis). When Mettinger headed for a back corner of the garage, he trusted the instincts that told him the man wanted to go there for a good reason and then kept shooting into the area to prevent it. When Mettinger laid down for cover behind the Honda, Borders skipped shots under the car. And when he realized that he was just about out of ammo, he took a deep breath, calmly brought his sights to bear on his target, and smoothly pressed the trigger for the most weighty shot of his life. Winners keep their cool by staying focused on what they need to do to win (another crucial quality in any crisis), as Borders so aptly proved in this case.

Closely associated with his unwavering focus on winning was how Officer Borders dealt with the belief that he was mortally wounded. Rather than dwell on or be frightened by it, he accepted what he believed to be the reality of his approaching death and then pushed on. He became determined to give his death meaning by saving Mrs. Mettinger's life and then used that commitment to drive him on to that goal. People who can overcome great adversity in the face of apparent hopelessness often possess this same quality. Like them, we can quietly accept our circumstances and then turn our focus toward doing whatever it takes to overcome any hardship in our lives.

Faith also played a crucial role in the way Officer Borders handled himself. Possessing a steadfast faith in God, the unwavering devotion to others that often goes with it, and less fear of death than many who do not possess faith, he was able to look beyond himself to his sworn duty to defend the weak. Armed with the firm belief that God had given him a job to do and that he was duty-bound to do it to the best of his ability, he ignored the danger and pressed on until Mettinger was no longer a threat. While it is not my intent here to preach spiritual beliefs, it would be a disservice not to mention that a strong faith system tends to be a prevalent trait among officers who handle themselves well in lethal encounters. This is not universally true, of course, but it happens often, and it makes sense that faith would bolster courage and devotion to others in the face of danger. Similarly, any of us who face grave fears or other severe challenges can use our faith to bolster our courage, especially when others are in danger or otherwise need our help.

Keith Borders exemplifies the best that law enforcement has to give. After literally throwing himself into the path of a blazing shotgun to save a helpless woman, he went on to defeat a relentless, apparently invincible adversary. He then graciously accepted the career-ending consequences of his actions as a fair price to pay for doing his duty. In the process, he saved an innocent life and taught us a great deal about how to persist and win against all odds. But his actions have a lot more to tell. They define the meaning of courage, self-sacrifice, and duty; and present us with an inspiring insight into a warrior's soul.

Police Officers as Warriors?

Note that I used the term "warrior" when discussing Officer Border's mindset and in this book's title as well. You will also find that it is used frequently in the coming pages. However, many police critics and others find the use of this term objectionable when referring to police officers. They claim that such references reflect a belief among police officers that they are at war with their fellow citizens, thereby encouraging police brutality. But do we object to those who say they are at war against poverty, injustice, drugs, or cancer? Do we object when those on the front line in these challenging endeavors call themselves warriors? Police officers and those who support them recognize that cops are at war against crime, drugs, and violence, but that doesn't mean they see their fellow citizens as the enemy. In fact, with very rare exception, they see themselves as individuals devoted to protecting their fellow citizens from these dangers, just as others see themselves as champions against the wrongs in our society today.

This begs the question: what does the term "warrior" mean when referring to police officers in America? In most cultures throughout history, warriors sometimes defended their country or tribe from invaders, but more often, they were invaders who attacked other groups for gain or oppressors who silenced anyone who dared to challenge their leaders. However, in a free society like ours, true warriors are far different. They are individuals who courageously and selflessly defend those who are unable or unwilling to defend themselves, no matter the risk. In police work, this often involves apprehending dangerous criminals, which sometimes necessitates justifiable force in self-defense. When that happens, the officer-warrior must fight to win because anything less will allow his assailant to continue his criminal behavior, thus putting others at risk. A warrior's foremost duty is to protect the innocent no matter what. That requires a strong will, never-say-die attitude, and willingness to use force decisively, but only when necessary. The officers whose stories appear in this book–and so many others across the United States–provide a superb example of today's selfless warriors in the never-ending battle against crime and violence.

CHAPTER 2

In Defense of Others:
The Eric Nelson, Luke Ross Case

"People sleep peaceably in their beds at night only because rough men
stand ready to do violence on their behalf."
—George Orwell

DESCRIPTION OF INCIDENT

Having just shaved his collar-length hair into a scraggly Mohawk, Sam T. Moore,
Jr. buckled the ammo-laden web belt around his camo fatigues, followed by a
bandoleer full of 12-gauge shells, picked up two long guns, and stepped out
of his apartment into the hallway. A hunting knife and black powder revolver
were shoved into his waistband, and one of the long guns he was carrying was a
12-gauge Remington pump. But all the damage would be done with his other
long gun—a semiautomatic MAK 90[1] rifle. The weapon was loaded with over
75 rounds of 7.62 X 39 ammunition in a drum magazine. Moore was carrying
another drum magazine and seven 30-round box magazines in pouches on the
web belt.

He moved down the hallway to the front door, stepped outside, and walked
across the lawn to the sidewalk on 22nd Street. Here, 22nd Street ran through
a quiet middle-class neighborhood, but it was lined with small businesses to the

---

1. The MAK 90 rifle is remarkably similar to the well-known AK47. The major difference between these
two rifles is that an AK47 can fire in either semiautomatic mode (one shot for each pull of the trigger) or
fully automatic mode (a three shot burst, or a continuous burst as long as the trigger is depressed), making
it a true assault rifle; whereas the MAK 90 can only fire in semiautomatic mode.

north, where it intersected Colhoun Street and then continued north into the adjacent commercial district.

The crisp autumn air carried the sounds of the city's afternoon rush hour as Moore quietly raised the MAK 90 to his shoulder. An instant later, the air erupted with the terrible crack of rifle fire as Moore strolled up and down the street, randomly shooting at anything that moved and sometimes at nothing at all. The deadly rifle repeatedly thundered at an even, steady pace, but aimlessly and without any significant effect. Then he spotted a Toyota cruising toward him on Colhoun. He opened fire, sending several rounds into the moving car, one punching its way through the windshield and spewing shards of glass in its path. The driver, a 28-year-old office worker named Emily Palmer, managed to avoid the deadly missile but not the glass. One piece struck her in the left eye and sliced its way deep inside. As she pressed her hands against the viciously damaged eye, her Toyota skidded into a boat storage lot at the southwest corner of the intersection. She braked a stop, bailed out, and scampered to the rear of her car. Terrified, she crouched down out of the gunman's line of fire and waited for help.

Fortunately for Mrs. Palmer, Moore had lost interest in her. But others wouldn't be so lucky. Moore quickly chose another target—a Ford approaching from the south–and opened fire. Rapidly cracking off one round after another, he sent a barrage of hot lead into the vehicle as its driver, a 56-year-old car salesman named Ken Nash, roared past him and continued north for another block to a service station on the left. Suffering from a bullet to the abdomen and bleeding profusely from a shattered left forearm and elbow, Nash pulled into the lot. With buildings now shielding him from further gunfire, he slid out of the driver's seat and rolled out onto the pavement.

As people on the streets scurried to cover and vehicular traffic began to stay clear of the area, Moore was starting to find it harder to spot targets, but that would soon change. The police department was being inundated with calls from terrified citizens, and officers from across the city were rushing to the scene. Moore would soon have fresh targets; targets who would willingly rush into his killing field instead of fleeing from it.

In the meantime, Moore had found another target. It was a pickup traveling south on 22nd Street, driven by Nick Russell, a 38-year-old off-duty firefighter. Moore opened up as the truck drove past, sending one round through its metal skin and the back of the driver's seat into Russell's back. With most of its energy now spent, the otherwise deadly missile mercifully penetrated only skin deep, and Russell was able to drive himself to the closest hospital for treatment.

Moore's next victim was 58-year-old Edward Tucker, who was driving a van northbound on 22nd. Again, the gunman began pumping rounds into the vehicle. As shattering glass and lead screamed past Tucker, pain sliced across the right side of his face and through one ear (Figure 1). He sped on and stopped after reaching the shelter of a nearby building. Though frightening, the wound wasn't severe and required nothing more than minor treatment at the scene.

Moore was expending a large amount of ammunition, having already emptied the drum magazine and at least one of the 30-rounders, but he still had plenty. As he looked for more new targets, he spotted one he had been waiting for—a patrol car.

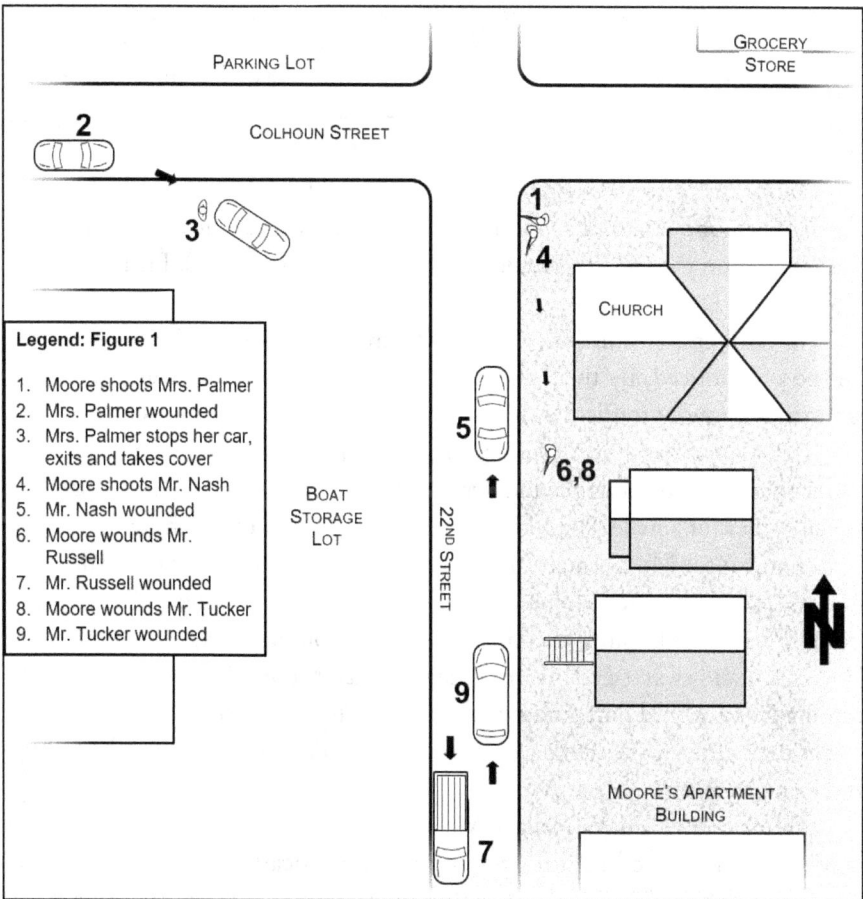

Legend: Figure 1

1. Moore shoots Mrs. Palmer
2. Mrs. Palmer wounded
3. Mrs. Palmer stops her car, exits and takes cover
4. Moore shoots Mr. Nash
5. Mr. Nash wounded
6. Moore wounds Mr. Russell
7. Mr. Russell wounded
8. Moore wounds Mr. Tucker
9. Mr. Tucker wounded

Figure 1: Moore wounds four motorists in rush hour traffic.

The unit, operated by a 27-year-old, six-year veteran of the department named Eric Nelson, was racing up 22nd directly toward him. Moore had the tactical advantage; he was standing in the lengthening afternoon shadows, and the unwitting officer was still too far away to see him. Moore ran to the refuge of some stairs leading up a steep incline to the front of a nearby residence. The steps were cut deep into the hill and lined on both sides with stone retaining walls, making for good cover and concealment. Moore waited as the speeding patrol car came closer.

Meanwhile, Sgt. Luke B. Ross, a 33-year-old, 11-year veteran of the department, was speeding to the scene from about four miles away. The dispatcher didn't have a specific location on the shooting or a good description of the suspect yet, but more details were coming in fast. Despite the confusion caused by the many calls from panicked citizens and anxious requests for information from responding officers, it eventually became clear that the gunman was wearing camouflage clothing, armed with a rifle, and near the intersection of Colhoun and 22nd Streets.

One of the officers asking for information had been Eric Nelson. There had already been one report of a wounded citizen, and just seconds after requesting clarification on the victim's location, he had added, "Disregard. I think I found him."

No further transmissions were heard from the young officer after that, but no one noticed. By then, the scene had become so chaotic, and the air so jammed with radio traffic that his silence was lost in all the confusion.

It appears that Officer Nelson had spotted one of Moore's victims. Mrs. Palmer had been kneeling behind her car on the boat lot, and he had apparently mistaken her for a male. With his attention now riveted on reaching the victim, Nelson didn't see Moore squatting, rifle at the ready, in the recess of the deep-set staircase. He had barely completed his last transmission when blistering fire from Moore's rifle began tearing into his cruiser from up ahead and to the right. He ducked and swerved to his left as he sped past Moore. The bullets were now coming from behind him, and two found their mark. He slumped down in his seat as the patrol car coasted onto the boat lot, slid into one of the parked boats, and came to rest.

After shooting Officer Nelson, Moore rose from his improvised bunker and headed for the rear of a church just north of his location. The church sat on the southeast corner of 22nd and Colhoun, and a sidewalk ran along its south wall to its back yard. Moore trotted down the sidewalk to the backyard, where he soon spotted another patrol car—this one driven by Officer Russ Abbott—speeding toward him from the east on Colhoun. After waving a couple of citizens through, Moore took aim on Abbott's vehicle and cranked off another hailstorm of bullets, peppering the cruiser with 7.62 rounds. Mercifully, Abbott remained unscathed as he wheeled his cruiser to the right, braked to a stop near the corner of a building, bailed out, and took cover. He could see Moore from where he stood, but he was too far away to take a shot. Instead, he called in the gunman's location and held his position.

Within moments of hearing Abbott's transmission pinpointing Moore's location, Sgt. Ross arrived from the north. Like the other officers pouring into the area, he didn't know Nelson was down. Nelson had been the only officer to approach the scene from the south on 22nd Street, and with everyone focusing on locating and neutralizing the gunman, it would be several more minutes before anyone noticed Nelson's bullet-riddled cruiser on the boat lot.

Ross parked a block north of the church and, with his mind focused on ending the violence, exited his car. As a member of the tactical team, he was well trained for the task. However, since department policy required that the team's rifles be kept at the station, he was poorly equipped to go up against Moore's MAK 90. Undaunted by the handicap, now well-informed about the gunman's whereabouts and hearing gunfire from the south, he ran to the rear of a grocery store across the street from the church. From there, he moved quickly along the east side of the store to its southeast corner, quick-peeked around the corner, and immediately spotted the gunman in the church's back yard. Moore held the rifle to his shoulder and was firing a steady stream of bullets in a northwesterly direction. Ross had seen a group of officers gathering on a parking lot northeast of Moore's location when he arrived, and he was targeting them.

Ross, his H&K[2] .45 already in hand, raised the pistol into firing position. It would be a nearly impossible shot for anyone except a competitive shooter—48 yards with a handgun—but Moore had to be stopped. Ross took careful aim, the .45's sights seeming to fill his entire field of view as he centered them on Moore's upper torso and pressed the trigger. A miss. Ross was a crack shot and not easily flustered. He re-centered the sights on his target and fired again, this time dropping Moore instantly (Figure 2).

Several other officers had been converging on Moore's position by this time, and they began approaching him from all directions as Ross moved cautiously

---

2. The initials H&K are an abbreviation for Heckler & Koch, a German gun manufacturer that makes high quality firearms that are often carried by police officers.

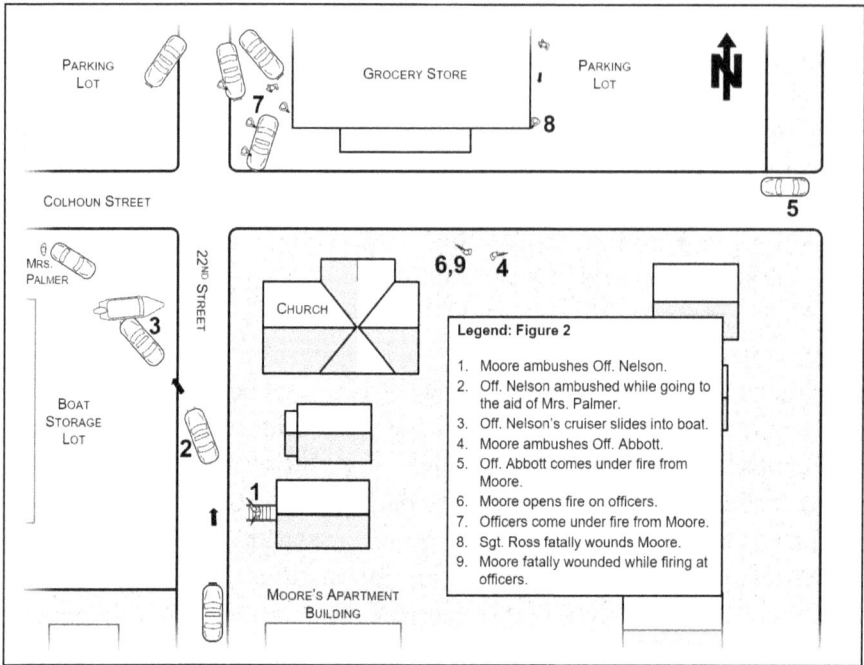

FIGURE 2: Moore ambushes Officers Nelson and Abbott and is firing at other officers when Sgt. Ross fatally wounds him.

forward to check the man's condition. As they moved in, it soon became evident that Moore's reign of terror had ended. Ross's second round had entered the right side of his head and penetrated his brain, killing him instantly.

THE AFTERMATH

Sgt. Ross had done his job well, but sometimes even the noblest efforts cannot prevent tragedy. During the gunfight's closing moments, a call had come in from a citizen who said he believed an officer had been shot. Even as the gunfire died away, an anxious search of the area began. Within minutes, Officer Nelson was found, still behind the wheel of his cruiser. He had died instantly from a gunshot wound to the head.

As tragic as it was to lose Officer Nelson, things could have been much worse. A heavily armed, mobile shooter with a nearly endless supply of ammo can do incalculable harm to unarmed citizens, and it was only because of Sgt. Ross's decisive action and the courageous response of every officer there that no citizens were killed. Except for Emily Palmer, who lost most of the sight in her eye, and Ken Nash, whose arm was permanently disabled, Moore's other citizen-victims fully recovered from their wounds.

Sgt. Ross, Officer Nelson, and seven other officers were later recognized for their courageous actions with various awards, including the department's Medal of Honor, the Medal of Valor from the Fraternal Order of Police, and TOP COPS award from the National Association of Police Organizations. Sgt. Ross is still with the department, where he continues to serve as a patrol sergeant and member of the tactical team.

It was later determined that Moore had expended 280-300 rounds of ammunition during his bloody rampage. He had no history of mental illness. And although he had a lengthy record of minor arrests, including one for a misdemeanor weapons violation (a knife), he had no priors to indicate a propensity for severe violence. Although his autopsy disclosed the presence of small amounts of THC and alcohol, it found no other explanation for his actions, and the subsequent criminal investigation was equally unrevealing. The cause of his irrationally violent behavior will forever remain a mystery.[3]

ANALYSIS

Training

It should be noted that this shooting occurred before mass casualty incidents (MCIs) became as prevalent as today. Consequently, Officer Nelson's medium-sized department was ill-prepared to deal with it. Regrettably, many, if not the great majority, of police departments today are still similarly ill-prepared. Most police departments provide some active shooter training, but it is far from adequate for the most part. The problem is that proper active killer training is too time-consuming and expensive for most departments to afford. If done correctly, every patrol officer must hone his shooting skills to a sharp edge and learn many new skills, tactics, and techniques. Command staff, supervisors, and telecommunicators must also learn complex new skills. These skills must be practiced and augmented with frequent reality-based training,[4] followed by

---

3. The incident recounted here is true, but the names were changed to ensure the privacy of those personally involved. Likewise, to preserve confidentiality and clarity, some facts have been altered slightly, but the essential elements of the story remain unchanged.

4. Reality-based training is training that immerses trainees in highly realistic, high-stress scenarios. The two most common of these are: 1) Training with AirSoft or paint ball guns in situations that require the trainees to confront roleplayers in difficult use-of-force encounters and other critical situations. 2) Computerized training that uses videos projected onto life-sized screens instead of roleplayers to thrust the trainees into the same kind of simulated situations..

honest, in-depth debriefings. These exercises must include large-scale simulations involving everyone likely to be involved in such events (e.g., 911 dispatchers, EMS, fire, neighboring police agencies, etc.) as well as every police officer in the department, which adds even more cost to the training. This is not to imply that any of this critical training should be curtailed. On the contrary, it is vital to public safety and well worth the cost. However, we also must accept the fact that the taxpayers will have to pay for it.

Patrol Rifles and Other Essential Equipment

This case highlights the importance of equipping every patrol officer with a patrol rifle. As a SWAT member, Sgt. Ross had been issued one and was well trained with it, but it was of no use to him because it was secured in a locker at the station. Like many departments at that time, his department viewed rifles as specialized weapons that should only be used by tactical officers and then only during SWAT operations. Fortunately for his citizens and fellow officers in the area, Sgt. Ross didn't need one to get the job done, but most officers would find it nearly impossible to make that shot with a handgun. If he had been any less proficient with his pistol, Ross might have hesitated to shoot or—more likely—been forced to get closer before firing, thereby exposing himself to greater danger and giving Moore more time to shed blood. Also, the officers who Moore was targeting when Ross arrived may have been able to stop him if one or more of them had been armed with a rifle.

Thankfully, most departments now issue rifles to all of their patrol officers and adequately train them in their use. However, some still do not, especially where the money is tight (rifles and their ammunition are expensive, and a considerable amount of costly training is needed to make officers proficient in their use). And many of the departments that issue rifles to every patrol officer limit their accessibility by storing them in the trunks of their cruisers. By their nature, emergencies require quick action, and a delay of even a few seconds can cost lives, especially during mass shootings. Since law enforcement's responsibility is to stop violence as quickly as possible, every officer must be appropriately equipped to make precision long-distant shots down long corridors and across open areas in schools, houses of worship, shopping malls, etc. This is of enormous importance because there are often many innocent citizens near the shooter, and there is usually no time or means for moving them out of the way before taking the shot. Rifles are essential under such circumstances, and they must be immediately accessible, which means one must be carried in the passenger compartment of every police cruiser, not the trunk.

Many police critics and others are critical of the police for carrying "assault rifles"[5] and using other military-style equipment like helmets, shields, and load-bearing vests.[6] The aggressive appearance of such equipment may be offensive to some, but it is vital to the safety of our citizens as well as our officers. As unfortunate as it may be, it is undeniable that today's mass shootings are ever-growing in their lethality and number, and terrorist attacks are also an ever-present possibility. Our police are the first line of defense against these mass tragedies, and our safety depends on their ability to rapidly, effectively, and safely respond to them.

For similar reasons, police departments should not be prohibited from possessing armored rescue vehicles. Despite their appearance, these vehicles are not armed and are designed for defensive purposes only. Although they have occasionally been used "offensively" to breach buildings, as in the Pulse Nightclub MCI and, more recently, the JC Kosher Supermarket MCI in Jersey City, such use can hardly be seen as militaristic attacks against the public. And far more often, they are used to transport officers to the scenes of active shooters, hostage situations, barricaded subjects, etc. Or, even more innocuously, to rescue wounded or trapped officers and citizens, as was done to great effect the just-mentioned Jersey City incident.

Moreover, these vehicles can be used to save lives when dealing with the threat of improvised explosive devices used by terrorists, other extremists, and even active shooters (active shooters sometimes set these devices to maim or kill first responders arriving on the scene). Today's ever-increasing rise in MCIs has added an entirely new dimension to police work. Our police officers must now

---

5. An actual assault rifle can fire in either one of two different modes: 1) semiautomatic mode (just one shot fired with each pull of the trigger) or 2) fully automatic (like a machine gun, in a rapid, continuous burst of gunfire for as long as the trigger is depressed or until the gun is empty). Some assault rifles will also fire in burst mode (a burst of three, or sometimes, two shots in rapid succession with each pull of the trigger). Many rifles, like the AR15 so often carried by police officers, are often mistaken for assault weapons, but actually they are not. Even though they have the distressing appearance of an assault weapon, they can only fire in semiautomatic mode, making them more similar to semiautomatic sports rifles than military firearms. They are, however, similar to assault rifles in their use of larger capacity magazines. Another major distinction is that true assault rifles are, with only a few exceptions, illegal to own or possess, whereas semiautomatic rifles are not. While police patrol rifles may be offensive in appearance to some, they are not military weapons.

6. Load bearing vests are vests with multiple pouches used to hold spare magazines and other essential equipment, including radios, trauma kits, etc. Many also hold body armor. Used primarily by the military and SWAT teams, they are now becoming increasingly more prevalent among patrol officers.

be able to protect their citizens under circumstances with many of the characteristics of a battlefield, and battlefield-like situations cannot be safely resolved
without militaristic weapons, equipment, and tactics. Some may not like their
appearance, but these things are necessary for everyone's safety and security.

It is also important to emphasize here that police departments and their
officers don't view their safety equipment as tools of war against their fellow
citizens, as some activists seem to believe. Instead, they see it as something
essential to their safety and effectiveness against violent criminals, mass casualty
events, and terrorists. There is no war against their community in their minds;
rather, their only war is against crime and violence. To say otherwise is an insult
to all the men and women in law enforcement. With rare exception, our police
officers are dedicated to protecting their citizens, and they are willing to put
their own lives on the line to do it.

Proficiency with Firearms and Other Critical Skills

This case also demonstrates the importance of firearms proficiency—an avid
shooter since childhood and highly trained tactical officer, Sgt. Ross possessed
not only the skill but, perhaps more importantly, the confidence needed to
make the precision shot required to neutralize Moore immediately. With
competence comes confidence, and confidence reduces stress, steadies nerves,
and clears thinking, all of which are crucial to decisiveness and accuracy under
stress. And it also increases mental flexibility, improves decision-making, and
enhances physical performance.

This is why our police officers need the best possible training in so many
of the critical skills they may need on the street, including firearms, self-defense
techniques, and even de-escalation, crisis communications, safety tactics, dealing
with emotionally disturbed persons, etc. Officers need to learn all these skills to
the point that they become second nature and then practice them under increasingly more stress. Only then will they possess both the competence and the
confidence to apply those skills under the highly stressful, often chaotic conditions on the street. Moreover, since things often fail to go as planned, officers
must possess a high degree of one of the most essential but challenging skills
to teach—mental flexibility under stress. Fortunately, confidence based on
competence significantly reduces stress and clears thinking, thus increasing the
mental flexibility they need to achieve the high level of performance their safety
requires and their public expects. Again, the necessary training to get this done
isn't cheap, but it is crucial to the safety of our officers and the citizens they serve.

Tactical Training for Mass Casualty Incidents

In this era of the ever-increasing prevalence of active shooters and the continuing threat of terrorism, patrol officers and even tactical teams need increasingly more training to effectively respond to these tragic events. They need to be concerned about such things as moving through the hot zone when approaching buildings, advancing down long corridors, making dynamic entries, etc. Such challenges require infantry-style tactics unfamiliar to most police officers, such as leapfrog tactics for moving through large open areas, proper utilization of various kinds of cover, movement to and from points of cover, etc. The public's expectations about how officers should deal with active killer incidents are also becoming more demanding, including a call for officers to make solo entries into the hot zone and administer trauma care to victims inside. While our citizens have every right to expect and even insist that police officers meet these demanding expectations, our officers need considerably more frequent and exhaustive training to do so. As with any other training needs, this training is expensive and time-consuming but essential to meeting the increasing demands of today's law enforcement.

Deadly Force in Defense of Others

In the great majority of cases when police officers use deadly force, they do so in self-defense, but sometimes duty demands that they take a life in defense of others. Unfortunately for the innocent targets of criminal violence, human beings are naturally much more reluctant to employ deadly force in defense of others than in defense of themselves or loved ones. We may kill out of an inherited or learned selfless concern for others, a sense of duty, etc., but our instinct for survival doesn't ordinarily come into play unless our loved ones or we are threatened.

Nevertheless, Sgt. Ross didn't hesitate to shoot Moore. This fact speaks directly to one of the noblest aspects of his character—his readiness to act in defense of others. He didn't pause to consider the "fairness" of killing a man who was no direct threat to him but was singularly focused on the need to stop the carnage.

He never doubted that he did the right thing. He understands that defending others goes to the heart of the law enforcement mission. Police officers are entrusted with the authority to use firearms because their citizens need well-trained armed defenders to protect them from predators like Moore. While it is true that—like every other citizen—police officers have an inalienable right to defend themselves, they have the *duty* to defend others. It takes a special kind of commitment to put your own life on the line in defense of others. Sgt. Ross and so many other devoted police officers have willingly accepted that responsibility. They don't want anyone's admiration or even a thank you, but they do deserve everyone's respect.

With the responsibility for our citizens' safety resting on their shoulders, police officers and their departments must leave nothing to chance. Law enforcement must train its officers to respond decisively to situations like the one faced by Sgt. Ross. They need to clarify that officers have the duty to defend innocent lives and then reinforce that point with appropriate policies and comprehensive training. Besides intensive classroom exercises, it is essential to conduct frequent reality-based training that includes increasingly difficult scenarios in which officers must decide whether to shoot to save others. This is the best way to ensure that officers can make proper lifesaving decisions when defending their fellow citizens.

It is also essential for police trainers to clarify to their officers that the law does not require officers to issue verbal warnings before using deadly force when engaging an active shooter. While it is generally preferable to issue verbal warnings in other armed confrontations, doing so is likely to add to the bloodshed in a mass shooting. When many innocent lives hang in the balance, police officers don't legally or morally owe the shooter any favors. They do, however, owe his potential victims their best efforts to protect them. By issuing a warning, they give the shooter the chance to flee, duck behind cover, turn his gun on them, etc. In that case, if he manages to escape or incapacitate the officer/s, they have failed their citizens and any officers who must confront him later. This is no time for fair play.

Winning Mindset

Besides his readiness to defend others, there were several other aspects of Sgt. Ross's mindset that contributed to his quick action in ending the bloodshed. First, like many officers who handle themselves well in high-stress situations, he had prepared himself mentally for the use of lethal force. He had role-played "what if" scenarios in his mind while on patrol and handling calls and used mental imagery[7] to "experience" armed encounters in preparation for the day when it may happen on the street.

---

7. Mental imagery is a mental exercise that enables you to use your imagination to practice how to respond to various situations without having to actually experience them firsthand.

Citizens can also use mental imagery to plan for dangers they may face, like becoming the victim of a home burglary, robbery, carjacking, fire, etc. We practice fire, tornado, earthquake, and even active shooter drills as part of our everyday lives, but we somehow avoid preparing in a like manner for other dangers. Like Sgt. Ross, we can plan for just about any threat by role-playing "what if" scenarios beforehand in our minds. This is best done by getting into a relaxed state and then imagining various scenarios as vividly as possible, start to finish, with an ending in which you successfully escape or otherwise deal with the threat. Elite military units, SWAT officers, professional athletes, and many other high-performing individuals frequently prepare in this way for the challenges they may face, and so can you.

Ross is also a man of strong faith, which is another common element of the winning mindset. People of faith are generally less afraid of death than others, which reduces stress and bolsters courage. Furthermore, faith helps create an outward focus on the needs of others. Shifting attention away from oneself enables one to ignore distracting self-centered thoughts and stay focused on the only thing that matters—saving innocent lives.

CHAPTER 3

Doing Something is Always Better Than Doing Nothing: The Herb Cuadras Case

"In any moment of decision, the best thing you can do is the right thing, the next best thing is the wrong thing, and the worst thing you can do is nothing."

—THEODORE ROOSEVELT

DESCRIPTION OF INCIDENT

Just about every department, precinct, or district of any size has at least one officer who attracts action like a magnet. These go-getters possess that rare combination of awareness, aggressiveness, and street smarts—with a measure of luck added to the mix—that always seems to put them in the right place at the right time. For them, the street is a crime-fighting goldmine. Officer Herb Cuadras was that kind of cop. The 27-year-old former marine had only ten months on the job, but he had already accumulated an impressive number of felony arrests, especially for the kind of community in which he worked. The city was a relatively affluent suburb with about 110,000 residents, primarily residential neighborhoods, a relatively low crime rate, and little violent crime. Even in this environment, Cuadras seemed drawn to serious crime, and he had the numbers to prove it.

Cuadras wasn't looking for any work tonight, however. A cool drizzle filled the night air, it was getting close to the end of his shift, and he was holding a lengthy report from a burglary arrest the night before. His sergeant had just cleared him to go to the station to finish the report, and he was heading that way when a robberyinprogress call came out. True to form, Cuadras was just passing the location, a restaurant that sat on the edge of a residential neighborhood.

The silent alarm wasn't a typical one. The broadcast was from a special alarm designed to apprehend a brazen holdup suspect who had been consistently robbing restaurants throughout the county for the past two and a half years, sometimes as often as once a week. The alarms were triggered by remote transmitters carried by many of the restaurant managers in the area. When tripped, they repeatedly broadcast the restaurant name and location until reset, and the transmissions overrode all other traffic on the police frequency. The robbery suspect was of particular concern, not just because of the number of crimes he had committed but also because they had become increasingly more violent. He had yet to kill anyone, but it appeared to be just a matter of time. At first, his M.O. had been the same as those in most small business robberies, but he now routinely kicked in the front door, fired several rounds into the ceiling, pistol-whipped the manager, and then fired several more shots before fleeing the scene.

One puzzling aspect of the robberies was that they had stopped suddenly about a year before. When they abruptly started up again about six months later, it was suspected that the perpetrator had been in jail, but there was no evidence to link any particular suspect to the crimes. As expected, it was later discovered that the suspect had, in fact, been incarcerated. James Carey, 24, had been doing time for a crime that resonated with hatred and contempt for the police. After being stopped for acting suspiciously, he had jumped and disarmed the officer who had stopped him, but the officer had managed to escape by jumping over a wall and ducking into the darkness beyond. Carey was later arrested, but in the meantime, he had mailed the officer's gun back to, with an ominous note that read, "You got away this time, but not the next time." A fingerprint had been lifted from the gun, and a hit was made identifying Carey through the local automated fingerprint system. Carey had been convicted just before the mysterious pause in the string of robberies but had received an outrageously short sentence and was released just six months later. As subsequent investigation would disclose, the attack on the officer had not been out of character for Carey—his foremost goal in life was to kill a cop. Tonight, he would get another chance.

Officer Cuadras had planned out how he would respond long before the alarm call came in. During earlier briefings on the robberies, the detectives had said the suspect usually left his car in nearby residential areas while committing the robberies. They recommended that officers respond to residential streets near the targeted restaurants and watch for the suspect as he tried to leave the area.

The first street Cuadras came to lead into the residential neighborhood behind the restaurant. He doused his lights, turned there, and immediately spotted a Monte Carlo up ahead. A shadowy figure was moving through the dark mist toward the car, and Cuadras instantly knew he had the right man. He kept his distance to give the suspect a chance to get into the Monte Carlo and drive away. His instincts had been correct, as usual. The man entering the Monte Carlo was Carey, fresh from robbing the restaurant. As Carey pulled away from the curb, he kept his lights off, apparently unaware of Cuadras' presence behind him. Cuadras was too streetwise to try to stop a holdup suspect alone, intending only to follow Carey until he could get some backup and make a high-risk stop.

Cuadras, cloaked in darkness, followed several car lengths behind Carey. Then, as they passed under a streetlight, he saw Carey glance at him in his rearview mirror. An instant later, the Monte Carlo's lights flicked on, and it leaped forward, busting through a stop sign as it sped away. The aggressive young officer was already pumped up and ready to go. He tromped on the gas, flipped on his roof lights, and called in the pursuit.

The Monte Carlo made a hard right at the next intersection. Cuadras followed, only to be surprised by the sight of the Monte Carlo stopped dead in the street in front of him. He braked hard and stopped short of the car, tense concern now gripping his chest. But then Carey pulled away again, this time slowly. Cuadras was puzzled. It was apparent the man in front of him didn't want to give up, but this was hardly your typical pursuit. He quickly concluded that Carey was looking for a better chance to make his escape. He called in his new location and waited expectantly for some sign that help was on the way. But it never came. The dispatcher never acknowledged his call, and no sirens were wailing in the distance or any other indication that he had been heard. Confused but not deterred, Cuadras continued to follow his slow-moving quarry.

Then, less than a block further on, the Monte Carlo took off again. Cuadras gunned his engine to keep up and close the distance when Carey suddenly made another right turn. Cuadras followed him and again found that Carey had stopped dead in the street. Cuadras braked to a stop just behind the Monte Carlo, now keenly aware he was in big trouble. He immediately sensed that there would be a shootout and visualized what it would be like. The realization brought tense fear, but Cuadras was not the kind of man to let fear immobilize him. Instead, he braced himself for the attack and quickly decided to do whatever it would take to win. At the same time, he planned a response. It wasn't a great plan, but it was simple, direct, and aggressive. As Carey started to pull away again, this time at an even slower speed than before—barely more than idle speed—Cuadras unsnapped his holster and tugged on his Smith & Wesson 9 mm to make sure it was ready to go. He knew exactly what he was going to do when Carey stopped again. He would immediately take cover in the V of his open driver's door, draw his gun, and get ready to fire.

Cuadras also knew this would be his last chance to let the dispatcher know his status and location. He grabbed the mic, made the transmission, and focused on the threat developing before him. He didn't have long to wait. He had barely hung up the mic when the Monte Carlo made a quick left turn and stopped abruptly—no brake lights this time—and its driver's door flew open. Though startled, Cuadras was instantly on the move. He flung his door open and scooted quickly to his left, drawing the S&W as he moved. Carey was already out of the Monte Carlo and moving fast. He spun toward Cuadras, a big .45 in his right hand, and whipped the gun up into firing position.

With the pistol's appearance, the scene shifted into dreamlike slow motion, and Cuadras could see every detail of his adversary's actions. Though this was unexpected and confusing, Cuadras felt like he now had plenty of time to think.

As if on autopilot, Cuadras thrust his gun up into the V of the open door as two great fireballs erupted from the muzzle of Carey's .45. Cuadras was already returning fire, sending two slugs toward the chest of the now-charging gunman who, with gun blazing, was quickly closing the short distance between the two vehicles. Oddly, the slow-motion scene was deathly silent—even the gunfire was muted—but the muzzle flashes from Carey's gun lit up the night like cannon fire.

Though bewildered by all this, Cuadras fought back unflinchingly. His quick initial actions had already saved him from two bullets. Carey's first two rounds, apparently meant to take him out while he was still behind the wheel, had blown through the windshield and whizzed harmlessly through the space he had just vacated. But then things got worse. None of Cuadras' shots were having any effect on his adversary. Without as much as a flinch, Carey kept firing as he advanced through Cuadras' vigorous return fire.

One of Carey's slugs sliced through Cuadras' right bicep. Mercifully, it missed bone and went unnoticed by the officer for the time being. Carey's next shot plowed into the rain gutter over the driver's door, fragmented, and sent a large chunk crashing into the center of Cuadras' forehead just above the hairline, causing a wound that could have been psychologically devastating to a less focused officer. Cuadras was also initially unaware of this wound but soon noticed blood flowing into his mouth from somewhere up above. Everything seemed to be going wrong, but he refused to let any of these setbacks affect his focus. He held his ground and pulled the trigger again.

Carey kept coming. He ran up to the driver's door, jammed the big auto-loader through the open window until it made contact with Cuadras' upper body, and fired! (Figure 1) Cuadras' left shoulder exploded with pain as the slug bore through it at a downward angle and exited at the shoulder blade. Cuadras grimaced in agony, but he couldn't worry about that now. Carey was coming around the open door for another shot, again thrusting the .45 forward for a killing shot into Cuadras' upper body. Cuadras twisted to his left, whipped his gun up into firing position, and fired. Simultaneously, excruciating pain seared through the hard-fighting officer's left elbow, and his body involuntarily recoiled from the blow. He felt himself falling hard across the front seat.

Though unaware of it at the time, his bullet had also found bone and liga-ment. The round had crashed into Carey's right elbow just before Carey pulled the trigger, causing the man's right hand to flinch and his gun to jam. Without realizing it, Cuadras had just taken Carey's gun out of the fight.

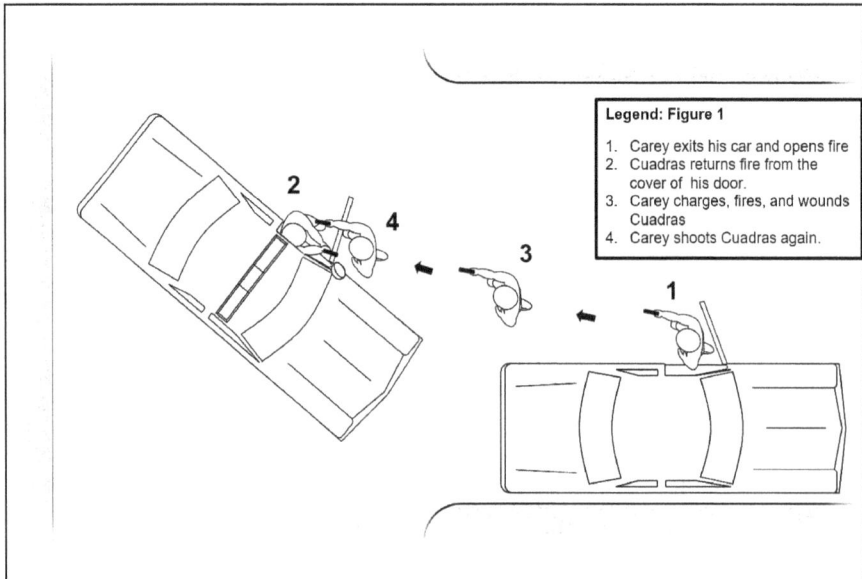

Legend: Figure 1

1. Carey exits his car and opens fire
2. Cuadras returns fire from the cover of his door.
3. Carey charges, fires, and wounds Cuadras
4. Carey shoots Cuadras again.

FIGURE 1: Carey charges toward Officer Cuadras and wounds him as Cuadras returns fire.

But Carey's last round had also had an unexpected outcome, and it wasn't good. As Cuadras landed inside the cruiser, his right wrist slammed against the front edge of the seat, knocking the gun from his hand. It hit the floor, tumbled away, and disappeared into the darkness under the dashboard. "Oh shit!" he thought. He felt naked and vulnerable but was determined to keep going.

Meanwhile, Carey dove to his right, rolled on the pavement, and jumped back up again near the back of the patrol car. He stepped around to a point just behind the left taillight, slipped a fresh magazine into the .45, and pointed it at Cuadras (Figure 2). Inexplicably, he didn't even try to clear the jam.

Cuadras knew how dangerous it is to do nothing when under attack, but he also knew Carey was waiting for him to move. Still unaware that Carey's gun had jammed, he wisely believed that Carey would open fire again if he tried to dig for his gun, back up his car to run over him, or take any other aggressive action. On the other hand, he was a bloody mess, and he knew he appeared to have taken several solid hits to vital organs, including the head.

After resolving not to let anything kill him, even if it meant having to take additional hits, he decided to risk playing dead. He remained motionless and waited. A few moments later, he felt the door, which had been resting against his left foot, come open. He mentally braced himself for the possible gunshot to follow, but it never came. After a wait of several long seconds, he felt his

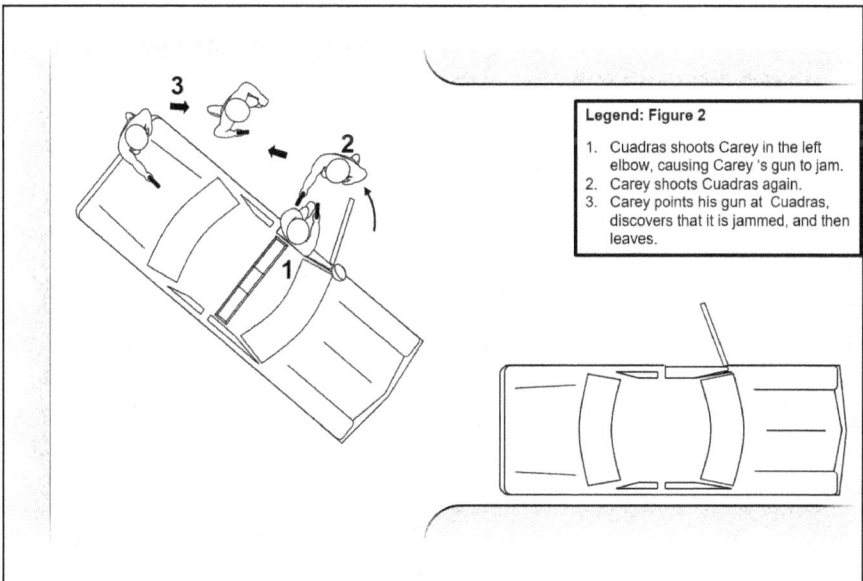

Legend: Figure 2

1. Cuadras shoots Carey in the left elbow, causing Carey's gun to jam.
2. Carey shoots Cuadras again.
3. Carey points his gun at Cuadras, discovers that it is jammed, and then leaves.

FIGURE 2: The gunfight ends; Carey's gun jams, and he flees the scene.

car start to ease forward. Without looking, he knew that Carey had driven away (Cuadras had not had time to shift into *park* before the shooting, and his car had crept forward until it had come to rest against the Monte Carlo's rear bumper).

Cuadras stayed where he was for several moments longer. He was in great pain and knew he had suffered at least one head wound of an undetermined nature. These wounds gave him cause for concern, but then he thought about his children and how much they needed him. His next thought was the memory of his officer safety instructor at the academy. The instructor, a dedicated trainer with an imposing command presence and powerful teaching style, had insisted that mindset was the key to surviving any wound. Cuadras remembered him standing face-to-face with the recruits and growling, "The only cop who dies is the one that wants to die. If you want to live, you will live."[i] This thought spurred Cuadras into action.

Carey was getting away, and he couldn't let that happen. He took hold of the steering wheel with his good right hand, pulled himself up into the driver's seat, spotted Carey's Monte Carlo about four houses away, and went in pursuit.

Again, Cuadras called for help, and again he got no response. He would later learn that the source of this dangerous and frustrating problem was an odd set of coincidences. The first time he called out, the restaurant manager had tripped the alarm again, which overrode Cuadras' transmission, and the subsequent two transmissions were overridden by traffic from another responding officer, who had spotted another suspicious vehicle leaving the area and covered Cuadras while following and stopping it. Then, as a final twist, Cuadras had unknowingly hit the frequency button on his radio when he fell across the front seat, locking out the police department frequency.

Though increasingly confused and frustrated by his unexplained inability to get help, Cuadras didn't falter in his determination to apprehend Carey. The thought of the man trying to kill him angered him deeply, and it made him even angrier to think about what Carey might do to the next person who got in his way. A moment later, he saw the Monte Carlo disappear while making a turn up ahead. He followed, but the car was gone. He scanned the area, looking deep into the wet darkness, and then he spotted it in the middle of a muddy field. Carey had spun out while trying to make the turn and was now stuck in the mud.

Cuadras knew he would have to back off if Carey wanted another fight, so he lit up the Monte Carlo with his spotlight and kept his distance. Once again, he called in his location, but this time he was rewarded almost immediately by the sight of a patrol unit from a neighboring city in his rearview mirror. The other officer stopped, stepped from his vehicle, and started to walk toward Carey's car. Obviously, the officer didn't know what was happening (as it turned out, he thought Carey was either drunk or had spun out on the wet pavement).

"Hold on!" Cuadras shouted, "That guy just shot me! He's a holdup suspect."

The startled officer immediately grasped the gravity of the situation. After drawing and taking cover behind his car, he waved Cuadras away. "Get outa here. I'll take care of this," he yelled back and then called for assistance on his walkietalkie.

"I gotta get to the hospital," Cuadras responded and took off.

It was a long way to the hospital—about seven miles—but Cuadras stayed calm and focused. He kept telling himself he would be alright as long as he got to the hospital in one piece. The last thing he needed was to get into an accident; so, he made a conscious effort to maintain a reasonable speed and be careful at every intersection. Although in great pain and bleeding heavily from his head wound, he focused on his driving and arrived at the hospital in good time.

THE AFTERMATH

The bullet to Cuadras' head had caused only a flesh wound, and none of the other wounds were life-threatening either, but his elbow had been mangled. Full rehabilitation seemed hopeless, and the doctors recommended that Cuadras take a medical pension. He refused. As determined as ever, he had the shattered elbow replaced with a plastic one, went through extensive rehabilitation, and returned to full duty within nine months. About two years later, he left the department to work for a larger neighboring department, where he recently retired as a patrol sergeant.

Carey's arrest and its aftermath provided the final bizarre twist to this incident. Though effectively unarmed because of his jammed gun, Carey refused to go easily. After he refused orders to exit the car, a nearby canine unit was called to the scene, and the dog was sent in. Carey fought the dog off and then had to be dragged out of the car kicking and screaming. Still unwilling to submit, he fought back as the officers handcuffed him and had to be forced into one of the awaiting patrol cars. While en route to the holdover, he managed to kick out one of the cruiser's windows and had to be subdued again. After he arrived at the holdover, he was placed in a holding cell to calm down. When an officer returned to book him about ten minutes later, he found him lying across his bunk in awkward stillness. Closer examination quickly confirmed what the officer already knew—the would-be cop killer was dead. His coat and shirt were removed, disclosing the wound to his right elbow and, although it had bled little, a hole in the center of his chest. A subsequent autopsy revealed that one of Cuadras' bullets had taken off the top of Carey's aorta. It was a mortal wound that should have killed him within three minutes.

ANALYSIS

Doing Something is Better Than Doing Nothing
Carey's erratic way of running from Officer Cuadras was an unconventional prelude to a common tactic used against unsuspecting officers during traffic stops and pursuits. The offender stops suddenly, often after disappearing around a corner, thereby forcing the officer to brake to a stop behind him. While all of the officer's attention and effort are focused on stopping before he crashes into the back of the vehicle, the offender jumps from his vehicle and opens fire, often while charging the officer as Carey did.

Today, most officers are trained to deal with this kind of attack, but this shooting occurred several years before such training was widely available. Still, despite this shortcoming, Officer Cuadras did an excellent job of quickly planning an impromptu response. Instead of freezing up or letting fear overwhelm him when he saw the attack coming, he simply accepted it and started to plan his counterattack. Of course, the plan wasn't ideal, but it enabled him to do something—and doing something—even if it isn't perfect—is far better than doing nothing. It allowed him to draw and move directly into the V of his open driver's door, which immediately gave him reasonably good cover and enabled him to return fire. Though not as effective as he had expected, this return fire may well have saved his life. Even though it didn't appear to have any effect on the man, the round to Carey's chest may have disrupted his physical performance in an indiscernible yet significant enough way to cause him to miss some shots that might otherwise have hit more vital targets. It may also have been a factor in Carey's decision to flee rather than continue his attack.

It is also interesting to note that some of Officer Cuadras' fellow officers criticized him for feigning death. But he had lost his gun and was trapped inside his car. He had also had the presence of mind to consider the fact that he was covered in blood, most of which was coming from an obvious head wound, which would make the ruse much more convincing. Moreover, even if he could have retrieved his gun, he would have had to sit up to use it, which would have exposed his head to Carey's gunfire. He wisely assumed that Carey would renew the attack if he dared to move, whereas feigning death might prevent further attacks. In addition, he had made up his mind that he would not die even if shot again, a remarkable never-say-die attitude that exemplifies the kind of mindset needed to overcome injuries, illnesses, or other dangers that might otherwise be fatal. Though it appeared on the surface that Cuadras had done nothing in the face of danger, he had, in fact, done something—he had made the astute decision to take a calculated risk that paid off.

The main thing to remember here is to do something when faced with any challenge, whether it is an attack, accident, illness, or anything else. Accept your situation, but don't dwell on it. Weigh your options, plan how to attack the problem, and then aggressively follow your plan. If your plan isn't working, as is often the case, don't just blindly keep going along the same path. Reassess and adapt your plan to the new situation or, if necessary, abandon it altogether and do something different. The importance of doing something cannot be overstated. Never surrender. Instead, let your determination drive you forward to win.

Resistance to Gunshot Wounds

Like several of the other shootings recounted in this book, this case highlights how ineffective gunfire can be in stopping a determined assailant. After the shooting, investigators learned that Carey's goal in life was to go oneonone with a police officer and kill him. Since the mind has an enormous amount of control over the body, this kind of hate-driven determination can be as effective as drugs, alcohol, or mental illness in enabling people to keep fighting after suffering incredible damage from gunshot wounds. But what made his case so remarkable was how long Carey lived and how much fight he had left in him after having the top of his aorta severed. It has long been known that a mortally wounded person can keep moving and fighting for 10-12 seconds, but Carey kept going for at least fifteen minutes. Incredibly, he also had the strength to put up a vigorous fight against a police canine and several officers and then kick out a window in the patrol car. We must always keep in mind that highly motivated or agitated people can display superhuman strength and endurance. Never assume they can be stopped easily, even when shot. If you are ever unfortunate enough to come under a lethal attack, keep fighting until your assailant is no longer a threat or you can escape to safety.

Exiting Your Vehicle During a Traffic Stop

This shooting provides a graphic example of why police officers respond so forcefully when a motorist steps from his vehicle rather than waiting behind the wheel for the officer to approach him. Even though Carey's hostile intentions were evident in this case, other dangerous offenders are far more subtle before they attack. They may approach the officer casually with their weapon concealed or exit their vehicle and then wait for the officer to approach. Every officer knows this, and they are also brutally aware that traffic stops are among the most dangerous things they do. They are well trained to handle traffic stops in a particular way that gives them maximum control over the vehicle's occupants and to go on high alert when anything out of the ordinary catches their attention. Remember, the officer has no way of knowing you are a law-abiding citizen with no intention of harming him, and he may even have information to indicate that you could be dangerous. For example, your car may meet the description of one that was used in a domestic disturbance, burglary, armed robbery, or even a shooting. In that case, quickly exiting your car to approach him might prompt an aggressive response. Depending upon the circumstances, the officer may even draw his gun and order you to stop and prone out, or even open fire if you unintentionally do something that appears to threaten his life. This is, of course, thankfully exceedingly rare; nevertheless, it remains a tragic possibility.

Even if you are being stopped for a minor traffic violation and exit your car without being told to do so, the officer will likely treat you in a way that may offend you or even appear unreasonable, especially if you start to walk back to his patrol car. In that case, it is vital to carefully follow his instructions to the letter, even if you don't believe they are necessary. If you feel the officer has stepped over the line, you can make a complaint or even file a lawsuit against him later, but don't risk your safety by resisting. Again, it is essential to remember that he probably has good reason to feel that you may be a threat to him, no matter how innocent your intentions may be. He may even have a good reason to believe you are an armed and dangerous offender.

There are several other rules that any motorist should follow when stopped for a traffic violation. First, pull over as soon as you can safely do so, and stop your vehicle as far off the roadway as possible to minimize the officer's danger from passing traffic. Stay in your seat with both hands on the steering wheel, and don't reach under your seat, into your glovebox, or anywhere else, *including your pocket or purse,* unless he tells you to do so. If the officer tells you to move in any way, do only what he tells you to do and don't make any sudden movements. If you don't understand his instructions, calmly ask for clarification. It is also within your rights to explain your perspective on the violation or ask questions about it, but you will not help your cause if you are rude, argumentative, insulting, threatening, etc. It never improves the situation when emotions flare, and it can even lead to your arrest under some circumstances, especially if you refuse to sign the ticket.

Similarly, if an officer stops you for any other reason than a traffic stop (e.g., pedestrian stop, suspicious person check, suspicion of shoplifting, other minor offense, etc.), your safety and as well as the officer's requires that you heed similar advice. Cooperate, maintain your cool, don't argue or resist, and don't make any sudden or furtive moves. Historically, officers have often been seriously wounded and murdered while handling suspicious person calls, investigating minor crimes, and handling other seemingly low-risk tasks. Their training and experience have taught them that people who are uncooperative or hostile can be dangerous. Also, sudden or furtive moves are often followed by an armed attack. Moreover, as with traffic stops, the officer may have received information that led him to believe you are an armed and dangerous felon. You may know better, but he doesn't. Under such circumstances, the situation can quickly escalate out of control, with tragic consequences for the officer, citizen, or both.

Winning Mindset

Officer Cuadras displayed many characteristics common to officers and others who possess a strong will to overcome danger and other obstacles. Instead of letting fear overwhelm him, he acknowledged it and then used it to focus on the need to plan and initiate an effective counterattack. Fear is an instinct meant to mobilize us into action when in danger, and when used in this way, it becomes a powerful asset.

At the same time, he refused to let his painful wounds distract him, choosing instead to focus on preventing Carey's escape. He was far from immune to the pain in his shoulder and elbow wounds (wounds that break bones tend to be much more painful than those that do not), but he didn't dwell on it or let it frighten him. He acknowledged the wounds and then continued to realistically assess the situation and do what he had to do to reach his goal. By contrast, someone who dwells on pain may intensify the effects of the injury, sometimes to the point that a relatively minor injury leads to shock or even death. Moreover, focusing on pain can distract you from taking action to solve the problem. For example, someone trapped in a burning building or injured in a car wreck after leaving a roadway in a remote place must focus on escaping the building or finding his way back to the roadway. If injured badly enough, he may have to stop the bleeding or immobilize a broken bone first, but he must not linger or let himself be overwhelmed by fear or pain.

Officer Cuadras also focused on what meant the most to him—his family. Such thoughts create a powerful motivation to overcome danger, and we must use them to our advantage. Focus on your family or something else that you treasure, and let these thoughts inspire you to keep fighting no matter what.

Finally, mental flexibility is also essential to winning, and Officer Cuadras possessed it to a remarkable degree. Carey's sudden attack didn't faze him. Nor did the lack of communications, the fact that his bullets seemed to be completely ineffective, or the loss of his gun. Each time, he persisted, reevaluated, focused on the threat, responded to it, and overcame. Even later, while driving himself to the hospital, he kept thinking and planning. Realizing that an accident would substantially delay his arrival, he made a conscious effort to slow down and use caution when approaching intersections. This kind of adaptability is crucial to winning against all odds.

CHAPTER 4

Taking the Fight to the Enemy:
The Joe Eagan Case

"Superiority, while useful, is not vital to the successful offensive
action. The fact that you are attacking induces the enemy to believe
that you are stronger than he is."
—GENERAL GEORGE S. PATTON, US ARMY

INCIDENT DESCRIPTION

Suddenly, the sound of running footsteps off to his right cut through the crisp
night air. Instinctively, Detective Sergeant Joe Eagan drew his gun and dropped
the binoculars from his eyes as he spun in his seat toward the sound. But his
draw came too late. His S&W 669 had barely cleared its holster when the
passenger door of his undercover car flung open to reveal the silhouette of
a man leaning inside, followed instantly with a white-hot muzzle flash, the
ear-splitting crack of a gunshot, and a hammerlike blow to his face. His ears
ringing, stunned by the pain and suddenness of the attack, and blinded by the
blazing light, he felt the gun fly out of his hand. It hit the floor and bounced
into the blackness beneath his dashboard.

As often happens when cops are shot, the attack had come as a complete
surprise. The night had started as apparently low-risk surveillance on a small
group of thieves who had been stealing catalytic converters in the medium-sized
suburb where Eagan, a 50-year-old, 25-year veteran of the department, worked.
Eagan and his detectives had identified the offenders, none of which had any
record of violent offenses or weapon violations. There was nothing in their

backgrounds to suggest they were anything more than small-time thieves who had found an easy, relatively low-risk way to make a lot of money.

Still, there had been a glitch even before they started. They served in one of the metro area's larger suburbs, located over 20 miles west of the core city, but the surveillance location was in a cluster of small, relatively high-crime suburbs just outside of the big city's western limits. Since they would be working in a rather dangerous and unfamiliar location far from home, they had arranged for several of the city's detectives to assist, but the assisting detectives had unexpectedly canceled at the last minute. This had left Eagan with only two detectives for the surveillance, and overtime restrictions had prevented him from calling in any off-duty personnel to help. With barely enough manpower to do the job, Eagan had been forced to man his position alone.

Though unknown to any of the detectives at the time, something else had also gone wrong. A multijurisdictional communications center dispatched for several departments in the area, and earlier in the evening, Eagan had advised the center of the time and location of the surveillance. But it was now almost 2:30 A.M., and no one on the evening shift had passed that information on to the overnight shift. Even though this mistake would not have any adverse effect on the outcome of the shooting, it would later cause a confusing delay that put Eagan and one of the other detectives at greater risk. Under any less fortunate circumstances, it could have made things a lot worse.

Eagan had set up on a vacant lot near the top of a hill not far from a motel where the offenders stayed, intending to follow them when they left. He was parked roughly facing the road that ran past the motel, with his lights out and the motel down the hill to his left. His car's position made it necessary for him to twist fully to his left—nearly to the point of turning around in the driver's seat—to maintain a clear view of the motel with his binoculars. The other two detectives were sitting together in an undercover van on the motel parking lot. Alone in the dark and focused on the motel, Sgt. Eagan had been unaware of his attacker's approach until he heard his running footsteps.

Reeling from the crushing blow to his face and virtually defenseless, Eagan could think of only one thing—ATTACK! He fully believed his ghostly assailant was going to kill him, but not yet; not before he got his now-empty hands around the man's throat and crushed his windpipe. If that failed, he hoped to at least leave his fingerprints there to mark him for positive identification later. He threw his door open, bailed out, and charged toward the back of his car, fully expecting the shooter to be circling from that direction for the kill. Still blind

from the muzzle flash, deaf from the blast, and with the taste of gunpowder filling his mouth, he kept moving in the burning hope that he would soon find his
assailant. Then it suddenly occurred to him that the shooter might be behind
him, and he started to brace for the bullet's impact.

But the shot never came. As soon as the shooter—a 21-year-old thug with
a lengthy and violent record named Evan Lockhart—saw his "helpless" victim
on the move, he turned and ran full speed into the night. He had been willing
enough to shoot when his victim was still defenseless, but he didn't have the
stomach for this. Just steps away were two of Lockhart's friends, but neither one
had any more interest in taking on this madman than he did. Like Lockhart,
they scurried away (Figure 1).

As Sgt. Eagan's vision returned, and he realized Lockhart was gone, he
grabbed his cell phone (he had no radio) and called the other two detectives
for help. Moments later, he heard the roar of their engine as they came closer,
followed shortly by the sight of their van turning, tires squealing, into the lot.

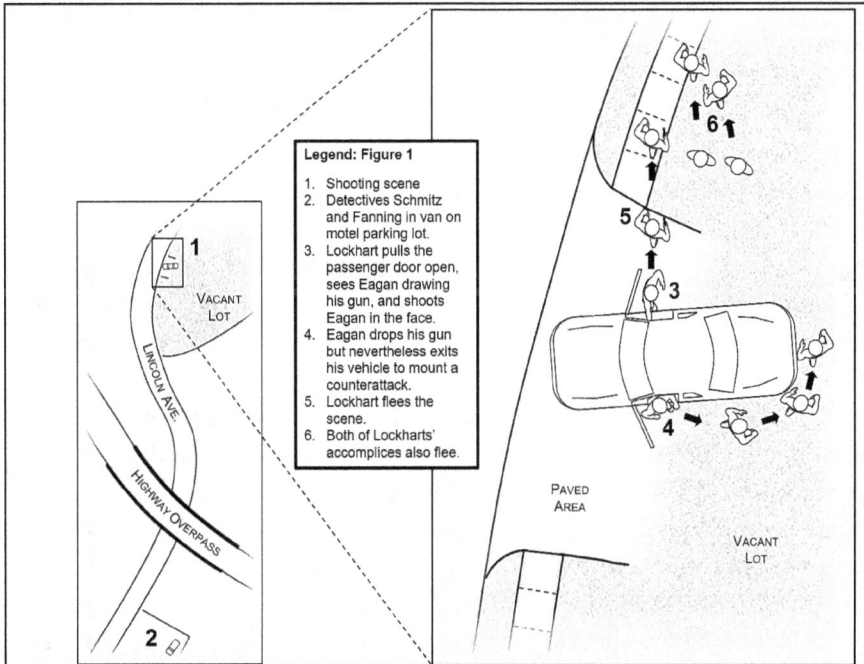

Legend: Figure 1

1. Shooting scene
2. Detectives Schmitz and Fanning in van on motel parking lot.
3. Lockhart pulls the passenger door open, sees Eagan drawing his gun, and shoots Eagan in the face.
4. Eagan drops his gun but nevertheless exits his vehicle to mount a counterattack.
5. Lockhart flees the scene.
6. Both of Lockharts' accomplices also flee.

FIGURE 1: Eagan starts to draw his gun when Lockhart attempts to carjack his vehicle, but is shot and loses his gun before he can complete the draw. He exits his vehicle to mount a counterattack, prompting Lockhart and his accomplices to flee.

Their arrival brought him comfort, but it was soon replaced with a rush of determination. "I'm not going to die," he thought, "Not on this shit-hole parking lot in the middle of the night, just before Christmas."

As the two detectives jumped from the van, Eagan took control and told one of them, Matt Schmitz—a 35-year-old, 15-year veteran of the department and close friend—to take him to the hospital. The stunned detective, shocked by the sight of his friend's torn and bloodied face, tried to argue with him. "Where is it? Where's the closest damn hospital?" he pleaded, "You need an ambulance!"

Despite his fearful wound, Eagan defaulted to his instinctive focus on concern for others. He knew he might well die, and he didn't want either of the detectives to feel any responsibility for his death. Asking them to make any critical decisions about his medical care would significantly increase that risk, and he refused to let that happen. "Don't worry," he said, "Just drive me there. I'll show you the way."

Then he turned to the other detective, 32-year-old Detective Sean Fanning, a 13-year veteran of the department, and said, "I hate to do this to you, but someone has to secure the scene. You have to stay here till we get you some backup."

"Sure, no problem," Fanning replied, "Get goin'! I can handle this."

Eagan was uncomfortable with leaving Fanning alone. It was in a high-crime area unfamiliar to the detective, but someone had to secure the scene. As he and Schmitz left the parking lot and raced down the ramp to the interstate that would take them to the hospital, he called the multi-jurisdictional communication center, told the dispatcher he had been shot and was on the way to the hospital, and asked her to send Fanning backup. She didn't believe him, and when he tried to convince her otherwise, she hung up on him. In frustrating disbelief, he called his dispatcher, told her to obtain assistance for Fanning immediately, and asked her to advise the hospital that he was on the way with a gunshot wound to the face. She called back a few minutes later, told him Fanning's backup was en route, and then added that the ER receptionist had hung up on her twice after refusing to believe what she said.

Meanwhile, Eagan was starting to feel the effects of losing so much blood when he noticed Schmitz glancing in the rearview mirror and letting his eyes linger there a bit too long. Before Eagan could ask what was going on, the detective announced, "Shit! There's a cop chasing us. What the . . ."

"Don't stop!" Eagan shouted, "Just keep goin'."

The pursuing officer was from one of the smaller suburban departments along the interstate and hadn't yet been told that a wounded officer in an unmarked van was racing through his town on the way to a hospital. But it wasn't long before he got the message and broke off the pursuit.

Meanwhile, Eagan's thoughts turned to his wife. He didn't want her to hear about the shooting from an officer sent to their home and knew she would worry less if she heard it from him. He called her, told her he had been shot, assured her that he would be alright, and asked her to come to the hospital.

Though driving at well over the speed limit, Schmitz had remained calm and in control of the van up to this point, but Eagan noticed that he might be overdoing it as they neared the exit to the hospital and asked him to slow down. The detective nodded and complied, but just enough to negotiate the exit without losing control. As they sped into the ER parking lot and up to the entrance, the absence of any hospital staff at the doors made it clear that their dispatcher's phone call was still being ignored.

Eagan was growing steadily weaker and needed help. Schmitz ran around to his door, helped him ease out of his seat, half-carried him to the entrance, and banged on its glass doors. The banging caught the attention of a pair of EMTs in the lobby, who ran out and helped drag the wounded sergeant inside and onto a gurney. As he was being wheeled into the closest available treatment room, Eagan heard a nurse express surprise that his dispatcher's phone call had been authentic, but the staff's lax attitude ended there. From that point forward, he received prompt, competent, and compassionate care.

THE AFTERMATH

Not long after his arrival, he discovered how lucky he had been. The bullet—either a .38 or .357 fired from what was later found to be a .357 magnum revolver[1]—had struck him just below the nose, traveled along the left side of his upper jaw, and exited just under his left temple. Though it had fractured his jaw in three places and shattered six teeth, it had failed to penetrate his skull. It was an excruciating wound requiring multiple complex surgeries to repair, but he left the hospital after six days and was able to return to work about six weeks later. He also learned that he had made the right decision when he decided

---

1. The diameters of .38 and .357 magnum cartridges are the same, but the .38 caliber cartridge is significantly shorter than the .357 magnum cartridge. Due to the different lengths of the cartridges they fire, the .38 caliber revolver cannot fire the longer .357 magnum ammunition, but a .357 magnum revolver can fire both the shorter .38 caliber and the longer .357 magnum ammunition.

not to wait for an ambulance. Because of the communications problems and other delays, an ambulance didn't arrive on the scene until 20 minutes after the shooting. His doctor later told him he would probably have died from blood loss if he had waited that long.

Sgt. Eagan was subsequently promoted to lieutenant and later to captain and is still serving with the same department. As further proof of his courage, love of the job, and commitment to his community, he still suffers considerable pain from his wound but refuses to take any pain medication because of the negative impact it might have on his work.

Lockhart was arrested two weeks after the shooting. He later pleaded guilty to assault of a police officer, attempted robbery, and armed criminal action and was sentenced to 30 years in prison. During the investigation leading to his arrest, it was discovered that he had carjacked another victim about three hours earlier and had run the stolen car out of gas just before the shooting. He and his two accomplices were attempting to find another vehicle to steal when they spotted Eagan and—apparently unaware that he was a police officer—decided to carjack him as well. Both accomplices were also arrested, convicted, and sentenced to ten years each.

ANALYSIS

Complacency
Complacency is an exceedingly common and dangerous problem for police officers in unknown-risk situations. In this case, the nonviolent nature of the suspects and crimes involved understandably helped lull the detectives into deciding to work shorthanded. As a result, Sgt. Eagan was working alone in a high-crime neighborhood under circumstances that required him to focus primarily on the motel instead of the secluded parking lot around him. Ironically, the suspects under surveillance had nothing to do with the shooting, but that doesn't change the fact that it was largely complacency about the surveillance that made Sgt. Eagan vulnerable to Lockhart's attack. This also highlights the reality that danger can come from unexpected sources that have nothing to do with the task at hand, which only increases the need to remain vigilant at all times.

Unfortunately, complacency is fundamental to human nature. When we repeatedly manage to deal with any given risky situation without suffering any negative consequences, we grow more comfortable doing so, which eventually causes us to let our guard down. The same is true when we become familiar with certain places or activities, like walking in our neighborhood after dark, even when we know it to be dangerous. Since we have never been threatened or assaulted so close to home, we tend to become lulled into complacency.

It is vital to our safety to eliminate or at least significantly alleviate this problem. The first step is to appreciate that anything that doesn't fit your surroundings and circumstances can be dangerous. Learn to look for anomalies and consider every one of them to be a sign worthy of further attention. Resist the temptation to base your assessment of potential dangers on your experiences, and don't try to rationalize your concerns away. This is not to say that you should overreact to danger signs; instead, use them to make you more vigilant and prepared in case they prove warranted.

Once we recognize the significance of anomalies, it is vital to enhance our ability to detect them and other danger signs. The best way to do this is to develop the Safety-First Habit. Make a game of continually scanning for things that appear out of place wherever you go and then asking yourself, "Is this something that could be dangerous, and if so, what can I do about it?" For example, if you see a person who stands out, watch him closely. Watch his body language, facial expressions, the location and movements of his hands, look for bulges or clothing that may indicate a concealed weapon, etc. What about the people around him? Is anyone shying away from him, is he paying too much attention to any of them, is there anyone else in the area who seems suspicious or appears to be acting in coordination with him? Depending upon the circumstances, you may want to leave the area immediately via the nearest exit, call the police, just watch him a little longer, etc., or you may decide that he no longer appears to be a threat. Similarly, if you start to enter a store and something seems strange (unusual silence, rushed movements or no movement at all, someone who looks like he doesn't belong, etc.), turn around, walk away and call the police if you feel it is necessary.

It is crucial to consciously engage in this indispensable mental exercise in everything you do, no matter how safe your surroundings may appear. Make a game of it, and encourage your family to join in by asking questions like, "If there was a fire in this restaurant, where would you go? Where is the closest exit and the best route to get there? What would you do if someone started shooting in here? Where is the closest cover? (Make sure they know that cover is something solid enough to stop bullets.) Where is the closest hiding place?" Don't worry about scaring them by talking about active shooters, as they will soon learn about them in school if they haven't already. It's regrettable that this is necessary, but active shootings are a terrible fact of life, and we need to be prepared to deal with them.

If practiced regularly over time, this Safety-First Habit becomes firmly ingrained in your subconscious mind. After that, it is still best to continue using it regularly at the conscious level, but your subconscious mind—which adheres to mental habits even when we are not aware it is doing so—will be playing it in the background even when you are not consciously thinking about safety. This provides a safety net when we are distracted by other concerns or otherwise not at our best.

This may appear to be a practice that could quickly lead to paranoia, but it generally has the opposite effect. As your mind becomes more adept at watching for danger signs, you develop expertise in threat assessment and start to realize that you have more control over what happens to you than you thought. This gives you greater confidence in your ability to detect and respond to danger, and as confidence grows, fear subsides.

Police officers use this habit, or ones similar to it, to maintain a high level of vigilance at all times. It can work just as well for anyone else who is concerned about his safety and the safety of his loved ones. It takes some effort, but the effort is well worth it.

Planning

In this case, a lack of planning resulted in the detectives having to work short-handed, which left Sgt. Eagan alone and highly vulnerable to Lockhart's attack. Also, it led to other problems that could have had severe consequences, including 1) dangerous confusion about the closest hospital; 2) failure to notify surrounding police departments that an officer was being conveyed to the hospital in an undercover vehicle, resulting in a high-speed pursuit and the risks it created for the officers and other motorists; and 3) a severe delay in the arrival of backup for Detective Fanning. Luckily, good fortune and Sgt. Eagan's coolheadedness after being shot kept these problems from negatively affecting the outcome, but it could have been worse.

Police officers are not the only ones who can benefit from planning. Preparation is crucial to everyone's safety. For example, it is advisable to maintain a supply of water, food, a first aid kit, and other essentials in case of an earthquake, tornado, hurricane, or other natural disasters. It is also a good idea to use security measures to keep your home safe from burglars, keep at least one fire extinguisher handy at home and preferably in your car as well, and practice fire and home intruder drills with your family. If you chose to carry a gun, you must become highly proficient with it, keep it safe from access by children, carefully follow all safety rules, and fully understand the law regarding the use of deadly force in self-defense and the defense of others. When walking or driving, always carry your cell phone, something you can use for self-defense, such as a firearm, pepper spray, a walking stick or golf club, or a pocketknife that can be opened quickly with just one hand. Teach your kids about stranger danger and other safety concerns, keep them close when taking them outside your home, and make sure to establish the kind of relationship with them that will encourage them to come to you with any fears or concerns they may have. In short, take your health and safety and that of your family seriously, and make sure you have plans in place in case the unthinkable happens.

Aiding a Seriously Injured or Ill Person
Since bleeding is the number-one cause of unnecessary traumatic deaths, everyone who is genuinely interested in helping others or protecting themselves and their families should seriously consider purchasing at least one C-A-T® tourniquet[2] and one trauma dressings for each of his vehicles. Besides providing life-saving medical gear for use in the unfortunate event of a severe car crash, these items can also help save lives in mass shootings, other shootings, stabbings, serious work and recreational injuries, natural catastrophes, and other medical emergencies.

Of course, it also imperative to be trained in how to use these implements properly. An excellent place to start is with Stop the Bleed® training. It is relatively inexpensive, and in most areas free, and provides all the basics of what one needs to know about properly applying tourniquets, dressings, and otherwise controlling life-threatening bleeding. Classes are relatively short (no more than three hours) and are accredited by FEMA, Homeland Security, National Association of Emergency Medical Technicians, International Association of EMTs and Paramedics, etc.

For more information on this lifesaving training, visit the Stop the Bleed® website at https://www.stopthebleed.org/training, and to sign up for a class, visit their Get Trained page at https://cms.bleedingcontrol.org/class/search.

---

2. C-A-T (Combat Application Tourniquet) is a brand name for tourniquets that are designed to be easily applied to oneself or another with one hand in the field. There are other brands of similar tourniquets, of course, and the use of the term CAT is meant here to be applied generically to any of them. However, it should be noted that the CAT is considered the best by many professionals.

Unfortunately, this training is not currently available in some parts of the country, but the website promises that more areas will soon be covered. It also suggests that visitors refer to the "Resources" tab for training materials regarding techniques you can use to control excessive bleeding. To access this resource, return to the home page by clicking on "Home" on the top bar, and then click on "resource hub." Stop the Bleed® can also be reached by phone at 312-202-5790 or email at stopthebleed@facs.org.

While it is crucial to help those suffering from gunshot wounds and other bleeding emergencies, we cannot forget those who are the victims of other more common medical emergencies like heart attacks, strokes, other serious illnesses, overdoses, fractures, burns, etc. Such medical emergencies occur far more often than significant bleeding and can happen at any time to any one of us, our loved ones, friends, neighbors, or fellow citizens. And it is relatively easy and inexpensive to prepare for them. The American Red offers training in first aid, CPR (cardiopulmonary resuscitation), and the use of AEDs (automated external defibrillators), which, when combined with Stop the Bleed® training, will enable you to provide lifesaving aid in just about any medical emergency.

To sign up for the Red Cross training, or for more information on their courses, visit their training website at https://www.redcross.org/take-a-class, click on the "Find a class" pull-down menu in the upper right corner, and then choose the "First Aid" option at the top of the list. If the city where you reside isn't already showing in the window to the immediate right of the "Find a class" window, enter it or your zip code, and click on the arrow to the right. This will take you to another page with a list of classes in your area and their locations, dates, and costs. Costs vary, but they are ordinarily in the range of $70.00-$130.00 for either the *Adult and Pediatric First Aid/CPR/AED* (preferable for younger parents and those who regularly deal with children) or the *Adult First Aid/CPR/AED* courses. In most areas, both of these courses are available as strictly in-class courses or, far more commonly, blended courses (an online portion followed by an in-class applied skill session). The blended courses (indicated on the webpage with the words "online + classroom" in the column to their right) are generally cheaper and require less time in the classroom, but the strictly in-class courses (indicated by the word "Classroom" in the column to the right) have the advantage of allowing more interaction with, and feedback from the instructor. The Red Cross can also be reached by phone at 888-232-9675, by email at support@redcrosstraining.org, or one of their local offices via an online search for "Red Cross."

Also, consider purchasing *The Street Officer's Guide to Emergency Medical Tactics* by Capt. Eric M. Dickinson,[3] or the *First Aid for Gunshot Wounds Pocket Guide*, by Rick Hammesfahr, MD, and Dwayne McBryde. The Street Officer's Guide can be purchase at https://www.amazon.com/Street-Officers-Emergency-Medical-Tactics/dp/1608850269 and The First Aid for Gunshot Wounds can be purchased at https://www.cheaperthandirt.com/u.s.-law-shield-first-aid-pocket-guide-for-gunshot-wounds/FC-9780692779644.html.

Emotional support for the victim is also vital when providing first aid to the severely sick and injured. For example, Det. Schmitz stayed calm while driving to the hospital and encouraged Sgt. Eagan by confidently assuring him he would be alright. His demeanor and actions highlight a vital point regarding medical aid to seriously injured people. Since the subconscious mind is highly susceptible to outside suggestions during a crisis and can hear what is being said even when the victim is unconscious, words can have a powerful impact on the victim's ability to overcome his injuries, regardless of his level of consciousness. If you appear frightened or discouraged, he may panic, experience shock, or even give up. By contrast, if you appear calm and confident about his ability to overcome his injuries, he is much more likely to pull through. Regardless of the seriousness of the victim's injuries, keep telling him that help is on the way, that he will make it, and that he can overcome his injuries. Such positive talk will give him indispensable reassurance and reinforce his will to live.

Also, if it becomes necessary to transport a victim to the hospital in your vehicle, it is best to have a third person on board to provide emergency medical aid as needed. In the case of a facial wound like the Sgt. Eagan's, for example, the victim should have his head elevated if he is lying down, and his mouth should be swept clear of blood as necessary. The wound should not be packed, and no hemostatic (i.e., blood clotting) agent should be applied, but a dressing can be gently applied to help stem the bleeding.[ii] The second person can ensure that all this is done. He may also help stabilize the victim's neck if necessary, gently turn him on his side to keep him from aspirating blood if needed, and provide any other assistance required. If the driver is the only other person in the vehicle, he can pull over to render this kind of aid if necessary, but this will delay arrival at the hospital and may be dangerous under some traffic conditions.

---

3. The author would like to thank Capt. Dickinson of the Vinton (IO) Police Department for his assistance in researching the resources listed here.

Taking the Fight to the Enemy

Sgt. Eagan was lucky that his wound wasn't as severe as it might have been, but luck wasn't the force that drove him to counterattack. That driving force was his winning mindset and warrior spirit. Instead of giving in to the overwhelming surprise and brutality of Lockhart's sudden assault and subsequent disheartening loss of his firearm, he unhesitantly went on the offense. By putting all his effort into taking the fight to Lockhart, he caught the man off guard and snatched the crucial initiative away from him. No longer the prey, he suddenly became the hunter, and Lockhart didn't know how to handle it. Instead of pressing his advantage against his unarmed, seriously wounded victim, Lockhart instinctively turned and ran. This same overriding willingness to fight back can be applied to any of the many grave challenges we may face in life, whether they involve serious illness, severe injury, crushing relationship or family issues, deep emotional problems, or anything else that threatens our wellbeing. Keep fighting back with all you've got and more, and keep at it until you win.

There are many things we can do to prepare for and mitigate human violence, such as preplanning, awareness, and mental flexibility, but the most important thing we can do once the attack materializes is to counterattack. It is the only way to regain the advantage and force your adversary into a reactionary mode of thinking and responding. Since action is always faster than reaction, this is where you want to be. Remember, when on the defense, the best you can hope for is a tie, and a tie is unacceptable when fighting for your life. Sgt. Eagan instinctively knew this and courageously acted accordingly.

Staying focused on fighting back to the exclusion of everything else can also play a crucial role when facing other adversities in life. Don't lay down and become a helpless victim. Instead, fight back against the illness that threatens your life, the injury that threatens your physical wellbeing, the emotional obstacles that threaten your happiness, or whatever other challenge comes your way. Keep fighting, no matter what.

Winning Mindset

Sgt. Eagan possessed other essential traits of a warrior, one of which was warrior optimism, or the ability to stay focused on the positive. Warrior optimism is more than just the overwhelming desire to win; rather, it ignores all things negative in favor of focusing entirely on how to best use one's existing resources, no matter how limited they may be, to win. As such, it is an especially valuable trait when the odds are against you. For example, Sgt. Eagan didn't worry about the severity of his wound, loss of his gun, or the fact that he was alone and in a poor position to defend himself. Instead, he focused on closing in on his adversary and using his only available weapons—his hands—to defeat him. He did, however, allow himself to consider the possibility that he might die, but even then, he focused on what he could do to help bring Lockhart to justice if he didn't survive. He knew his fingerprints might be left behind if he could get his hands around Lockhart's neck, and he wanted to put them there in the hope that they could help identify the man after his death. No matter how remote the possibility of success, he optimistically did whatever he could, no matter how small, to redress his own murder.

Another essential element of the warrior mindset displayed by Sgt. Eagan was mental flexibility. Though fearfully wounded, he kept thinking on his feet. He didn't freeze up, hesitate, or remain in Lockhart's line of fire by groping around for his gun in the dark. Instead, he immediately exited the hot zone and went on the attack. When Schmitz and Fanning arrived and became confused about where to take him for treatment, he coolly decided for them, remembered to leave Det. Fanning behind to guard the scene, and then tried to call in backup for him. When the skeptical dispatcher hung up on him, he overlooked his frustration and anger and told his department's dispatcher to straighten out the problem. After juggling all these matters, and despite the fearsome amount of blood spilling from his painful facial wound, he thought to call his wife so she wouldn't have to hear the frightening news from someone else.

In the same way, mental flexibility and warrior optimism can be applied to other serious problems we may face in life. Fortunately, you can help develop and enhance these mental skills by developing the Safety-First Habit discussed above (pp. 55–56) and even by deep reading the incidents presented here. Try to anticipate what might happen next as you read through the various chapters, and make a point of asking "What" questions at key points as the stories progress: "What positive things can the officer do to win the fight?" "What mental and physical options does he have to be successful?" "What should the officer do if the offender does so and so?" "What could the officer have done differently to change the outcome?" "How can I apply what I am learning here to challenges in my own life?" This will train your brain to be more flexible and optimistic when dealing with whatever challenges come your way. It is not panacea for solving all our problems, but it will help you approach them with the right mindset.

Sgt. Eagan's concern for his wife's feelings, fear for Det. Fanning's safety and decision not to allow anyone else to make any crucial decisions about his care demonstrated another one of his warriorlike qualities—selflessness. True warriors don't put themselves in harm's way or use violence for the thrill of it; they do it because it has to be done to protect themselves or others. If we rightly define courage not as the absence of fear but the willingness to act despite it, it becomes evident that selflessness is the force behind courage. It inspires warriors to push aside their survival instinct for the sake of others, even those they don't know. Selflessness is so essential to courage that courage can hardly exist without it. Though Sgt. Eagan never got the opportunity to demonstrate his selflessness by putting himself in harm's way for someone else, his concern for others despite his wound proves that he possessed it in abundance.

CHAPTER 5

Tragedy Averted:
The Nick Ekovich Case

"If anything worthwhile comes of this tragedy, it should be the
realization by every citizen that often the only thing that stands
between them and losing everything they hold dear . . .
is the man wearing a badge."

—GOVERNOR RONALD REAGAN, SPEAKING ABOUT THE
INFAMOUS NEWHALL SHOOTING[1]

DESCRIPTION OF INCIDENT

Officer Nick Ekovich wasn't particularly concerned as he pulled up to the curb
next door to the beauty salon. 911 hang-ups were even more common in his
city than in most venues, and they were cleared as unfounded almost without
exception. Unfounded 911 hang-ups were so common, and the workload so
heavy due to recent deep manpower cuts, that the officers had gotten into the
habit of canceling their backup as soon as they were dispatched to them. Even
though the field supervisors had recently stopped this practice, no one took 911
hang-ups very seriously. In this case, it was especially easy to take the call lightly
because Ekovich had cruised past the salon a short time before, and nothing had
appeared out of the ordinary. It was also mid-afternoon—hardly a peak time
for robberies or other violent business crimes. And it was also the Friday before

---

1. The Newhall shooting occurred during a traffic stop by two California Highway Patrolman on April
6, 1970 in the unincorporated city of Newhall, California. Both of the officers who initiated the stop and
two other officers who assisted them were killed during the gunfight, making the incident one of bloodiest
shootouts in the history of American policing.

Labor Day, a popular time for small businesses to close early. Ekovich had pretty well concluded the call was unfounded, an assumption that was bolstered by what he saw when he arrived. All the lights in the front room were dark, while the lights in the back were still burning. The salon was about to close from all appearances, and the staff was cleaning up in the back.

Nevertheless, Ekovich, 51 years old and a 25year veteran of the city police department, knew better than to take any unnecessary risks. He stepped out of his cruiser and eased up to the salon's far left window. Stopping just to the left of the window, he leaned over and looked inside. It was a clear, warm day, and plenty of the late summer sunlight shined through the window to lighten the otherwise darkened front room. Ekovich paused to give the scene a good look and saw a young woman walking across the hall that led to the back door. She appeared to have come from a room on the right and headed towards a door on the left (later determined to be the color room and bathroom, respectively).

The young woman looked at Ekovich. Her face wore a calm expression that didn't change as her eyes met his. Without pause, she continued across the hallway and walked through the bathroom door. Nothing in the woman's appearance gave Ekovich any cause for alarm, and her manner and dress led him to believe she was an employee. Ekovich remained there a moment longer to check for signs of trouble. Seeing nothing out of the ordinary, he moved over to the front door and pulled it open to go inside.

The woman Ekovich had just seen was not an employee but a customer named Grace Finley, and her calm expression belied the excruciating fear in the pit of her stomach. She was living a nightmare and was too terrified to alert the officer at the window to her plight.

Just a few minutes earlier, she had been in the color room with her two-year-old son, waiting for her hair treatment to set in while the beautician cleaned up the front room. She had heard someone come into the salon and engage the beautician in conversation. When the conversation dragged on, and the beautician failed to return when expected, she walked up front with her son to investigate. The first thing she saw was a large, husky man talking to the beautician. The man instantly turned to look at Finley and then pulled a gun from his waistband and pointed it at her.

"Get over here!" he demanded.

Fear threatened to make Finley's knees buckle, but she complied. Holding tightly to her son's tiny hand, she haltingly walked toward the gunman.

The beautician was a young woman named Rita Kline. Kline was no fool, and she knew how to keep her head in a crisis. She had noticed the large man hanging around outside earlier, and something about him had made her apprehensive, prompting her to grab the cordless telephone. She had watched him closely, and when he started to move toward the front door, she punched a "9" and then a "1" into the phone. Holding the phone face down to keep the man from seeing its On light, she approached him and asked if she could be of any assistance. Though he offered no explanation for being there, he showed no interest in leaving either. Hiding her mounting concern, Kline had tried to talk him into leaving, but then Finley had shown up, and the man had pulled the gun. Then, before the gunman could turn his attention on her again, Kline punched in a second "1" and held her fingers over the earpiece to keep him from hearing the call go through.

Later, the robber, identified as James Morgan, a 35-year-old meth user with a growing and increasingly more violent arrest record, didn't look like a man to be fooled with. Like Finley, Kline didn't hesitate to cooperate. She held the muffled telephone down by her leg as Morgan herded them into the color room. Once there, Morgan spotted the phone. "Gimme that phone!" he demanded.

Devastated by this loss of her lifeline but too wise to argue, she pushed the Off button and handed the telephone over.

"Wait here!" Morgan commanded and returned to the front of the salon. The two women could see the lights go out in the front room, followed by the sound of the front door closing. Dark despair fell over them as they heard Morgan returning. A moment later, he stepped back into the room, "Gimme all your money!" he growled, "Jewelry, credit cards—everything you got!"

As the two frightened women emptied their purses, pulled off their jewelry, and started to hand all of it over to Morgan, they heard someone enter the salon through the front door. "What's goin' on here? Where is everybody?" came the voice of the salon owner, Dana Schmitt, followed shortly by her appearance in the doorway.

Morgan was already moving toward the door. He grabbed Schmitt by one arm, announced the robbery, and ordered her to hand over all her valuables. Without argument, she nervously complied with the request as Morgan stuffed his pockets with the booty. "Is this all you got?" he asked in a threatening tone.

"That's everything," Kline said as the other two women nodded their heads in agreement.

"O.K., everybody in the bathroom!" Morgan commanded as he motioned across the hall. Then, looking at Kline, he said, "You first!"

Kline sensed the danger of being cornered in a confined area. But she could see no alternative to compliance and headed for the bathroom. Morgan was no longer holding the gun, but she was sure he still had it close at hand. With her senses numbed by dread, she stepped into the bathroom, followed almost immediately by the owner with Finley's son in tow. As the two women stood waiting for Finley to enter the room, Kline realized there might be some safety in moving as far out of Morgan's line of fire as possible. She suspected he intended to kill them and didn't want to be caught out in the open. She stepped into the toilet stall, climbed up onto the bowl, and hunkered up against the wall. Finley came in at just about the same time, stepped up to the two women, and excitedly whispered, "There's a cop outside! I think he's comin' in."

In the meantime, Morgan had also spotted Ekovich. He snatched one of the spare smocks off its hook, pulled it on, and headed for the front room.

Ekovich didn't feel threatened as he stepped through the front door, but he knew better than to let his guard down. Still scanning for anything unusual, he unsnapped his holster, wrapped his fingers around the grip of his .45 caliber Glock, and left his hand there as he stepped inside. Almost immediately, he spotted someone coming down the hallway from the back room. It was a rather large man in his 30s, wearing a smock. "Must be another employee," he thought as he eyed Morgan closely.

Morgan didn't seem nervous or uncomfortable about Ekovich's presence. "We got a 911 hang-up call here," Ekovich said, "Is everything OK?"

"Everything's fine," Morgan answered pleasantly.

Morgan had approached casually, his movements unrushed and calm, and his attitude didn't change as he kept walking at the same unhurried pace. He turned to his left, strode over to one of the nearby workstations, and stepped up to a small table with a black fanny pack resting on top of it. He casually reached into the fanny pack as if to retrieve identification from inside. It wasn't especially unusual for people to get their ID without being asked, and Morgan's mannerisms gave no indication that he had anything else in mind.

Suddenly, Morgan's hand flashed back into view. It held a Smith & Wesson 9 mm that belched flame almost before it cleared the top of the fanny pack. The muzzle flashes bloomed savagely in the darkened room as Ekovich drew his gun and returned fire. Ekovich hadn't expected this, but the surprise didn't delay his response as he fought back. It seemed unlikely that either man would miss at this range, but Ekovich felt no impact or pain from Morgan's bullets, nor did he worry about it. His focus was on Morgan, who wasn't going down under the barrage of the.45 caliber slugs spewing from his Glock. The big man was advancing toward him, still shooting and showing no signs of giving up!

"I have to shoot him in the head," Ekovich thought to himself.

He raised the Glock, pointed it at Morgan's head, and snapped off another round. Morgan flinched and then crumpled to the floor (Figure 1). Ekovich immediately looked at his gun and saw that its slide was forward. Now confident that he had at least one round left,[2] he kept the .45 trained on Morgan and backed off to the front door for cover. Morgan lay there in motionless silence. Ekovich had witnessed death many times in his long career and had no doubts that Morgan was dead.

After backing out of the front doorway, he holstered his Glock and reached for his shoulder mic with his left hand—or at least tried. His left arm refused to move. He looked down and saw the arm hanging limply by his side, drenched in blood. Morgan had fired five times, and three of those shots had hit Ekovich's

---

2. The slide, or upper portion, of semiautomatic handguns slide back after a round is fired, and then forward to their original position again to ready the weapon for its next shot. This occurs with each shot until the final round is fired, at which time the slide stays to the rear, thereby indicating the gun is empty.

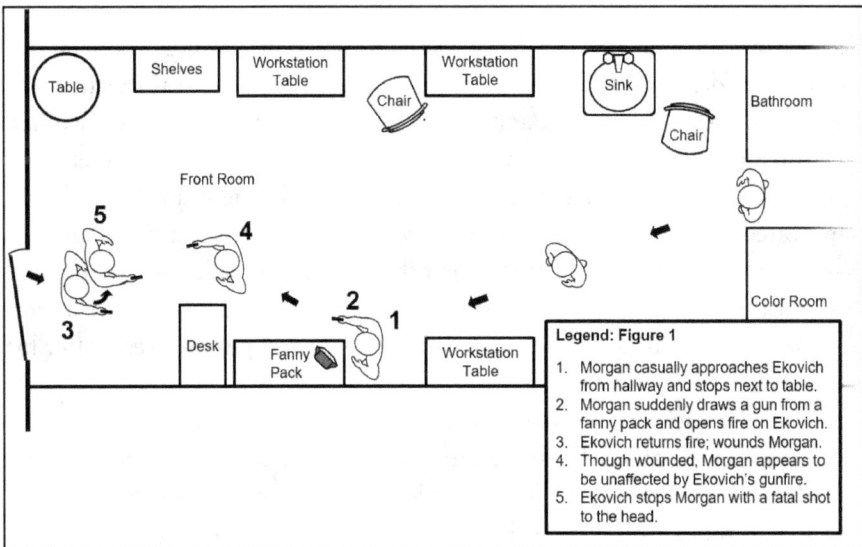

Legend: Figure 1

1. Morgan casually approaches Ekovich from hallway and stops next to table.
2. Morgan suddenly draws a gun from a fanny pack and opens fire on Ekovich.
3. Ekovich returns fire; wounds Morgan.
4. Though wounded, Morgan appears to be unaffected by Ekovich's gunfire.
5. Ekovich stops Morgan with a fatal shot to the head.

FIGURE 1: Morgan pulls a gun from a fanny pack and opens fire on Officer Ekovich. Ekovich returns fire and fatally wounds Morgan.

left arm. One had slammed into the upper arm, fracturing the humerus, and the other two had struck the forearm, cracking the ulna and tearing a path along the radial nerve. Morgan's remaining two rounds had also landed on target, and if it had not been for Ekovich's body armor, they would have inflicted devastating, if not fatal, wounds. Though both had struck center chest, they had caused nothing more than the deep bruises common to body armor hits. It is believed these were Morgan's first two shots.

Ekovich's arm was now useless and bleeding profusely, but he didn't let it bother him. Instead, he focused on what he had to do next. Using his good right hand, he keyed his shoulder mic and called for help. That done, he knew it was time to tend to his wounds. He leaned against the doorframe, eased himself down into a sitting position, and began to apply direct pressure to the brachial artery to stop the bleeding. It was then that he noticed the Glock at his feet. He had unwittingly missed his holster and let the gun drop to the floor. Keeping an eye on Morgan, he made up his mind to grab the gun if he saw any movement and then kept up the pressure on his bleeding arm. Moments later, one of the women showed up with a towel, which he used to help control the bleeding while awaiting backup.

THE AFTERMATH

Backup officers and an ambulance were not long in coming. Morgan was pronounced dead at the scene, as expected. Ekovich had fired thirteen of the fourteen rounds in his Glock, and all but two had found their mark. Two had hit Morgan in the right arm, one through the heart, seven in the other parts of the torso, mostly in vital areas, and the last one in the head. Ekovich was transported to the hospital, where he began his long recovery. The damaged nerve eventually regenerated itself, the other injuries healed, and, after a year of extensive rehabilitation, he returned to work. He went on to retire after a 30-year career on the street but regretfully passed away just two years after his retirement.

While Ekovich was in the hospital, Finley's husband came to visit him. He told the wounded officer he wanted to thank him for saving his wife and son's lives. He was probably right. The investigation had revealed that Morgan was planning to murder his victims, including the Finleys' young son, after robbing them. Officer Ekovich had done his job superbly well.

ANALYSIS

Danger Signs

The "routine" nature of police work can lead to some highly dangerous assumptions. Time and time again, silent alarms, 911 hang-ups, and other potentially dangerous calls are unfounded. Consequently, officers tend to dismiss them as false unless there is clear evidence to the contrary. This makes for a perilous blend of dangerous assumptions and complacency.

Closely associated with the problem of dangerous assumptions is the tendency of all human beings, police officers included, to miss danger signs. Though most danger signs are subtle and easy to miss if one is not looking for them, it is extremely rare for any attack—or any other threat to our safety for that matter—to occur without at least some forewarning. In this case, for example, despite the upcoming holiday weekend, it was still early for the salon to be closed, and Mrs. Finley's neutral response to Ekovich's presence was rather unusual. Most people react with surprise, concern, puzzlement, or even alarm when an officer unexpectedly shows up. In retrospect, it appears that Mrs. Finley was afraid to betray any emotion, which is a possibility any officer would do well to consider in any similar situation. Finally, it was also unusual that Morgan walked directly to his fanny pack without asking permission or explaining why. Although not unheard of, this kind of behavior was rather unusual and indicated that Morgan was highly focused on a particular course of action. Such single-minded focus is often associated with a committed intention to attack.

None of these danger signs alone were strong enough to set off alarm bells or necessitate extreme defensive measures. This is a common problem for police officers and citizens alike because most subtle danger signs turn out to be unfounded, desensitizing us to all but the most obvious ones. Moreover, since we are taught from an early age to suppress our more basic instincts (e.g., the instinctive urge to punch others who anger or frighten us, to urinate in public, to wait for one's turn to eat when hungry, etc.), we learn to ignore our ambiguous fears as well.

All officers are well aware of these deadly phenomena, of course, which is why they are so careful to combat them by using street-proven precautionary tactics (e.g., approaching citizens cautiously, using cover, watching people's hands, etc.) and issuing what may appear to be unnecessary commands (e.g., ordering citizens to keep their hands out of their pockets, stop moving around, stay in their vehicles, etc.). It is not hard to see why citizens are sometimes offended when officers firmly assert control by their words and actions. However, it is important to understand that they are trained to maintain firm control of street encounters to prevent things from escalating into violence. True, it can be unpleasant to be treated in this way, but these precautions are necessary for the safety of both the offended party and the officer.

A dramatic example of why such precautions are indispensable to the safety of citizens as well as officers comes from this author's personal experience. Many years ago, I stopped a young man for running a stop sign, obtained his driver's license, and returned to my cruiser to check his license and conduct a routine check for wants and warrants. This was several years before police cars had onboard computers, and a few minutes later, the dispatcher told me the driver was an armed and dangerous escapee.

I immediately exited my car with my shotgun, took cover behind my car door, charged the shotgun, released the safety, and leveled it at the young man. Then, I ordered him to open his car door and slowly exit the vehicle. He readily obeyed without comment, and I could see his left hand. It was late at night, but there was a streetlight slightly behind me and to my left, and it illuminated most of the driver. However, his right side and hand were hidden in deep shadows. As he moved—thankfully slowly in obedience to my instructions—his right hand came into view. It was holding a shiny black object in a manner that extended forward of his fist like a handgun. My trigger finger immediately came to rest on the shotgun's trigger and started to tense in readiness to pull it to the rear. But I knew I was well-armed and in a superior tactical position that would enable me to fire the first shot if he pointed his "gun" at me. I distinctly remember thinking, "You have the advantage, Brian. You don't have to shoot yet. Just hold off for a little longer to make sure that is actually a gun."

Then, as the "gun" came further into the light, I saw a crease along its top edge. It was a wallet, but he was holding it with just two or three fingers on the side away from me and his thumb resting along the side facing toward me, much like one would hold the grip of a pistol with its frame and barrel pointing forward. Relieved, I arrested the young man without further incident and took him to the station for booking. Before I had finished, the dispatcher called to tell me he had made a mistake. The young man was not the wanted subject. After I released my "prisoner" with my deepest apologies, he told me he was a college student coming home from a date.

Under the circumstances, it is doubtful I would have been charged with a crime or successfully sued if I had shot him. But I would have had to live with what I had done, and a fine young man would have been severely wounded or worse. Many times since then, I have thanked the good Lord that I issued the appropriate commands and was in a good enough tactical position to hold off just a split-second longer before pulling the trigger.

Trusting Your Instincts

While the rest of this book focuses on what we can learn from the officers whose stories are told here, we must not ignore Rita Kline, the young beautician who so heroically dealt with the nightmare unfolding around her. She trusted her instincts when she saw Morgan lingering outside and did something about it. Even though she couldn't put her finger on exactly why she was suspicious, she took the wise precaution of dialing "9-1" and holding the phone face down to hide its light from Morgan. She then kept her cool as she tried to talk him into leaving, and she might have succeeded if Ms. Finley hadn't appeared when she did. Later, when Morgan noticed the phone, she punched in the final "1" and held her fingers over its earpiece to prevent him from hearing the call go through. This was a magnificently wise and brave thing to do, and it probably saved everyone's life by bringing Officer Ekovich to the scene in time to prevent their murders.

The key here is that Kline didn't question her instincts but used them to summon help instead. The fear instinct is a natural survival tool that warns us of danger, often even before we know why, and it should never be ignored or explained away. Like Ms. Kline, we usually don't need to do anything drastic when we feel uneasy or afraid, but we need to acknowledge what it may mean to our safety, stay calm, and plan what to do next. By her courageous example, she showed us how to use our natural warning system to stay safe.

Unsafe Subconscious Reactions

As crucial as trusting our instincts is to our safety, it is also beneficial to resist the urge to panic or otherwise react to them inappropriately. For example, if Ms. Kline panicked instead of keeping her cool, it is quite possible that Morgan would also have panicked or reacted with anger, with tragic consequences.

This problem can be alleviated by developing the Safety-First Habit discussed in the previous chapter (pp. 55–56). By teaching our brains to stay focused on safety as we continuously scan for and analyze possible danger signs, we develop threat assessment expertise. But more than that, we develop confidence in our ability to protect ourselves, and this confidence also helps us stay calm under pressure, which leads to better decision-making when in danger.

Using appropriate tactics and safety protocols can also help. When we do this, it helps us stay focused on safety, which keeps us from responding entirely on instincts during an emergency. For example, be a responsible gun owner. Memorize the four primary rules of gun safety,[3] secure your guns when not in use, and carefully follow all range safety rules when practicing. And if you carry a gun in public, don't be satisfied with what you learn in your state-mandated concealed carry training. Practice hard and often until you become proficient because you don't want to hit an innocent bystander if you are ever unfortunate enough to get into a gunfight. It is also worthwhile to thoroughly learn how to handle the firearm to prevent fumbling with it under stress and avoid accidental discharges. Finally, learn common firearms tactics, like the use of cover and concealment, maintaining a safe distance, escaping the hot zone, shooting from various positions, shooting with the support hand only, reloading under stress, etc. And then visualize using these tactics to precondition your mind to use them in an emergency.

Similarly, follow good safety protocols when driving. Drive carefully and defensively, obey all traffic laws (as corny as it may sound, they are there for everyone's safety), maintain a high level of awareness, and never text, drink or take drugs while driving. The same care in following safety procedures should be applied to everything you do at home, work, and play. Accidents can occur at any time, and there is no way to turn the clock back after tragedy strikes.

Sudden Attacks

This case provides a vivid example of the speed at which most attacks against police officers occur. Officer Ekovich barely had time to spot Morgan's gun before the man opened fire, let alone time to pull his gun and return fire. Like the vast majority of police gunfights, the entire gun battle lasted mere seconds. As also happened in this case, they almost always come as a surprise, especially

---

3. These four rules are: 1) ALWAYS treat all guns as if they are loaded, 2) NEVER point a gun at anything you are not willing to destroy (i.e., keep all guns pointed in a safe direction), 3) ALWAYS keep your finger off the trigger and outside the trigger guard until you are on target and ready to shoot, and 4) ALWAYS be sure of your target and what is behind it. There are other safety rules as well, especially regarding storage, and every gun owner should know them as well.

when the officer is handling an unknown- or questionable-risk incident[4] or has no clear warning of danger. This puts police officers at a severe disadvantage when attacked. The only effective way for them to lessen this danger is always to be ready for anything, which sometimes requires them to say or do things that may offend some citizens.

Officers use various mental tools to enhance their ability to spot and respond to danger signs quickly, and these tools can be used by other citizens as well. First, they frequently remind themselves that danger signs are often subtle and are usually followed by more danger signs. They also make a practice of learning what to watch for. A lot of this comes from their police experience, but any citizen can make a point of identifying cover and escape routes when they are out in public, watching for telltale bulges that may indicate someone is carrying a gun, going online to research body language that warns of a possible attack, etc.

Like police officers, citizens can also make a habit of constantly scanning for anything that seems out of place, no matter how subtle it may be, and then doing something about it. This is not to imply that you need to overreact because it is usually enough just to slow down or scan for other possible danger signs, all the while thinking about how you will respond if your suspicions prove correct. Even in more serious cases where you feel more is needed, you can often deal with the problem by simply avoiding it. For example, if a suspicious character is lurking nearby as you walk down the street, turn around and go the other way, otherwise change your route, go to a safe, well-lit place like a filling station or store, etc. And, of course, call 911 if your gut tells you it may be necessary. Don't be reluctant to call the police. They don't mind, and in fact, most officers relish the opportunity to help citizens who are afraid or otherwise in need of their assistance.

In some mercifully rare situations, your suspicions may alert you to a danger that occurs so quickly that you don't have time to call the police, thus compelling you to use force. If that happens, act decisively without warning, with as much force as the law allows, and whenever possible, use your defensive response to distract your assailant and allow you to escape. Then, move far enough away to remove yourself from immediate danger, call 911, and if possible, move to a safer location. There is one exception to this advice, however. If you are ever unfortunate enough to be compelled to use deadly

4. A questionable-risk incident is one that is carries less risk than a high-risk incident (e.g., in-progress burglaries or robberies, man-with-a-gun calls, etc.), but greater risk than unknown-risk activities (e.g., accident and crime reports, traffic stops for minor traffic violations, etc.). 911 hang up calls fall into this middle category.

force[5] in self-defense, move to a place as close to the scene as safety allows, and then wait there for the police. This is critical because leaving the scene would make it appear that you were hiding something. Even if you could offer a reasonable explanation for leaving, this would make it harder to defend your actions in court.

Watching the Hands

Officer Ekovich reacted quickly to Morgan's surprise attack, but he probably could have reacted even faster if he had been able to watch Morgan's hands more closely. This is beneficial for other citizens as well. The hands are the most dangerous part of any assailant's body. They hold weapons, and even empty hands can cause severe injuries and even death, especially when the attacker is a skilled fighter or exceptionally strong. Make a point of watching any suspicious person's hands, and be extra wary if you see any telltale bulges or other indications that he may be armed. Also, be especially suspicious if he appears to be trying to keep his hands out of sight, as he may be trying to hide the fact that he is holding a weapon.

And don't hesitate to move to safety and call 911 anytime you see someone holding an unholstered handgun or uncased long gun, unless he is a police officer, of course. Most states currently allow law-abiding citizens to carry concealed firearms, and many also allow open carry (i.e., guns not concealed from view). However, that doesn't mean they can legally brandish them without good cause. For some inexplicable reason, people sometimes fail to call the police as soon as they see someone approaching a location with a gun in hand. Perhaps, they are so busy fleeing or trying to hide that they forgot to call or don't want to look foolish if it proves to be a false alarm. But we can't afford to ignore the possibility of a mass shooting in today's culture. Remember, the sooner the shooter is stopped, the fewer lives will be lost.

Post-Shooting Tactics

Any citizen unfortunate enough to be compelled to seriously injure or kill an attacker in self-defense can learn invaluable lessons from how Officer Ekovich

---

5. Deadly force is any force that can be reasonably expected to kill or seriously injure another person, regardless of the actual results of its use. For example, shooting a firearm at someone is deadly force, even if the bullet doesn't harm him or anyone else. Also, since pushing someone cannot be reasonably expected to seriously injure or kill under most circumstances, it is not generally considered deadly force, even if the person falls, strikes his head, and dies. This would still be a homicide, but probably not murder. However, if the person was obviously in frail physical condition, standing on the edge of a cliff, etc., the offender would probably be charged with murder.

handled the immediate aftermath of his shooting. Often, the natural human tendency is to go to the downed person's aid, shift your attention to your wounds, stand transfixed in dismay or disbelief, etc., but such behavior can be catastrophic. As noted elsewhere in this book, multiple hits to vital organs cannot be relied upon to stop a determined attacker immediately. Even someone who appears dead or otherwise fully incapacitated may still have the ability to launch one final deadly attack suddenly.

It is far safer to follow Officer Ekovich's example by immediately retreating to cover while keeping your attacker at gunpoint (make sure to remove your trigger finger off the trigger and place it outside the trigger guard first). Next, while continuing to stay behind cover with your gun drawn, take a few deep breaths to calm down, and then think about your next move. You will have to call 911 as soon as possible, but since the police may arrive at any moment with drawn guns, it is imperative to decide the best way to protect yourself from being mistaken for the "bad guy." Move as far away from your assailant as you can, holster your gun, and keep a wary eye on him—preferably from behind cover—while you call 911. Tell the dispatcher you have just been involved in a shooting. Give your location and description, your assailant's description and condition, and any other information you deem necessary to your safety. Then carefully follow the dispatcher's directions as you wait for officers to arrive. If possible, ask a bystander to meet the officers when they arrive and inform them about the situation, including your description, location, and the fact that you are not the offender. Finally, ask him to escort the officers to you so that he can point you out.

As soon as you hear/see the police show up, raise your hands, don't make any sudden moves, and slowly do exactly what they say. Remember, they may rudely order you to lay face down or even, in some extreme cases, shove you to the ground. And you can count on being handcuffed until the situation is clearly under the officers' control. As unpleasant as this may be, don't resist. You can always complain later if you feel you were unjustly manhandled.

Also, keep in mind that it is not uncommon for several officers to issue loud, sometimes conflicting commands simultaneously. One of the perceptual distortions that occur in human beings during chaotic, high-stress situations is auditory exclusion, or the failure to consciously hear many of the voices and other sounds around us. As a result, they may not hear the other officers shouting commands, or they may be so focused on issuing their commands that they ignore others.[6] This makes it all the more necessary to stay calm, not make any sudden moves, and not argue.

However, there may be a time when you cannot holster or move away from your assailant, either because he is still mobile with his firearm within easy reach or for some other reason. In that case, it is imperative not to have your back to the police with your gun drawn when they arrive because they may startle you as they approach, causing you to turn toward them with your gun still in hand instinctively. Regrettably, that can have tragic consequences if the officers mistakenly believe you are the offender turning around to shoot them. So, try to determine from which direction they will come and watch closely for their arrival while still keeping one eye on the gunman. If you are in a poor position to do this, quickly move to a better one that preferably gives you cover from your assailant and be ready to move again if the police approach from an unexpected direction. As soon as you see them approaching you, slowly lay your gun on the ground unless the risk of being shot by the offender outweighs the danger from the police. Fortunately, it is exceedingly rare that you will have to keep your gun trained on your assailant, but if that happens, immediately remove your finger from the trigger and place it solidly against the frame of the gun. Then raise your free hand and, in as clear and calm a voice as you can muster, tell them you believe the downed gunman is still dangerous. They may tell you to drop your gun, in which case freeze in place while calmly verbalizing that you will fully obey their commands and mean them no harm. Then, with your finger off the trigger, slowly lower the gun to the ground and let go of it. Of course, if it appears that they mean you drop the gun rather than lower it onto the ground, do it. The cost to repair or replace it is not worth risking your life. Again, follow their orders explicitly.

As you can see from the foregoing discussion, there is a lot to consider before carrying a firearm. Guns offer the absolute best defense against lethal threats, but they also entail some serious risks that many fail to recognize. If you chose to carry a gun, make sure to consider all the risks, and please don't be content with the minimal training required to carry it. Train until you are highly proficient with it, totally familiar with all gun safety rules, have obtained a full understanding of the laws related to the use of deadly force, and can handle the gun in a responsible and tactically sound manner. This includes

6. Since it takes a great deal of training to override this and other natural physiological human tendencies, few if any officers are adequately trained to overcome this problem. Police trainers may eventually find a way to do it affordably, but as with other severe deficiencies in police training, it will probably be a long time coming.

post-shooting tactics, tactical approach and positioning, malfunction drills, reloading, drawing and reholstering the firearm, decision-making under stress, and many other essential skills.

Never forget that you assume a grave responsibility by carrying a gun with severe moral, legal, financial, and emotional consequences if you use it irresponsibly. If you chose to carry one, train hard and train often.

Rights versus Responsibilities

Every person who chooses to carry a firearm regularly must carefully consider what that means. With every right comes a responsibility to use it properly and in a way that benefits others as well ourselves. A firearm has an enormous capacity to kill and otherwise negatively impact others, and it is the duty of every lawful gun owner to take that awesome responsibility seriously. If you chose to exercise your right to bear arms, never abuse it by forcing your will on others, for selfish gain, or, most significantly, in a manner that threatens the lives of other innocent citizens.

Finally, do some soul searching about the incredible power for good that this constitutional right offers you. Carrying a gun gives you the ability to protect others from unthinkable harm. It can, of course, be used to protect you and your family, but what about others? In today's world of ever more mass violence and the continuing threat of terrorism, lawfully armed citizens can provide the first line of defense. Sadly, even the best-trained police officers can seldom arrive in time to stop the killing. Harsh experience has taught us that, by the time someone calls the police, the police are dispatched, and officers arrive on the scene, many innocent lives will be lost. Only someone on the scene when the shooting starts can stop the violence soon enough to make a truly significant difference. When in the right place at the right time, an armed citizen with the skill and willingness to go into harm's way for others can fulfill that momentous role. All of us who are willing to take that risk must make a solemn commitment to intervene to the best of our ability if we are ever thrust into the middle of a mass casualty incident.

Physical Conditioning

Officer Ekovich faithfully maintained a rigorous but not overly ambitious routine of running and weightlifting, even when he wasn't in the mood for it. He did about 45 minutes of heavy weightlifting every other day and light weightlifting followed by a three-mile run on the alternate days. Besides building strength, stamina, and improved reaction time, this kind of training fosters a winning mindset, aids in recovery from injuries, and helps the body stand up to blood loss. All these factors played a crucial role in Officer Ekovich's ability to win the encounter and overcome his injuries. Good physical conditioning can do the same for you when facing injuries, illnesses, and other serious challenges in your life.

Winning Mindset

It was not his good physical condition alone, however, that made Officer Ekovich a winner. He also had an especially positive and healthy attitude. He was dedicated, determined to win no matter what, and made a point of pushing himself hard. This last point is vital. Perseverance is a habit, and, like any other habit, it can be developed through repetition over time. By forcing ourselves to persist in everything, no matter how unpleasant it may be, we can eventually become habitually persistent. For example, when it comes to regular exercise, we must make a point of sticking to our routine even when we don't feel up to it. This conditions us to overcome our natural tendency to give up on unpleasant things, which can be a fatal flaw in a lifeanddeath struggle.

Officer Ekovich's positive mindset also helped him cope with the emotional aftermath of the shooting. He views police officers as defenders of the innocent and justified deadly force as a necessary part of that role. He recognized that Morgan's actions, not his, made it necessary for him to apply deadly force, thereby putting the responsibility for the shooting where it rightfully belonged—on Morgan himself. This is a healthy attitude that others would do well to emulate.

Self-Sacrifice

Officer Ekovich's perspective on his severely wounded arm provides an inspiring insight into his view of police work. Instead of focusing on the pain he suffered and the challenges he faced during his recovery, he saw the ordeal as a privilege. As a true servant-warrior, he considered it an honor to suffer for the sake of saving Mrs. Finley and her son from a terrifying death. Few police officers are ever given the opportunity to make such a sacrifice, but many would feel the same way. Police work is about protecting those who cannot protect themselves, and all officers know that protecting others sometimes requires sacrifice.

CHAPTER 6

Unarmed Lethal Encounters:
The Mark Elliott, Allen Beckman Case

"The day-to-day reality of modern policing is that the police are
increasingly the first point of contact with those suffering from
mental illness, who come to our attention not because they are evil
but because they are hurting. When . . . that hurt exceeds their
capacity to cope, it is expressed through maladaptive behavior that
becomes a problem the police must manage. And sometimes that
maladaptive behavior has terrible outcomes."

—ALTHEA OLSON

DESCRIPTION OF INCIDENT

"Al," Officer Mark Elliott said as he looked over to his right, "Look at that guy!"

Elliott and his partner Allen Beckman had just stopped for a red light at
the busy intersection while en route to a residential alarm call. Elliott and Beckman didn't usually ride together, but their regular schedules had been adjusted
to allow them to attend a couple of hours of training earlier in the evening, and
the change had made it necessary for them to partner for the rest of the shift.
Although they had only known each other for about six weeks, they got along
well. Elliott was new to the agency, but Beckman was a twelve-year veteran of the
large urban department who had worked in many of the city's toughest districts.
Elliott respected his experience and trusted him explicitly.

Though on his last night of probationary status, Mark Elliott was no stranger
to law enforcement. Before joining this department, he had spent twelve years

in the US Air Force Security Police as a patrol officer. Now 34, he was of only average height, but his solid frame held 190 pounds, and he was in good physical condition. He had wrestled in high school, received an above-average amount of defensive tactics training throughout his career, and independently obtained martial arts training. He also took training more seriously than most and had made a point of mentally preparing himself for the possibility of having to fight for his life. He had also dealt with his share of resistive individuals in the Air Force, but his precinct was one of the city's slowest, and he had yet to encounter any serious resistance. It had been a relatively uneventful first year, but that was all about to change.

The man he had just pointed out to Beckman was Ross Harris, a powerfully built 22-year-old seaman from a nearby Navy base. At six feet, three inches, Harris weighed in at 235 pounds of solid bone and muscle and was obviously in a highly agitated state of mind. Until just a few moments earlier, he had been a stable sailor with no outward signs of emotional issues or mental illness. However, while leaving a store about a block away, he had suddenly burst into a flurry of bizarre, irrational behavior. After running to the intersection, he had raced through passing traffic and was now standing on one of the concrete medians, furiously shaking his fist and screaming at cars as they sped by. The intersection was one of the busiest in the area. Even at this late hour—almost midnight—Harris had plenty of targets on which to vent his sudden anger. Neither officer could hear Harris' words above the din of the rushing traffic, but his body language made it clear he was highly distressed.

The officers watched with wonder as Harris ran frantically through the busy intersection, cars whizzing past him in both directions. They had been stopped facing eastbound on the larger of the two streets, a major nine-lane thoroughfare, and Harris had been standing in the median of the four-lane cross street, just south of the intersection. Ignoring the north and southbound traffic, he now ran across the intersection again to a Ford Taurus stopped for the light in the westbound lanes. He stopped next to the Taurus, screamed at its occupants in a frenzied voice, and banged on its roof with his huge fists.

As Beckman, who was driving, shifted into *park*, Elliott radioed in their location and advised the dispatcher they would be out with a mentally disturbed subject. As Elliott hung up the microphone, Harris turned away from the Taurus and dashed brazenly into the intersection again. Running at full tilt through the traffic toward the officers' side of the intersection, he crossed about a car length in front of their cruiser and headed straight for a Chevrolet

Impala that was passing the officers on the right. By this time, the light had changed, east-west traffic had started again, and the Impala was moving full speed through the intersection. Harris crashed solidly into the Chevy's left side while simultaneously smashing one massive fist into its side. The collision of flesh and bone into speeding steel and glass flipped Harris, as big as he was, into the air and spun him around like a twig. He crashed to the pavement as Elliott leaped from the patrol car.

Elliott had barely put one foot on the ground when Harris bounced back to his feet, seemingly unfazed by what had just happened. He looked directly at the stunned officer, threw his fists into the air, and shrieked, "You want some of this? I'm gonna f__kin' kill you!"

Instinctively, Elliott drew his 9 mm Smith & Wesson Model 469 and pointed it at Harris. "Stop right there," he commanded, "Get down on the ground!"

Harris didn't seem to hear. Instead, he kept screaming, lowered his head, and charged full speed toward Elliott. Second thoughts about pulling his gun now shot through the startled officer's mind. His opponent was obviously unarmed and didn't yet present an immediate lethal threat, but things were coming dangerously close to that point. In the meantime, Elliott's gun was thrust out in front of him, unsecured and almost within reach of a charging madman. Elliott knew he would have to do everything within his power to stop him without gunfire. But he had to secure his gun first.

Using a skill that had become second nature to him through years of practice—and with a rapidity fueled by adrenaline—he slipped the Smith & Wesson back into its holster. At the same time, he drew his pepper spray with his left hand and, while backing up and circling away from the patrol car to get away from Harris, shot a burst directly into the man's eyes. Harris didn't break stride, slow his pace, or even blink. Now within range, he threw a tremendous right hook at Elliott's head. Elliott instinctively threw his left hand up to block the blow, but too late. Harris's ham-like fist crashed into the left side of the officer's head, sending him stumbling backward and knocking the pepper spray out of his hand. A barrage of stunning blows followed as Harris grabbed Elliot by the shirt collar with his left hand and pummeled his face and head with his right.

Though still standing, Elliott was growing weaker and more disoriented with every blow. He lifted his left hand, grabbed Harris by the collar of his sweatshirt, stepped back, and pulled in an effort to pull the man off balance and take him to the ground. The collar ripped, but Harris didn't budge. Elliott used the opportunity to deliver a punch with his right. It landed solidly on the man's face but with no effect. Harris punched back, and they stood there, toetotoe, trading punches for several moments. Elliott was growing weaker by the second, and Harris was still impervious to the officer's blows. Elliott pushed away, drew his expandable baton,[1] and hit Harris twice in the legs with everything he had. Harris swung again, and Elliott countered by blasting him in the hand with the baton. Still no reaction. This had become a life and death struggle–there was no longer any doubt that he could use deadly force. Holding back nothing, he swung the baton at Harris' head with all the force he could muster.[2] The blow landed solidly on target, but even that didn't faze the man. Harris kept swinging (Figure 1).

---

1. Baton is the technical term for what is also called a nightstick, and an expandable baton is one that collapses down to a length that allows it to be carried on an officer's duty belt without dangling down along his leg, where it can get in entangled in the seatbelt or otherwise get in the way.

2. Deadly force can justifiably be used by a police officer–or any other citizen for that matter–when the individual under attack reasonably believes it is necessary to prevent him or another from death or serious physical injury. Since it had now become clear that his life was in jeopardy, Officer Elliott had the legal right to use deadly force in self-defense, including baton blows to Harris' head, even though such blows can cause death or serious bodily harm.

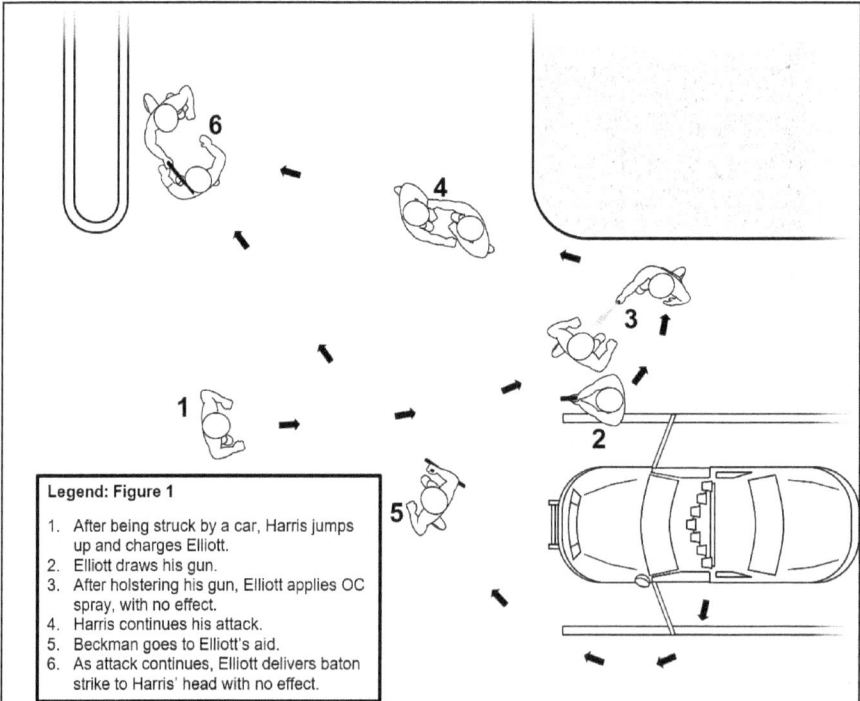

Legend: Figure 1

1. After being struck by a car, Harris jumps up and charges Elliott.
2. Elliott draws his gun.
3. After holstering his gun, Elliott applies OC spray, with no effect.
4. Harris continues his attack.
5. Beckman goes to Elliott's aid.
6. As attack continues, Elliott delivers baton strike to Harris' head with no effect.

FIGURE 1: Officer Elliott uses pepper spray against Harris to no effect, and a fight ensues. Elliott then employs his baton against Harris as Beckman arrives to assist.

Elliott could now see Officer Beckman coming up behind Harris with his PR24[3] held along his right forearm. Beckman leaned forward and slammed the baton into the back of Harris's head. This finally got the enraged man's attention, and he turned away from Elliott. As Harris turned to face Beckman, both officers struck him repeatedly with their batons. Again, the blows had no visible effect on Harris. Harris turned back to Elliott and punched him so hard in the head that it knocked him to the ground and caused the baton to fly out of his hand.

Elliott lay sprawled in the roadway, dazed and in severe pain, for several moments of sluggish semi-consciousness (Figure 2). Then, as he started to drift back into full consciousness, he made up his mind to get back into the fight. Through sheer willpower, he forced himself to stagger to his feet, only to see Harris pressing his attack on Beckman.

---

3. A PR-24, otherwise known as a side-handled baton, is a type of baton that has a short perpendicular handle extending out from the main body. The officer grips the perpendicular handle while holding the main body along his forearm, and then strikes with the baton by swinging it in an outward arch parallel to the ground as he releases his grip on the perpendicular handle just enough to let it spin in his hand. The PR-24 is an effective and highly versatile impact weapon, but is seldom used by the police today, as it has been replaced by the more compact collapsible baton.

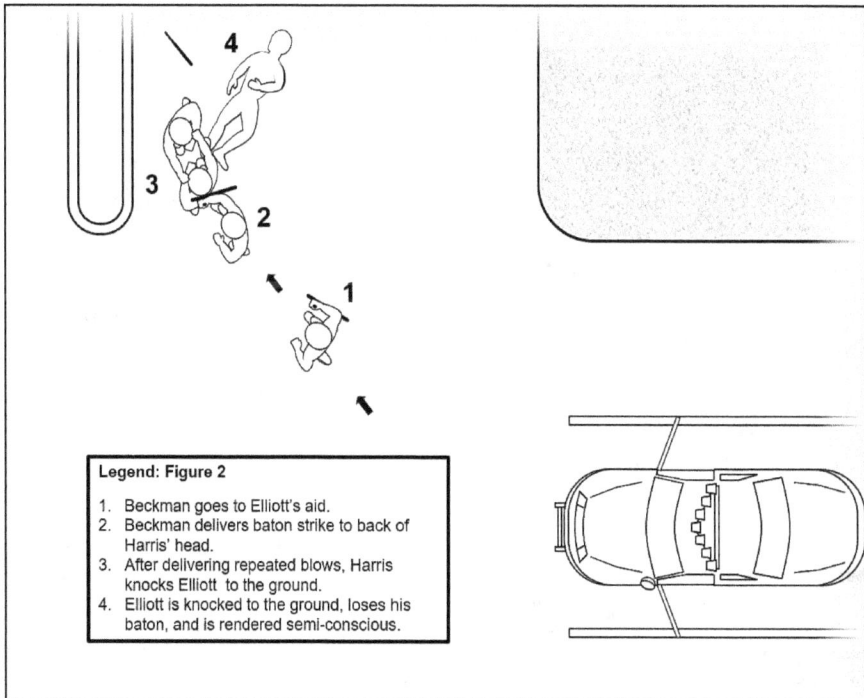

Legend: Figure 2

1. Beckman goes to Elliott's aid.
2. Beckman delivers baton strike to back of Harris' head.
3. After delivering repeated blows, Harris knocks Elliott to the ground.
4. Elliott is knocked to the ground, loses his baton, and is rendered semi-conscious.

FIGURE 2: As both officers strike Harris with their batons, Harris turns and hits Officer Elliott, rendering him semiconscious.

Beckman was backing away from Harris while striking him repeatedly with his PR-24. Ignoring the baton strikes, Harris punched Beckman again and again until one tremendous blow knocked him down. Though Beckman managed to kick Harris from the ground, Harris was unfazed. He bent over the now highly vulnerable officer and began kicking him in the head.

Elliott pulled himself erect and drew his gun again. He staggered painfully toward Harris. His vision was blurred, tunnel vision was closing in, his head was throbbing, and he had to fight to stay conscious. He knew he would have to shoot Harris, but he was concerned about hitting his partner or one of the many bystanders who had gathered to watch. He shouted at Beckman to stay down and then repeated the warning several more times as he moved forward.

Beckman stopped moving. Elliott knew he was unconscious—or worse—but he had no fight left in him. He was physically incapable of helping his motionless partner by any other means than gunfire. Following his training, he repeatedly ordered Harris to stop as he moved closer. He forced himself to look past Harris to make sure no one else was in his line of fire. He also made up his mind to fire just one shot and then reassess the situation before deciding whether to take another.

Harris turned, gave Elliott a blank stare, and took one step forward. Elliott squeezed the trigger. The 9 mm made a puny sound in Elliott's mind, like a .22 popping, but the sound of its impact was starkly different—like a sledgehammer slamming into Harris' chest. Unlike all that had transpired up to this point, the effect of the bullet was instantaneous. The man, who had seemed oblivious to everything the officers had thrown at him up to this point, slipped to the ground without a sound (Figure 3).

Elliott lowered his gun to low ready[4], cautiously approached Harris, and looked down at him. A small patch of blood about the size of a quarter stained his shirt near the center of his chest, and he showed no signs of life. Elliott knew he was dead. He lowered his hammer[5] and reholstered, both shocked by the tragedy of what had just happened and relieved that it was over.

---

4. The "low ready" position is a position in which the shooter extends his firearm toward his opponent, but keeps it pointed at the ground just below the target. This position enables the shooter to immediately raise his gun into firing position in case the target unexpectedly becomes a lethal threat.

5. Unlike revolvers and many other semiautomatic pistols, semiautomatic pistols like the one Elliott carried have a hammer that stays cocked after each shot is fired. Since a firearm is much more likely to be accidentally discharged when the hammer is cocked, such semiautomatics have a lever on the side of their slides that safely lowers the hammer to a safe position. (Single-action semiautomatics like the well-known Colt 1911 are a rare exception, as they use a safety lever to safely lock the hammer back in its cocked position).

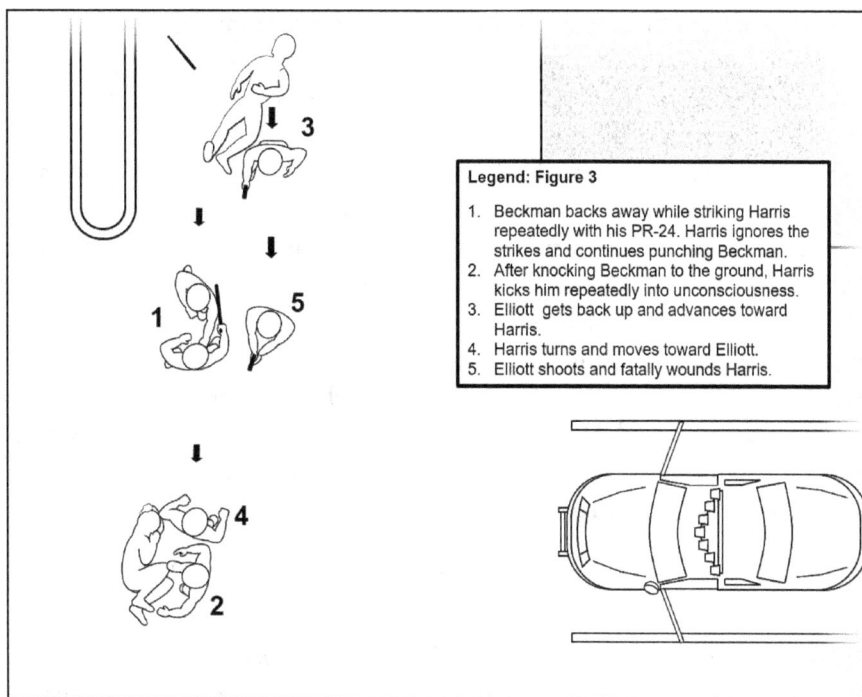

Legend: Figure 3

1. Beckman backs away while striking Harris repeatedly with his PR-24. Harris ignores the strikes and continues punching Beckman.
2. After knocking Beckman to the ground, Harris kicks him repeatedly into unconsciousness.
3. Elliott gets back up and advances toward Harris.
4. Harris turns and moves toward Elliott.
5. Elliott shoots and fatally wounds Harris.

FIGURE 3: Officer Elliott gets back up and, upon seeing Officer Beckman lose consciousness, shoots and fatally wounds Harris.

Elliott turned his attention to his partner as he grabbed his portable radio and tried to call the dispatcher. The radio didn't seem to be working, but Elliott was immensely relieved to see Officer Beckman conscious and getting to his feet. Beckman's nose was bleeding, and one eye was swollen, but he otherwise appeared to be in reasonably good shape. As Beckman reached for his radio, Elliott got his working and called for help and an ambulance.

THE AFTERMATH

Officer Elliott's single bullet—a 147-grain Hydra-Shok™ [6] —had hit Harris just right of center chest and then passed through his heart before zigzagging through his torso. After penetrating both lungs, the liver, and one kidney, the bullet had come to rest in his left hip. He had died almost instantly. Investigators later learned that Harris had suffered a rare form of mental illness that causes

---

6. Hydra-Shok™ is a brand of hollow-point ammunition considered to be one of the best rounds for use in self-defense, and is therefore often issued to police officers.

the abrupt onset of highly bizarre behavior without forewarning. Tragically, he had been a normal, well-respected member of the US Navy until just a few short minutes before the attack. The autopsy revealed no evidence of alcohol or drugs in his system at the time of his death.

Both officers were remarkably unscathed, considering the intensity and duration of Harris's attack. Officer Beckman received the more serious injuries. He suffered a serious concussion and a hairline fracture in one orbital lobe and was burdened with severe headaches for at least eight months after the incident. Elliott was luckier. Although he had received a mild concussion and his injuries were disorienting and painful, he had no broken bones and received no permanent disabilities. He did suffer painful headaches and some hearing loss for three months afterward, but these were not debilitating. Despite their lingering headaches, both officers were able to return to full duty within 30 days, even though neither one fully recovered until several months later.[7]

ANALYSIS

Police Encounters with Emotionally Disturbed Persons
This case presents a heartrending example of the challenges officers face when dealing with emotionally disturbed persons. No one wants to hurt someone suffering from mental illness, but police work requires officers to interact with these unfortunate individuals. And, like Officers Elliott and Beckman, they sometimes have no choice but to use lethal force.

Nevertheless, there can be little question that training can help officers handle these difficult situations more effectively and with a reduced risk of having to resort to force. In response to this need, many police agencies train CIT (Crisis Intervention Team) officers with special psychological training and require them to be dispatched to all calls involving emotionally disturbed persons. However, since officers are usually called only after the situation has reached a crisis point beyond others' ability to handle, this is often not enough. The scene may also be chaotic, or even unfriendly, and well-meaning, but distraught family or friends may be present to add to the problem. Even a highly educated psychologist who regularly deals with emotionally disturbed persons would find it difficult to do help under such circumstances. Yet, at best, a CIT

---

7. The incident recounted here is true, but the names were changed to ensure the privacy of those personally involved. Likewise, to preserve confidentiality and clarity, some facts have been altered slightly, but the essential elements of the story remain unchanged.

officer with far less training and experience than any psychologist will respond to the scene. And in many instances, it will be an average beat cop who is even less prepared. Remarkably, however, police officers usually get by without resorting to force using common sense and their well-honed people skills. There are some tragic exceptions to this rule, of course. Every one of them is heartbreaking for everyone involved, including the officer who must suffer the trauma of having taken a life under such circumstances. The only way to reduce these tragedies is to give officers far more and better training.

Many police agencies have been addressing this problem with more training, either because they recognize the need for it or because their state mandates it. This is long overdue, but it also comes at a price. With limited training budgets and the cost of such training, other essential training has to be eliminated or reduced to pay for it. Unfortunately, training in many areas essential to the safety of our police officers and citizens is already dangerously inadequate, and cutting back their funding will only aggravate the problem. Unless more money becomes available, we have to make some tough choices about spending our limited tax dollars for police training.

Drawing on an Unarmed Offender
Immediately upon making contact with Harris, Officer Elliott found himself in a dangerous predicament. He knew the confrontation could quickly turn deadly and instinctively reacted accordingly. Without conscious thought, he drew his gun and only then realized his mistake. The threat had not yet reached the point where he could legally or morally pull the trigger, he was now at great risk of being disarmed, and there wasn't much time to effectively secure his gun, let alone draw his pepper spray or expandable baton. Fortunately, unlike many officers, he was well trained in reholstering his firearm and switching to pepper spray instead. This enabled him to switch to a less-lethal option in time to avoid being disarmed, or more lives may have been lost.

Armed citizens may also find themselves in a similar predicament, and unfortunately, so many factors can come into play that there are no universally applicable rules for dealing with it. Generally, it is best not to draw your firearm until it is obvious that you need it, but several other crucial factors may need to be considered. These include your distance from the person confronting you; the likelihood that he is armed; his size, apparent level of physical fitness and quickness relative to yours; the presence of obstacles between the two of you; the availability of cover,[8] the presence of other potential assailants; and of course, the immediacy and seriousness of the threat.

Anyone who carries a gun should give this problem serious forethought. Think through how you would respond in various difficult situations and visualize in detail being involved in each one. Training in the skills you may need if faced with this decision can also help prepare you to handle it properly. For example, just as it is vital to practice drawing your gun, it is also important to practice holstering it. Start slowly, focusing on smoothness and proper technique rather than speed. This will allow speed to develop naturally as your technique improves. Another important component of this training is to keep looking forward, not down at your holster. This will enable you to watch your assailant closely for any threatening moves after he is down (people can still be dangerous after collapsing), or, as in this case, you must quickly reholster after you realize you have drawn your gun without enough legal justification to use it.

Consider carrying and thoroughly practicing with pepper spray or some other nonlethal option in case you are ever involved in a dangerous but nonlethal threat. Practice drawing it, properly employing it, and reholstering it to a high level of proficiency, just as you would your firearm. Then practice reholstering your gun and then switching to your pepper spray. As mentioned earlier, Officer Elliott's training in this skill helped him avoid being disarmed, and it can do the same for you. It is also imperative to emphasize that it is vital to your safety and the safety of others to never practice these drills with a functional gun anywhere except the range. Even then, only nonfunctioning guns should be used until you become proficient with these techniques. Fortunately, inert plastic training guns, AirSoft[9] guns, and barrel blocking devices[10] can be purchased for this purpose. They are relatively inexpensive and are more than adequate for practicing drawing and holstering, as well as many other valuable firearms drills, including dry fire practice[11]

---

8. Cover is anything that will protect you from gunfire. It is often confused with concealment, which can also be helpful in an armed encounter. However, concealment is simply any item or condition (e.g., shadows, bushes, running out of the assailant's view, etc.) that hides you from your assailant's view, while cover must have the ability to stop bullets.

9. An AirSoft gun is a gun that fires low-velocity plastic pellets with an exceptionally low potential for causing injuries, unless they strike someone in the eye. For this reason, it is essential that everyone participating in training with these weapons wear adequate eye protection.

10. These safety devices are inserted into the gun's barrel and firing chamber to block any ammunition from entering the firing chamber. For further information, search the internet for "barrel block dry fire."

11. Dry firing is a highly effective way to learn and refine one's ability to pull the trigger smoothly while also minimizing movement of the gun's barrel. In fact, competition shooters regularly dry fire to keep their marksmanship skills sharp. However, even professionals sometimes make mistakes and, unless the gun is rendered inoperable there is always the possibility that a live round will be left in the firing chamber. For this reason, it is vital to only practice dry firing with inoperable guns or expensive special training guns specifically designed for that purpose.

Also, keep in mind that nonlethal assaults are far more common than lethal ones, and it is crucial to be adequately prepared to deal with them as well. Therefore, both armed citizens and those who choose not to carry a firearm should also seriously consider carrying and thoroughly training with one or more less-lethal weapons[12] for self-defense. Moreover, anyone concerned about his safety should seriously consider taking some form of martial arts training, or at least a few self-defense classes. Besides providing you with valuable self-defense skills, this kind of training builds your self-confidence, which is essential to clear thinking, mental flexibility, and good decision-making. And it is good for your physical and emotional health as well.

Tasers[13]

It should also be noted that this encounter might well have been resolved without fatal results if either officer had been armed with a Taser™. These less-lethal weapons are not 100 percent effective, of course—no weapon is—but they are often highly effective against mentally disturbed individuals like Mr. Harris. Other less-lethal weapons like beanbag and rubber projectiles can also be effective in many of these cases, but Officers Elliott and Beckman were not equipped with them. And even if they had been, it is doubtful they could have gotten them out of their trunk in time to use them in such a dynamic situation. By contrast, Tasers can be carried on the gun belt, where they can be accessed immediately. This makes them much more practical for everyday duty use than bulkier, less-lethal weapons.

Unfortunately, Tasers have received bad press and undue criticism from police critics in recent years. They are often maligned as dangerous, often lethal weapons that should not be used except under the most extreme circumstances. While it is true that Tasers have occasionally been deemed to be the cause of death or–more often–a contributing factor in some deaths, this is exceedingly rare. Furthermore, every less-lethal weapon, and even many unarmed defensive measures, have been known to cause some deaths. Anytime someone engages in any kind of struggle, there is a risk of death or serious bodily harm, and Tasers are no different. However, many police trainers, including this one, are

---

12. Less-lethal weapons are weapons designed to incapacitate combative individuals without causing serious injury or death. It is important to note, however, that no weapon can be said to be entirely nonlethal, because anything used to incapacitate a person, no matter how carefully designed to cause only minimal injury, carries some risk of causing unexpected harm, especially to individuals who have underlying medical conditions and/or who overstress themselves while resisting apprehension.

13. Taser™ is actually the brand name for the most common electronic control device (ECD), but it is used generically for all ECDs, regardless of the brand. ECDs are less-lethal weapons that are quite effective at bringing resistive individuals under control. They use an essentially harmless electric charge to temporarily incapacitate the individual.

convinced that Tasers are considerably safer than any other less-lethal weapon or unarmed self-defense measure, except pepper spray. In addition, they also tend to be more effective in subduing combative offenders than any other less-lethal weapon or technique, thereby reducing the chances that the confrontation will escalate to a more dangerous level. To severely restrict their use would be dangerous not only for our officers but probably even more so for the public.

It should also be mentioned here that Taser™ makes a civilian model of their Taser. It is essentially the same as the law enforcement version, except its charge lasts a full 30 seconds after striking its target, and then automatically shuts off, whereas the law enforcement version shuts off after just five seconds. Like the law enforcement version, the civilian model is a valuable defensive weapon with little chance of causing serious harm to anyone, but it has its limitations. Also, if you plan to purchase one, make sure they are legal to own and carry in your state, county and city.

Control Tactics

Even though Officer Elliott was better trained in control tactics than most officers, nothing he tried had any visible effect on Harris. He later pointed out that the fight was too close, fast-moving, and furious to allow for the appropriate application of any established control techniques. It was, in his words, a "street brawl with no rules." The pepper spray was completely ineffective, as were his baton strikes to Harris' legs. Elliott was trained in delivering the highly effective strikes to the legs and had used them successfully on the street before, but he had already received several telling blows. He was tiring fast when he brought his baton into action, which probably reduced its effectiveness. Eventually, he was forced to resort to baton strikes to Harris' head, but even this extreme technique failed to slow the man down.

The purpose of this discussion is not to downgrade the value of police control tactics. They often work well, but they have their limits in the real world, especially when the assailant is hellbent on severely injuring or killing the officer. Nothing works all the time. Some people are immune to pepper spray, others are oblivious to pain, and even bullets can be unnervingly ineffective at times, sometimes failing to stop attackers even after a remarkably large number of hits to vital areas. For police officers, this means they must be mentally flexible enough to quickly change tactics and techniques as necessary, proficient with various techniques, and unshakable in their determination to defend themselves.

Another shortcoming in police control tactics is the difficulty in teaching them to officers. The problem here is that the number of techniques officers need to learn are numerous, including defense against multiple assailants; weapon retention; ground fighting; handcuffing; use of the baton, pepper spray, Tasers; hand, knee, and foot strikes, and many more. Also, many of these techniques are rather complex or hard to learn, and all of them are highly perishable (i.e., not easy to retain in the long term). Lastly, although learned in a controlled environment on level safety mats, in the real world, they must be executed on concrete, hard floors, or uneven ground cluttered with debris, furniture, trees, broken glass, and other dangerous objects; in closed-in spaces; and made slippery with just about any substance, including mud, filth, oil, rainwater, snow, ice, or even blood. Many fine trainers have worked hard to overcome these difficulties with considerable success, but there is still much more to be done. Training that genuinely prepares officers to effectively apply control tactics under the extreme pressure of a "street brawl with no rules" is costly in both time and money.

This case also explicitly highlights how quickly and brutally a nonlethal police encounter can escalate into deadly force. Far too often, officers must resort to deadly force because they are unable to control their adversary at lower levels of force. This is because control tactics are remarkably prone to failure when applied improperly or with too little force, which is likely to do nothing more than make the offender angrier and more aggressive. Also, with increased anger comes a higher tolerance to pain and increased aggressiveness. As a result, the officer must increase his level of force, which escalates the encounter even further.

Meanwhile, it is also likely to increase the officer's fear and stress, thereby clouding his thinking and possibly degrading his ability to make good decisions. This makes for a dangerous mix that often leads to the use of deadly force that might well have been avoided if the officer had been better trained, especially in those tragic, highly controversial cases in which the offender is unarmed. This rapid escalation of force has also led to the unnecessary deaths of police officers, most often by disarmings, but also by beatings, offenders accessing their own concealed weapons while struggling with the officer, etc.

Too many officers and citizens have died and suffered serious injuries because of the inadequacies in police control tactics training. Our officers must receive far more and far better training in these essential skills. We have countless police trainers with the ability and dedication to do it. The only thing lacking is our society's willingness to spend the money.

For citizens, this case demonstrates how dangerous an unarmed person can be and the need to be wary of anyone who appears to be highly agitated, in great emotional crisis, or dangerously aggressive. For one's physical, financial, and legal wellbeing (every violent encounter carries the possibility of civil or criminal action against the victim, regardless of how clear it is that he acted in self-defense), it is best to avoid such people and call the police to handle them instead. Also, be aware that no less-lethal weapon is completely reliable, and all have their limitations. If it is necessary to use such a weapon, the best way to employ it is to refrain from threatening your assailant with it. Rather, keep it out of sight until you need it. That way, if he starts to attack, you can surprise him by suddenly deploying it as a distraction and then running to a place of safety. Or in extreme cases, you can use the distraction to shift to a highly aggressive and violent counterattack, such as powerful blows to the throat, eyes, groin, or other vital areas. Remember, however, that such blows can be considered deadly force in some instances; therefore, they should be reserved to situations where you reasonably believe you are in danger of death or great bodily harm. Also, you may have to explain why you were not able to retreat because some states require victims to make every reasonable effort to retreat before using deadly force in self-defense.

Finally, if the situation is serious enough to require the use of force of any kind, it is no time to be shy about using it. Your goal should be to end the fight as quickly as possible, before it can escalate to a higher level. Punch as hard as you can, or if you must use a nonlethal weapon, use it as it is designed to be used (e.g., don't hit someone in the head with a steel pipe unless he is trying to kill or seriously injure you), but without hesitation or timidity. Similarly, if you are in a desperate enough situation that you must use an improvised weapon (e.g., a hammer, screwdriver, pipe, etc.) don't be afraid to use it. As long as you can legally inflict the level of injury that the particular weapon in question is reasonably likely to cause, use it with maximum power and enthusiasm.

As you can probably see from this discussion, it is vital to know and clearly understand the laws on use of force in self-defense and the defense of others, especially if you regularly carry a firearm or other deadly weapon. It is not enough to have just a passing knowledge of these laws. Instead, strive to understand them well enough to be able to apply them in the real world, quickly and under the incredible stress of combat. At minimum, study them carefully while paying close attention to every detail, and check the internet for definitions of common terms used in use-of-force law, especially "reasonable" and "totality of circumstances." If you want to take your study a step further, visualize various dangerous situations in which you must make one or more quick use-of-force decisions, and then follow up with a self-critique of the decisions you made. Were they good or bad choices? What other decisions could you have made? What might have happened if you made those decision instead? Then, go through the same process with difference scenarios. This builds mental flexibility and self-confidence in your ability to make good decisions. Also, if you have family or friends interested in this subject, you can go a step further by brainstorming or even role playing various scenarios with them

Decisive Use of Non-Lethal Force

It is easy to be shocked when viewing an officer using non-lethal force, or even when hearing about it, and to assume that he was too quick to act or too forceful in his use of force. But real-life violent encounters are never pretty. They are quick, unpredictable, chaotic, and messy. Often, the first person to land a solid blow is the winner. Police officers, whose safety depends upon ending the fight as quickly and effectively as possible, realistically view resisting offenders as a great threat to their wellbeing. If an officer hesitates too long, allows the offender to get the upper hand, prolongs the fight to the point of exhaustion (an all-out fight can bring about total exhaustion in less than one minute), the consequences can be severe. At best, the offender will escape, saving the officer from further injury but at the cost of having failed to do his duty. But there is also a significant possibility that the assailant will continue his attack with increased brutality, or even worse, disarm and shoot the officer.

Another example of the dangers of an officer using too little force can be found in the murder of a deputy sheriff in an attack that trainers have long used to emphasize the importance of decisively applying force. In that case, the deputy used his baton in an attempt to stop a motorist who had suddenly and inexplicably charged directly at him in a fit of rage but with too little force to bring him under control. Rather than submitting to arrest at that point, the motorist became angrier, marched back to his pickup truck, removed a rifle from its cab, and shot the deputy to death with nine shots to his body and a tenth through his right eye. This is but one example of how quickly a situation can escalate out of control to the point that someone dies. No doubt, non-lethal force applied with full force early in a non-lethal violent encounter is often ugly, but in the final analysis, it the best way to minimize the possibility of unnecessary serious injury or death.

This principle applies to citizens, as well as police officers. Obviously, this is not to imply that one has the right to use deadly force to defend against a nonlethal threat. For example, it would be illegal for a large, muscular young man to punch a frail older person with enough force to crush his jaw unless the older person was attempting to use deadly force against him. On the other hand, it would accomplish little, and perhaps be dangerously counterproductive, to be half-hearted about striking someone in a fistfight in which you are legally justified in defending yourself. The safest course of action in such a case would be to hit him hard and often enough to stop the attack before it can escalate into something much worst. This is a judgment call, of course, but as long as you don't overdo it or continue to strike him after he is no longer a threat, you have a right to defend yourself or another from an unlawful attack. Also, unless a particular less-lethal weapon is illegal where you live, you may use it to defend against a nonlethal attack, as long as you use it as it is designed to be used. For example, it would be illegal to bash an assailant's eye with a can of pepper spray unless he was threatening to kill or seriously injure you, or in most states, attempting to commit some other violent felony against you, such as rape or kidnapping. The bottom line is to be reasonable but not shy about using sufficient force to defend yourself or others.

Legal Survival
Officer Elliott was fortunate not to be sued for using deadly force against Mr. Harris. This is not because the shooting was anything less than completely justified, but because of the image of unfairness created when someone shoots an unarmed person or even one armed with a knife, club, motor vehicle, or anything besides a functional firearm. Furthermore, the fact that Harris was mentally ill also increased Officer Elliott's vulnerability to a lawsuit, as did two other unusual features of this incident: Harris had displayed no outward signs of mental illness until just before the incident occurred, and the injuries to both officers, though rather significant and long-lasting, were barely visible. Many officers and law-abiding citizens are not so lucky.

If you are ever unfortunate enough to be compelled by circumstances to use any force—especially deadly force—you must exercise your right to remain silent. In the emotional aftermath of a serious force incident, you are likely to say something that can make you appear guilty, even when it is otherwise clear that you acted in self-defense. Cooperate with the police, but politely tell them you choose not to say anything without your attorney present. And then call an attorney as soon as possible. This may be difficult because you may be eager to explain why you were forced to defend yourself, but it is unwise to speak in the highly emotional aftermath of a deadly encounter.

Post-Shooting Concerns

Furthermore, never forget that you are in danger of being shot by the police anytime you draw a gun, and even more so if you wind up shooting someone with it. Even experienced police officers are under stress when responding to a shooting or man-with-a-gun call, and they have no way of knowing that you are a law-abiding citizen. The scene will likely be chaotic and noisy, and human beings tend to have trouble hearing under stress. This means officers may not hear bystanders telling them who you are, and you may not hear their orders to put your gun down. In all the confusion, it is also possible that you will not see them coming, especially if your back is to them when they approach. Therefore, holster your gun as soon as possible, position yourself in a place and manner that enables you to face the officers' likely avenue of approach, and then focus on watching and listening for them. If possible, ask a bystander to meet the officers when they arrive to tell them the circumstances and guide them to your location. Or, if that isn't possible, call the police yourself, briefly tell the dispatcher that you had to shoot someone in self-defense, give him a description of yourself and what you are wearing, and carefully follow his directions. Once the officers arrive, immediately identify yourself as an armed citizen and carefully follow their commands.

Especially in today's world of active shooters, your safety may well rest on knowing what to do when the police arrive, and that will probably depend on your training. Luckily, this doesn't have to depend on formal training, but you can use mental imagery[14] to train yourself. Get into a relaxed state, and visualize what you should do in the aftermath of a shooting. Visualize various scenarios in detail and do your best to imagine they are occurring in real life. Then critique your actions and thoughts by asking yourself what you did well, what you could have done better, and what else you could have done if things had been different. This improves mental flexibility, which is critical in high-stress situations, and builds self-confidence, which is also crucial to improved performance. You can also get together with like-minded family members or friends to brainstorm about post-shooting tactics or even develop and conduct roleplay scenarios to enhance this vital skill further.

---

14. Mental imagery is a mental exercise that enables you to use your imagination to practice how to respond to various situations without having to actually experience them firsthand. It is regularly used by special forces, SWAT members, and elite athletes to practice skills when away from the gym or range, and more importantly, to mentally prepare for various challenges they may face in the field.

CHAPTER 7

Winning Mindset/Warrior Spirit:
The Ronald Griffin Case

"If we don't keep the warrior in the mix, we become glorified
social workers with guns. We will fail at our ultimate
responsibility; saving innocent human lives."
—Anonymous police officer

DESCRIPTION OF INCIDENT

The first thing Sgt. Ronald Griffin noticed about the man walking directly toward him was the intensity of his features. Then he saw the man's hands shoved into his jacket pockets. Griffin, a 40-year-old, 18-year veteran of the police department, quickly put his prisoner into the back seat of his patrol car and closed the door as he turned to give the interloper a closer look. Believing the man to be high on drugs, Griffin anticipated that he would have to arrest him. But instead, he was just moments away from the fight of his life, with the lives of several others hanging in the balance.

The incident had started with a call for a shoplifter at a discount store. Griffin, who had a 17-year-old cadet named Nick Anderson riding with him, volunteered to take the call. Griffin, who was enthusiastic about helping his department's cadets learn as much as possible, knew he could give Anderson some easy exposure to the arrest process by arresting the shoplifter.

After contacting Security Officer Tony Unger, 27, in the loss prevention office, Griffin learned that Unger had taken an 18-year-old shoplifter named Vicky Irving into custody after she tried to use a forged receipt to obtain a refund. Unger also mentioned that Irving's boyfriend had been in the store earlier but had left shortly after her arrest. He mentioned that the boyfriend had what looked like jailhouse tattoos on his neck, leading Griffin to suspect he was a parolee and probably a doper.

Irving seemed rather hostile but offered no resistance as Griffin cuffed her and escorted her outside, accompanied by Anderson and Unger. As they walked, Griffin, who was not one to go blindly into any situation, asked Irving, "Does your boyfriend have any weapons?"

"No," she answered.

"Do I have to be concerned for my safety?"

Again, Irving said no, but her voice hinted of insincerity. Griffin kept his senses on alert as they stepped out into the chilly night air.

Irving's boyfriend, a 35-year-old ex-con named Lewis Nolan, was waiting outside on the dimly lit parking lot. He lingered in the shadows until he saw the group moving toward Griffin's cruiser and then headed toward them. A member of a violent white supremacist gang who had spent most of his adult life in prison, Nolan already had two strikes against him and had bragged that he would never go back to prison. He had already murdered once when, as a teenager, he had brutally stabbed an elderly man to death during a robbery. Now on parole, he was also wanted for home invasion and was probably about to commit another robbery, or worse. In his car parked nearby were five home-made bombs.

Griffin knew nothing of all this, of course, but his instincts told him he would have his hands full. He moved off to his right, away from the others, and immediately addressed his greatest concern.

"Take your hands out of your pockets!" he commanded.

Nolan ignored him and kept coming, "Why is she in there?" he demanded as he glanced toward Irving in the back seat.

"I said, 'Take your hands out of your pockets!'" Griffin repeated.

"Why?" Nolan snapped.

"Because I'm concerned for my safety. What do you have in your pockets?"

"I have a knife."

Nolan was now just two or three steps away, his forward advance accented by an alarming movement of his left hand, still hidden in his coat pocket. Griffin couldn't see what was in his hand, but he knew it wasn't empty.

Griffin, his reactions fine-tuned from years of martial arts and defensive tactics training, sprang forward. He grabbed Nolan's left wrist and trapped it inside the pocket, but only briefly. Nolan was fighting hard to complete the draw, and Griffin knew he had to control him before it was too late. He pulled hard as he stepped to his right, cranked the arm straight out at a right angle away from Nolan's body, and twisted hard until he felt the crunch and snap of cracking bone and tearing tendons.

This should have done the trick, but Nolan was uncontrollable. A glint of bright metal flashed across his chest. It was a snub-nose[1] .38, coming straight for Griffin's face! Then, before the startled sergeant could do more than flinch, a blazing flash and scorching lead tore into his left cheek.

Stunned by the blow but not one to surrender, Griffin held on and slammed Nolan into the hood of a parked car. The next moments were a blur of vicious hand-to-hand combat. More shots rang out, and the valiant officer felt more bullets smash into his body. The exact sequence of shots was never determined, but two of them punched into Griffin's body armor, where—had it not been for the vest—they might well have inflicted mortal wounds. But the other two hollow points[2] struck hard, one drilling through Griffin's right arm and the other slamming into his left side (Figure 1).

Meanwhile, the two men had rolled onto the ground, where Griffin continued his desperate fight despite the grueling punishment from Nolan's gun. Then, help arrived from an unexpected source. Security Officer Unger, though unarmed, had seen enough. Imbued with a sense of duty that transcended his survival instinct, he slammed into Nolan from behind and hammered his fist into the side of the man's head. Reaching down, he grabbed the gun, wrenched it free, and pressed the muzzle against the side of Nolan's head. He pulled the trigger, but the hammer landed with an impotent click. He tried again with the same results. Now realizing the gun was empty, he chucked it into a bush and started punching Nolan again.

But Nolan also had a fixed blade hunting knife in his left hand. Switching the weapon to his right hand, he turned it on Unger as Griffin sprang back into

---

1. A snub nose is a small revolver with a short barrel (i.e., three inches or less). Larger caliber (.38 and .357 magnum) snub noses were almost universally carried used by police detectives in the past, when virtually every police officer carried a revolver. They are still popular among many officers as off-duty guns because of their compact size, easy concealability, reliability, and ease of operation.

2. Hollow point bullets are called by that name because, instead of a rounded or flat nose, their noses are hollowed out to improve expansion when they hit their target. The result is an expanded surface area as the bullet penetrates tissue, which causes a larger wound channel, thus more damage. This in turn improves the bullet's ability to quickly and reliably stop one's attacker. Contrary to common opinion, hollow points are not illegal. In fact, they are by far the most common type of bullet used in law enforcement today, because they are more reliable in stopping violent assailants, and also tend not to over-penetrate, which decreases the likelihood of an officer's bullet striking a bystander.

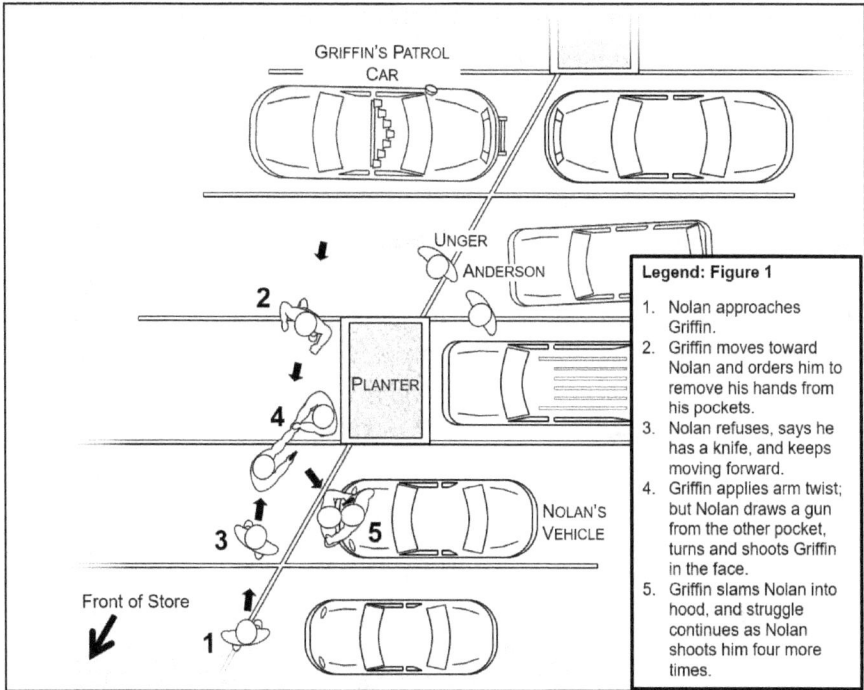

FIGURE 1: Nolan attacks Sgt. Griffin, shooting him in the face, Sgt. Griffin slams him into the hood of a car, and Nolan shoots him four more times.

the fight. Before Griffin could stop him, he drove the blade into Unger's left chest, ripping open a gaping hole that exposed the lung. Unger, now bleeding freely from the fearsome knife wound, crawled away as Griffin continued the fight.

"I've got to stop this now," Griffin thought. A headshot was his best bet, and he sent the draw command to his right hand. Nothing happened!

Suddenly, Nolan broke free and headed for the patrol car. He jumped into the front seat, closed the door behind him, and began reaching around inside. Oddly, he made no effort to free his girlfriend or drive away. Just seconds later, it became clear that he knew exactly what he was doing. There was a Remington 870 in the trunk and a full-auto[3] HK33 assault rifle[4] in a rack above the prisoner

---

3. The phrase "full auto" is an informal way of referring to a fully automatic firearm, or a gun that has the capacity to fire in a rapid, continuous burst of gunfire for as long as the trigger is depressed or until the weapon is empty.

4. The HK33 assault rifle, made by Heckler & Koch, is of the same caliber as the well-known M16 (i.e., 5.56X45 mm) but, unlike the AR15, it can also fire in fully automatic mode (see footnote above).

cage. Both were accessible using hidden switches on the dashboard, and either one could do incalculable damage.

The parking lot was full of shoppers. Tony Unger had crawled between two parked cars, bleeding so profusely that it appeared he would soon die, and Cadet Nick Anderson was still somewhere nearby. With so many citizens in grave danger, Griffin was more determined than ever to act. Again, he commanded his right hand to draw the .40 caliber Beretta 96G at his side, and again the hand refused to budge. Glancing down, Griffin saw the unresponsive limb hanging at his side, twisted into an ugly angle and pumping blood down his sleeve. He reached for his holstered pistol with his left hand, but that hand wouldn't work either. A quick look told him why: it was drenched in blood, and there was a wicked, two-inch tear between his fore and middle fingers. He had suffered wounds that threatened to doom his chances of stopping Nolan's murderous rampage!

Griffin believed he was dying, and nothing seemed to be going right. Yet, nothing could stop him from doing his duty. His keen mind, unhampered by fear or frustration, flashed through his options. Then he thought of the young cadet.

Anderson knew the rule against getting involved if an officer was attacked, but he had refused to stand by and do nothing. After taking cover behind a car, he had remained there and waited for an opportunity to help. Griffin didn't know Anderson's exact location, but he knew he hadn't gone far. "Nick," he shouted, "Come here!"

Anderson emerged from the dark and stood behind Griffin, who was now kneeling on both knees. Griffin glanced back at him and gasped, "Take my gun out and put it in my left hand!"

Anderson knew the gun was secured inside its holster with only a top snap, but he felt rushed and anxious. After releasing the snap, he realized he couldn't draw the gun as easily as he had hoped. Nevertheless, he persisted and soon managed to remove it from the holster. He placed it into Griffin's left hand and stepped back.

Though his wounded hand had prevented him from drawing his pistol, Griffin was able to hold the weapon firmly enough to get on target and pull the trigger. Nolan's center mass was solidly behind the closed passenger door, but Griffin knew modern handgun ammunition had a good chance of penetrating the door. Raising the pistol to eye level, he pointed it at a spot on the door directly in line with Nolan's body and fired twice. Though both shots hit where he aimed, they failed to pierce the door. However, they immediately caused Nolan to turn toward the sound. A startled look crossed his face as he stared down the dark muzzle of the Beretta.

So much for shooting through the door, Griffin thought. He raised the gun higher and pulled the trigger. Glass exploded from the window frame as Nolan's head jerked back violently, and Griffin fired again. Nolan went limp and slumped down into the front seat (Figure 2).

The gunfight was over, but there were still things to be done. Griffin had to get help for Unger, himself, and anyone else who may have been hurt. He told Anderson to call for assistance and tell the dispatcher several people were down.

Griffin knew he was badly wounded and losing blood fast. Fearing he would soon bleed out, he focused on deep breathing to lower his blood pressure and calm himself down and then stoically waited for help to arrive.

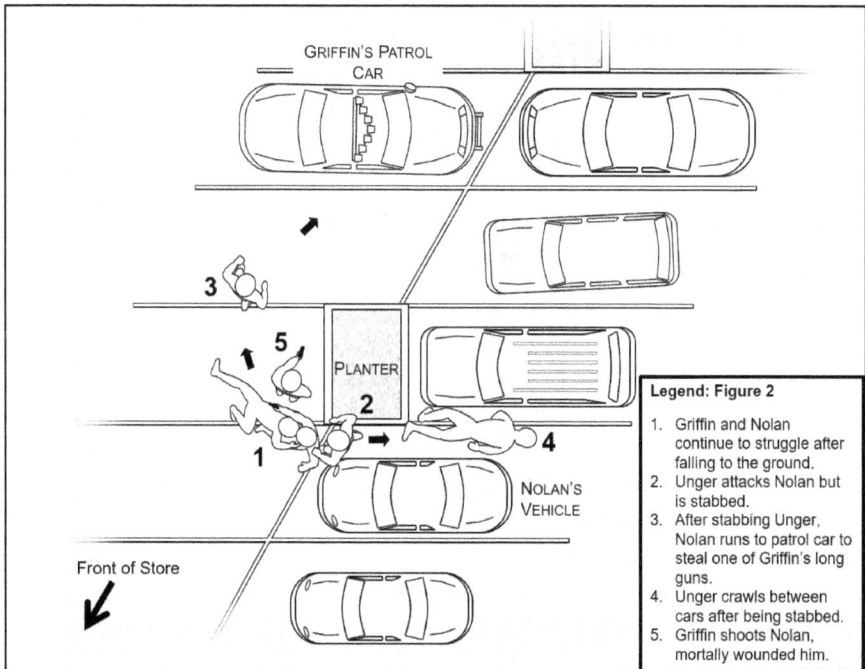

FIGURE 2: Nolan stabs Unger after Unger intervenes to stop him from attacking Griffin. Nolan then tries to retrieve Sgt. Griffin's rifle from his cruiser, prompting Griffin to shoot and mortally wound him.

THE AFTERMATH

Sgt. Griffin had been shot three times besides the two rounds in his vest. One round had struck him in the left cheek and exited the back of his neck near the base of the skull, mercifully missing the spine by a hairsbreadth. Another had shattered his right arm, and the third had hit him in the back portion of his left side, just above the side panel of his vest and in front of the shoulder blade, zipped horizontally across his back, and exited near the spine. Unfortunately, Griffin's wounds eventually forced him to retire, but he made the most of the situation. He went on to earn his master's degree and now teaches police science at a local college. He also lectures extensively about the shooting so other officers can learn from his experience.[5]

Tony Unger recovery completely but later left his security job to move out of state with his family. He, Nick Anderson, and Sgt. Griffin all received numerous local and state awards for their actions and Sgt. Griffin was also awarded several national awards, including the Presidential Medal of Valor.

Griffin's third shot had struck Lewis Nolan in the forehead, but the bullet had hit at an angle and skirted his skull, causing only a flesh wound. Nevertheless, he had also flipped down into the front seat so that his buttocks protruded above the lower edge of the window frame. Griffin's final round had hit him in the right buttock and torn its way up the entire length of his torso, causing extensive internal bleeding before stopping in his neck. He was dead on arrival at the hospital.

ANALYSIS

"Routine" Calls

This case once again proves that there is no such thing as routine in police work. Shopliftings and other minor offenses occur regularly, but that doesn't necessarily make them routine events. A shoplifter can be anything from a youngster stealing a cheap toy on a dare to a junky hungry for a fix, from a professional booster to an armed felon desperate to avoid prison. In this case, Irving was wanted on a felony stealing charge, which was unlikely to result in serious jail

---

5. The incident recounted here is true, but the names were changed to ensure the privacy of those personally involved. Likewise, to preserve confidentiality and clarity, some facts have been altered slightly, but the essential elements of the story remain unchanged.

time in our justice system, but she was not alone. Nolan was a dangerous man whose actions make it clear that he was looking for an excuse to kill a cop.

Hardened killers like him are a rarity in our society but, because of the nature of the work police officers do, they cross paths with them far more often than ordinary citizens do. Therefore, they must be ever vigilant, regardless of the call's seemingly routine nature, and always ready to deal with the worst of society's predators. As a result, they are trained and conditioned through experience to treat everyone with a certain amount of suspicion, which some people view as rude or threatening. This is unfortunate because that is not their intent; rather, police officers are simply exercising their right to stay safe and their duty to keep everyone else safe. This requires establishing and maintaining control of every street contact they make, no matter how seemingly routine or innocent it may appear to be.

How to Respond to Police Commands

When Sgt. Griffin saw Nolan's hands in his pockets; he did what every officer does under such circumstances—he ordered him to remove them. This is a good example of the kind of "rude" behavior mentioned above. Some critics would say such behavior unnecessarily treats law-abiding citizens like criminals, but police officers have no way of knowing what people are thinking. Most of them learn from experience how to identify pre-attack indicators,[6] and some even receive formal training on the subject, but such knowledge doesn't mean they can afford to let their guard down. Many violent offenders are remarkably adept at hiding their dangerous intentions. Moreover, pre-attack indicators often don't appear until the officer has spent some time interacting with them. Consequently, safety-conscious officers make a point of remaining reasonably skeptical for the duration of their contact with every citizen.

Sgt. Griffin's efforts to make Nolan show his hands also highlights another key point that every citizen should be aware of—how to behave when an officer tells them to show their hands or otherwise orders them to do something that seems unnecessary, overly aggressive, or even offensive. First, never forget that police officers don't issue such commands without good reason. They see things from an entirely different perspective than the average citizen. Their training and street experience have taught them to alert on things that you would never

---

6. Pre-attack indicators are body language, facial expressions and other behaviors that indicate someone is planning to attack. Similarly, some officers learn to identify the behaviors of individuals who are carrying concealed weapons.

consider to be danger signs (e.g., reaching for a wallet or into their glovebox without being asked, etc.). And they frequently have information unknown to you (e.g., the knowledge that your car meets the description of one used in a recent holdup, related to a call of suspicious circumstances, etc.). Since, as previously mentioned, police officers cannot know what others are thinking, it is dangerous to assume they will recognize your innocent intentions. Also, considering that you may be nervous, confused, or frightened, your voice and body language may inadvertently telegraph that you are hostile toward them, trying to hide something from them, or even dangerous.

Since it is difficult to think clearly or make good decisions under such high stress, the best thing you can do is take a couple of deep breaths and focus on following the officer's orders to the letter. If you are unsure what to do, don't move, don't reach for your wallet or anything else, and in as calm a voice as you can muster, tell the officer you want to follow his commands but are not sure what he wants you to do. Police officers are used to operating under stress. They don't want to hurt anyone unnecessarily, but they are also concerned about their safety and have perilously little time to weigh their options before responding to apparent threats. The safest way to handle any encounter with the police is to slow down, calm down, don't make any sudden moves, and carefully follow their instructions. If you are offended or feel like you were not treated fairly, make a complaint or even file a lawsuit later, but remember, this is not the time to argue or voice your anger.

And, for heaven's sake, please don't do anything foolish. Perhaps the closest this author ever came to shooting an innocent citizen—or anyone else for that matter—was in response to an unexpected encounter with an intoxicated man in a hotel lobby. I had just finished handling a false holdup alarm at the motel and was getting information from the clerk when I suddenly heard someone behind me shout, "Hey!" Startled, I turned around and saw an older, unkempt man with his hands in the pockets of his tattered coat. He was just coming into my view when I saw him whip his right hand out of his pocket, point at me, and yell, "Bang!" Without conscious thought, I started drawing my pistol and had almost raised it to shooting level before my brain realized his hand was empty and ordered my finger not to pull the trigger. The old guy seemed amused at first—he was smiling—but I quickly set him straight with a tirade fueled by terror over what I had almost done. I doubt that he ever fully realized how close he had come to a violent end, but I will never forget it.

People sometimes do enormously foolish things during encounters with the police. Fortunately, this rarely results in tragedy, but we must never forget that there are no second chances when tragedy strikes. If you are ever unlucky enough to be confronted by the police under tense or frightening circumstances or thrust into any other dangerous situation for that matter, please think before you act.

Training

Sgt. Griffin credits his training for his success at stopping Nolan. His firearms training had included shooting from awkward positions and under adverse conditions, including shooting from the ground when wounded and a considerable amount of practice shooting with his support hand. All these came into play in the gunfight, and they gave him the skills and confidence he needed to defeat Nolan. The confidence that comes with good training is especially consequential to winning on the street because it lowers the stress of combat, which leads to clearer thinking, greater mental flexibility, and improved decision-making.

Griffin is also a blackbelt in Shorinryu karate, had trained others in the art, and served as a departmental defensive tactics instructor and field training officer. He also took training very seriously. To him, training was preparation for the day when he would need it on the street, and he infused every practice session with meaning and emotion as if it were the real thing. His rigorous training and positive attitude had taught him how to take punishment, and his experience as a trainer had taught him to view his actions and those of others with a critical eye, which had further developed his ability to think flexibly under pressure.

Anyone who engages in any dangerous or high-stress activities, whether at work, play, or for self-protection, can similarly benefit from Sgt. Griffin's example. Training for high-risk activities must be thorough, realistic, frequent, and intense enough to build a high level of competency and the confidence that such competency creates. Simply learning the basics of any crucial task or skill is not enough, especially if applied in the real world under stress. This is why police trainers are always striving to make their firearms and other crucial training ever more realistic, with special emphasis on conducting the training exercises under increasingly greater stress. And it is also why so many officers follow Sgt. Griffin's example by taking their training earnestly. They train as often as possible, as hard as possible, and with a positive attitude based upon the realization that it is preparing them for the harsh realities of the street. Many even go so far as to attend training from private sources on their dime because they know it is often more advanced than their department has the money and resources to provide.

Likewise, considering the grave dangers and responsibilities associated with carrying a firearm in public, no lawfully armed private citizen should ever settle for just the training mandated by their state. Intense training in safe gun handling, drawing from a concealed holster and various body positions, marksmanship, tactics, the legalities related to the use of deadly force, and more are crucial for anyone who carries a gun in public. Remember, the key to maximum performance under pressure is confidence based upon proficiency. Proficiency gives you the skills you need, and confidence gives you the mindset to execute those skills calmly and effectively under pressure.

Similarly, anyone who engages in extreme sports does a dangerous job, drives for a living, or must make crucial decisions under pressure should train to a higher competency level than required if they hope to stay safe and be successful.

Winning Mindset

Lewis Nolan was one of those rare individuals with the instincts of a predator and the soul of a killer. Fortunately for everyone else on the parking lot that night, he was met by a man who possessed the instincts of a winner and the soul of a warrior. Ronald Griffin was up to the challenge, and, with the help of two other like-minded warriors–Tony Unger and Nick Anderson—he held his ground and stopped the rampage. This is the unique role police officers play in a free society. They serve the public in other valuable ways, to be sure, but only a well-trained, properly armed defender with the will to put others' safety first can truly defend the innocent.

True warrior that he was, Sgt. Griffin understood this, and he proved it by his actions. When Nolan suddenly turned a seemingly routine arrest into a deadly confrontation, Griffin instantly countered with an aggressive attempt to disarm him. When that failed, and Nolan shot him in the face at point-blank range, Griffin fought back. When Nolan continued to pour lead into him, Griffin continued to fight back. When Nolan stabbed Tony Unger and then tried to arm himself with another, far more devastating weapon, Griffin ignored his wounds and went for his gun. When his shattered arm and torn hand made that impossible, Griffin refused to surrender. He stayed focused on his duty, assessed the tools at his disposal, and used his only available resource—Nick Anderson—to help get the job done.

These actions dramatically exemplify many of the traits common to the warrior spirit. They proved Ronald Griffin's commitment and capacity to stay focused on doing his duty. Others were depending on him, and that was the only thing that mattered. He refused to let anything—not even his fearsome, disabling wounds—stop him.

Sgt. Griffin also possessed the ability to keep thinking on his feet. Such mental flexibility is essential to winning because most lethal encounters are fluid events that have a bad habit of taking unexpected turns for the worse. Warriors must quickly adapt to these sudden changes and counter them with shrewdness and ferocity.

Closely associated with mental flexibility was Sgt. Griffin's optimistic perspective, or what can be termed Warrior Optimism. Instead of concerning himself with all that had gone wrong, he focused on what he could do to succeed. He searched out his assets, found one with the best possibility of success, and put heart and soul into making it work.

These interrelated traits are what enables and drives warriors to succeed against seemingly impossible odds. They are what makes warriors stand out above all others, and they explain why their fellow citizens look to them when all they hold dear is threatened.

These same warrior traits are also crucial to anyone else's survival and happiness when confronted with the dangers and other challenges that life throws at us. No matter how bad things get, we must stay focused on the fight, quickly adapt to changing circumstances, and remain optimistic about what we can do to succeed.

One final note: As has already been mentioned, Sgt. Griffin credits his training with much of his success and gives the rest of the credit to Tony Unger and Nick Anderson. While his praise of others is well justified, it only tells part of the story. With the humility of a true hero, he refuses to give himself any credit. Moreover, he also possessed a selfless concern for others and a deeply emotional obligation to protect them at all costs. The telltale mark of his noble character comes through, despite his best efforts to conceal it, during an interview on *America's Most Wanted*. When discussing Nolan's efforts to access his patrol rifle, this unassuming man talked about his inability to draw his gun. He had shown little emotion throughout the rest of the interview, but when he explained this growing threat to the safety of Anderson and the others, he began to choke up in a voice cracked with emotion. The message, though unintentional on Sgt. Griffin's part was clear. This warrior's greatest concern was for those he had sworn to protect, and the prospect of almost failing them tore at his soul.[7]

---

7. The author would like to thank Dr. Alexis Artwohl and Sgt. Brian Willis, (Calgary Police Service, retired), for their invaluable assistance in this analysis of Sgt. Griffin's outstanding performance in this incident.

CHAPTER 8

To the Sound of the Guns: The Jake Laird, Tim Conley, Pete Koe Case

"When the will defies fear, when duty throws the gauntlet down to fate, when honor scorns to compromise with death—that is heroism."
—ROBERT INGERSOLL

DESCRIPTION OF INCIDENT

No one knows exactly what set Kenneth Anderson off, but it most likely had something to do with his beloved guns. He had amassed a virtual arsenal—including numerous assault-style rifles, handguns, and vast amounts of ammunition—but the police had seized them after his mother told them about his schizophrenia and deep hatred for the police. Even though he had managed to get them back after a brief legal battle with the police department, it is believed that his resentment over having lost them in the first place made him snap.

Several months later, Anderson's brother inexplicably received a late-night call from Anderson summoning him to their mother's home. When the brother arrived, Anderson met him at the door, escorted him to their mother's bedroom, and showed him their mother's body. Her midsection was drenched in blood from two gaping bullet holes inflicted by one of the weapons from Anderson's arsenal—a 7.62 X 39 mm SKS rifle.[1]

---

1. The SKS is a Soviet-made semiautomatic carbine (short barreled rifle) chambered for the same 7.62X39mm round used in the well-know AK47, but with a somewhat less threatening appearance. The 7.26X39 mm cartridge is considerably larger than the .223 caliber cartridge used in the AR15, and is thus capable of causing more severe wounds.

"It was me. I shot her," Anderson announced, and then pulled a .357 magnum from his waistband, handed it to his brother, and asked him to shoot him.

In stunned horror and disbelief, the brother fled the house as Anderson cried out behind him, "Stick around and see what happens next!"

The meaning of Anderson's remarks soon became clear. Leaning against the kitchen wall were the SKS and six fully loaded magazines. He picked up the rifle, crammed the magazines into his coat pockets, and stepped outside. The brisk midnight air erupted with the rattle of rapid gunfire as he cranked off one round after another. He wasn't aiming at anything in particular but seemed satisfied with randomly shooting up the neighborhood.

Calls of "a man with a machine gun" began flooding into the dispatch center, and several officers were dispatched to the scene, followed almost immediately by every available officer in the city's South district. Among the responding officers were Officers Timothy "Jake" Laird, a 31-year-old, four-year veteran of the department and former Marine, and Officer Tim Conley, 43, with eight years of service.

Conley was the first to arrive. He had doused his headlights and couldn't see much in the murky shadows lining the street as he cruised along looking for the gunman. Then, just before he reached Mrs. Anderson's home, a storm of gunfire began peppering his cruiser. Throwing his transmission into reverse and gunning the engine, he sped backward to escape the barrage, but not before one of Anderson's 7.62s tore into his stomach. He kept going and then tried to make a hard right onto the first intersecting street. But he missed the intersection, jumped the curb, and slammed into a chain-link fence. He bailed out, moved to cover alongside his cruiser, radioed in that he had been shot, and—now relatively safe from Anderson's gunfire—stayed there until help arrived.

Other units were soon pouring into the area, and Anderson turned his attention to them. With the gunman now distracted and the help of two other officers, Conley was able to withdraw to a safer location, from which he was soon transported to the hospital by ambulance.

The din of battle permeated the air as Anderson continued his rampage, but none of the officers could see his muzzle flashes. Blanketed in darkness, constantly moving and firing from concealed locations with a flash suppressor on his rifle, Anderson seemed invisible. The result was a growing number of officers—none of whom were armed with a rifle—who found themselves in the dire predicament of taking fire from a mobile adversary they couldn't see or contain. Unable to advance, unwilling to retreat, and too well disciplined to put others at risk by returning fire, the only thing they could do for now was hold their ground and endure the long wait for SWAT.

But one of the members of the tactical team was already en route. Officer Pete Koe, 41, a 16-year veteran of the department and former RECON Marine, had been at headquarters when he overheard Conley's desperate call for help. After hurriedly making his way back to his squad car from the building's top floor, he covered the 4.3 miles to the scene in record time. The traffic was surprisingly light for this time of the night, and even the traffic signals seem divinely manipulated to assist his lights and siren in clearing the way. All twelve of them along the route were either green or turned green as he approached. And his greatest concern—the possibility of colliding with one of the many other units rushing to the scene—proved to be no problem, as he saw no other patrol cars along the way.

Nevertheless, tragedy struck elsewhere as Koe sped toward the scene. Officer Laird, arriving just a few minutes behind Conley, stopped his cruiser almost 200 yards south of Anderson's location and got out to take cover. As he started to crouch down behind his vehicle, one of Anderson's bullets slammed into his left clavicle and sliced downward through his torso before coming to rest in his right hip. "I'm hit," he gasped into his mic and then crumpled to the ground. The deadly missile had penetrated almost every one of his major organs, causing a devastating wound. Though carried to safety almost immediately by three officers who desperately tried to save him, there was nothing anyone could do to help. He was dead within minutes.

Koe heard Laird's call and then the frantic "officer down!" calls from the officers nearby, and his heart sank. He knew Laird and Conley well, now both of them were down, and this latest radio call had an especially ominous ring. Like a bad dream, the powerful engine under his hood seemed just to creep along as he rushed the rest of the way to the scene.

As he drew closer to the scene, he saw three ambulances and a squad car in an intersection just two blocks from Mrs. Anderson's home. A single officer was trying to corral the ambulances into an organized group, and he could now hear the distinctive sound of gunshots even with his windows closed. The realization that the ambulances could not enter the hot zone to aid the wounded until the gunman was stopped, coupled with the crack of gunfire, added an even greater sense of urgency to the situation. Koe's natural inclination to help others—already running high—was stirred to its highest pitch. There wasn't time to wait for SWAT. He would have to go it alone.

Koe had heard enough on the radio to realize no one had located the gunman yet. Since there is no way to deal with a threat that can't be seen, he would have to find a way to draw Anderson out into the open. To do that, he would have to enter the eye of the storm. Anderson's gunfire was coming from the south, so he headed that way. He was close enough to proceed on foot, which would have been safer, but since his white patrol car was more likely to draw Anderson's attention, he chose to drive instead. Koe had barely gone a block when he overheard another officer notify dispatch that a resident had just spotted the shooter walking toward his location in an alley less than a block away. He was in an ideal position to intercept Anderson as long as the man didn't change directions. He stopped his car and headed for the trunk where he kept his M4.[2]

Two other units pulled to the curb behind him. The officers driving them—Officers Leon Essig, 35, a three-year veteran of the department, and Andrew Troxell, 25, a two-year veteran—had seen him heading into the hot zone and decided to follow. Both exited their vehicles, ran up to him as he opened the trunk, and asked him what he needed them to do

Koe grabbed his rifle, inserted a magazine, chambered a round, and started to answer as he switched on its optical sight.[3] Suddenly, the air was filled with scorching lead and the roar of gunfire. Koe dropped to the pavement behind the trunk for cover, brought the M4 into firing position, and started scanning for a target, but the other two officers were unable to react as quickly. Startled and caught further away from the open trunk, they were both hit in the barrage—Essig in the arm, shattering the bone in two places, and Troxell through one hand. They wisely withdrew into the darkness.

Though behind decent cover, Koe was at the vortex of the firestorm. Shards of metal, shattered glass, and flying asphalt crashed all around him, and he still had no target. He was looking for a muzzle flash or even a hint of movement in the shadows to help him locate the shooter when a chunk of metal—probably a bullet fragment or piece of metal from his left rear wheel—crashed into the top of his head. It gouged a nasty hole into his scalp and sent blood gushing

---

2. The M4 is a rifle remarkably similar to the better-known AR15. The major difference between these two rifles is that the M4 can fire in either semiautomatic mode (one shot with each pull of the trigger) or three round burst mode (three shots in rapid succession with each pull of the trigger), making it a true assault rifle; whereas the AR15 can only fire in semiautomatic mode. Semiautomatic rifles like the AR15 are legal to possess, but M4s and other assault rifles are not. Law enforcement officers are an exception, of course, but only when the assault rifle is not their personal property but owned by their agency instead.

3. An optical sight is an electronic sight that displays a small glowing dot on a clear screen that enables the shooter to aim without using the firearm's metal sights. This allows the shooter to aim faster with greater accuracy, and since the dot glows, much greater accuracy in low light conditions.

down into his eyes (see Figure 1). He knew it couldn't be anything too serious because he was still conscious and alert, but the blood made it harder to see. He rolled onto his left side, got up onto one knee, and kept looking for his invisible assailant. It was then that he took another round, this time in the right knee. There was a telephone pole just a few feet away, and it would make better cover than the patrol car. He rolled over to it, stood, shouldered the M4, and once again began looking for the gunman.

Amazingly, even though the bullet had hit Koe's femur straight on, it had merely punched a hole through it without breaking the bone. There was no pain, but the realization that he had been hit again made Koe acutely aware of how vulnerable he was. However, he felt no fear, only deep concern about his inability to finish the job if the next round penetrated his body armor and mortally wounded him. He remembered from his SWAT training that human beings could often live for as long as 12 seconds after being mortally wounded. Then he knew what he would do if severely wounded: He would move forward, find his target, illuminate him with his weapon-mounted light, and keep moving and shooting until the threat was terminated.

Using the sound of Anderson's gunfire as a guide, Koe looked over to his right toward the backyard of the house on the other side of the intersection

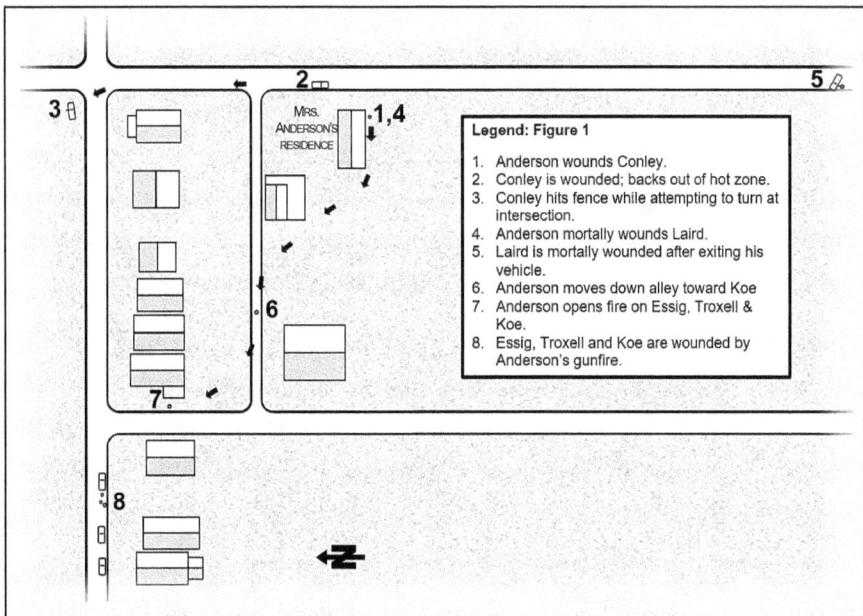

Legend: Figure 1

1. Anderson wounds Conley.
2. Conley is wounded; backs out of hot zone.
3. Conley hits fence while attempting to turn at intersection.
4. Anderson mortally wounds Laird.
5. Laird is mortally wounded after exiting his vehicle.
6. Anderson moves down alley toward Koe.
7. Anderson opens fire on Essig, Troxell & Koe.
8. Essig, Troxell and Koe are wounded by Anderson's gunfire.

FIGURE 1: Anderson wounds Conley, kills Laird, and then wounds Essig, Troxell, and Koe.

in front of him. There was a small garage in the yard, and he could see a hint of movement and dark contrast against its light-colored wall. He pointed his rifle at the spot and switched on its flashlight, instantly flooding his target in its beam. Anderson, a massive man whose stance conveyed a message of angry determination, was still firing the SKS at Koe, but now with greater vigor and less accuracy. It was just the chance Koe had been waiting for, and he answered the gunman's rifle fire with two quick, well-placed shots of his own.

Anderson's torso twitched with each round, confirming that both had hit center mass, but he didn't go down. Instead, he darted off to the left and started moving toward the front of the house. He was heading toward a Jeep Wagoneer parked in the driveway, and his route took him past a well-lit window that briefly silhouetted him in its light. The movement gave Koe another ideal opportunity to get multiple rounds on target, but he realized that someone might be sitting just inside the window and held his fire.

Koe later learned that the homeowner had been sitting inside the window. The man had been watching a war movie on television at the time, and its sound had drowned out the real-life gunfire just outside his window, making him oblivious to the danger. Koe's exemplary firearms discipline may well have saved the man's life.

This wasn't the last time Koe exercised such discipline. Well trained, confident in his abilities, and deeply conscious of his duty to protect others, he never lost sight of the danger posed by his gunfire. Even now, as Anderson took cover behind the Jeep and opened up on him again, Koe was conscious that other officers were down the street behind the man. Still, Anderson had to be stopped, and Koe was the only officer in a position to do it. Lowering the muzzle of the M4 to alleviate the risk to the officers downrange, he targeted Anderson's lower body and legs. It worked. Anderson slumped to the ground, landing on his back with his head pointing toward the Jeep's rear.

But he was still moving, holding the rifle, and growling incoherently. Koe stepped from behind the pole and advanced, firing as he moved. His M4 went empty just before he reached the Jeep, but he couldn't stop now. Aware that it would be harder for Anderson to shoot him if he approached him from the direction his head was pointing, Koe moved around the rear of the Jeep and approached him from there. Anderson's right hand was still holding the SKS, finger on the trigger, and in his left hand was a .357 Magnum revolver.

Koe moved in closer and ordered Anderson to drop the weapons, but he ignored Koe's command and started to lift his rifle. With his rifle now empty,

Koe had to improvise. He swung the M4 hard, connecting solidly with the side of Anderson's head. Anderson dropped the SKS but then started to lift it again. Again, Koe ordered him to drop the gun, and again Anderson ignored him. Koe countered with another butt stroke, this time shattering the man's jaw and causing him to drop the gun. But Anderson wasn't finished yet. He lifted the magnum toward Koe, and once again, Koe crashed the rifle butt into his face, smashing his eye socket.

The blow seemed to take the fight out of the amazingly resilient madman. He lowered the revolver. But then, in a sudden burst of fury, he thrust it up towards Koe's face. Koe instinctively dodged his head as flame thundered from the muzzle, sending a slug whizzing past his left ear. Koe kept moving, drew his Glock, and fired three .40 caliber slugs into the gunman's chest and head. Anderson had seemed unstoppable, but no one could stand up to these last rounds (Figure 2). The nightmare was over.

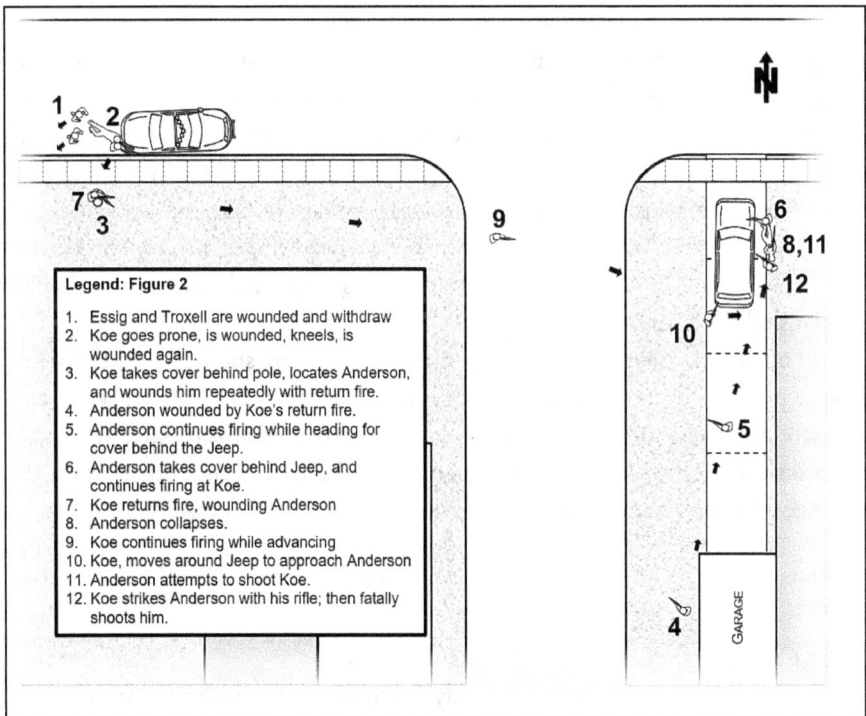

Legend: Figure 2

1. Essig and Troxell are wounded and withdraw
2. Koe goes prone, is wounded, kneels, is wounded again.
3. Koe takes cover behind pole, locates Anderson, and wounds him repeatedly with return fire.
4. Anderson wounded by Koe's return fire.
5. Anderson continues firing while heading for cover behind the Jeep.
6. Anderson takes cover behind Jeep, and continues firing at Koe.
7. Koe returns fire, wounding Anderson
8. Anderson collapses.
9. Koe continues firing while advancing
10. Koe, moves around Jeep to approach Anderson
11. Anderson attempts to shoot Koe.
12. Koe strikes Anderson with his rifle; then fatally shoots him.

FIGURE 2: Koe locates, engages, and wounds Anderson. As Koe moves forward, Anderson attacks him again, prompting Koe to wound him fatally with three shots from his sidearm.

THE AFTERMATH

Every officer had done his job with courage and conviction, and Officer Koe's selfless actions had finally brought the bloody rampage to a close, but no one could turn the clock back. Anderson's fury had cost others dearly: Officer Laird, a promising young officer who had devoted his life to serving others, first as a Marine and then as a police officer, was gone, leaving a wife and seven-year-old daughter behind. Anderson's mother was dead, and his brother was left behind to deal with the tragic loss of both his mother and brother, not to mention the horror of what his brother had done.

Anderson's other victims were more fortunate. Officer Conley's wound was the worst and most difficult from which to recover, but he was eventually able to return to work and is still with the department. Despite the wound to his knee, Koe also made a full recovery and suffered no permanent injury except hearing loss in his left ear. He is still with the department, continues to serve on its tactical team, and speaks to law enforcement groups on the lessons learned from this incident. Officers Essig and Troxell were also fortunate enough to suffer no permanent disabilities from their wounds and are still with the department.

As tragic as this incident was, we can take some comfort in the fact that Officer Laird died courageously while selflessly rushing into harm's way to protect others. The wounded officers acted with similar courage and commitment, as did every officer who responded to the scene. Officer Koe, in particular, acted with selfless disregard for his safety and distinguished himself by using his special skills and resources to stop the carnage.

In our current world of growing threats from active shooters and terrorists, today's police officers must be unswerving in their readiness to deal with mass violence and their commitment to keeping their fellow citizens safe. With very few exceptions, they have proven to be up to the task, as is evident from the courage and commitment displayed by every officer in this case.

ANALYSIS

Mass Casualty Incidents (MCIs)

As long as Anderson was just randomly firing his weapon, the situation, while serious enough to require a rapid response, was not yet so urgent that it was necessary to take extraordinary risks or abandon sound tactics. However, this had changed dramatically by the time Officer Koe responded to the scene. Officers Conley and Laird had been shot, other officers were under fire, and the threat had to be stopped without delay, even if it meant taking unusually high risks to do it. This concept is a drastic departure from law enforcement's traditional view of how officers should deal with violent crimes in progress, which focuses on a cautious approach to danger and the prudent use of deadly force. While these concerns remain critical to the police mission, there are times when the need for rapid intervention is so urgent that officer safety and delays in the use of deadly force (e.g., issuing warnings and considering lesser options before neutralizing the shooter) must be relegated to second place.

As Officer Koe is quick to point out, responding to an MCI is "more like a military firefight than a police shooting," which requires "a whole new perspective on the way police do their jobs." Included in this new perspective is the acceptance of the increased likelihood of multiple police casualties, ignoring severely injured officers and citizens to find and neutralize the shooter as quickly as possible, and shooting the offender on sight (i.e., without warning and as soon as he is identified, which is usually, but not always, obvious). In short, officers must shift their mindset from the judicious guardian of the peace to a military-like hunter, which is not an easy transition. It requires a great deal of training, self-confidence, and selfless devotion to protecting others, especially now that law enforcement is finally beginning to accept the necessity of making immediate solo entries into the scene.

The importance of solo entries during MCIs rests in the brutal reality that the police simply cannot respond fast enough to stop the killing. By the time someone calls 911 (usually 3-6 minutes), the dispatcher dispatches cars to the scene, officers arrive (usually another 3-6 minutes), enter the scene, and neutralize the killer (another several minutes), it is usually too late to save lives. The killer has stopped killing by then and has either left the scene, committed suicide, or decided to surrender. Of course, the police can still help stop the bleeding and remove victims to safety, but they can rarely do anything to stop the bloodshed. Remember, even the remarkably rapid response of the Dayton Police on August 4, 2019, was not enough to save nine innocent lives or prevent the wounding of at least 17 others. Nevertheless, the heroic Dayton officers undoubtedly saved countless lives, thereby reinforcing the importance of intervening as quickly as possible. Solo entries cannot entirely solve this problem, but since stationing an officer at every soft target across the country is a financial and logistical impossibility, it is the best the police can do.

Regrettably, some critics have accused police trainers of trying to mold police officers into overly aggressive "warriors" by telling them to hunt down aggressively and neutralize active shooters. Most likely, this is because they don't understand how an MCI is different from other violent police encounters. The offender in a conventional officer-involved shooting is not actively killing defenseless men, women, and children. The officer can thus afford to respond in his traditional role as a guardian. But the fast-paced bloodbath perpetrated by active killers can only be stopped by officers with the mindset of a warrior. When police trainers emphasize the need to shift to this radically different mindset when dealing with MCIs, they are not telling their officers to take the same approach to other dangerous encounters. They are doing the exact opposite by stressing the distinct differences between the two approaches and the importance of instantly shifting into the "hunter" mode when entering into the hot zone searching for an active killer.

"Militarization" of the Police

Similarly, officers are sometimes criticized for being too militaristic in their appearance and equipment. This author agrees that military-style load-bearing vests[4] filled with rifle magazines and other equipment make officers appear unnecessarily militaristic for regular patrol work. However, since any officer may be called upon to respond to an MCI or terrorist attack at any time, they must have quick access to necessary military-style equipment at a moment's notice. Therefore, every patrol car should be equipped with a rifle and extra magazines in the cab, and other military-style equipment like heavy body armor, a helmet, trauma kit, etc., in the trunk. The patrol rifle with several magazines is especially valuable because an officer armed with nothing more than a pistol is at a severe disadvantage when going up against an active shooter with a high-capacity semiautomatic rifle. Besides the danger posed to the officer, this significant difference in weaponry also puts others at grave risk. Since there are often innocent citizens in the shooter's immediate vicinity, and the responding officers are often required to shoot at atypically long distances, they must be able to shoot with great accuracy. And since rifles are far more accurate than pistols, all responding officers must be armed with patrol rifles, especially at longer ranges.

---

4. Load bearing vests are vests with multiple pouches used to hold spare magazines and other essential equipment, including radios, trauma kits, etc. Many also hold body armor. Used primarily by the military and SWAT teams, they are now becoming increasingly more prevalent among patrol officers.

Exiting the Hot Zone

Officer Conley's patrol car made him an easy target for Anderson's ambush. Trapped behind the wheel while under a heavy barrage from an unseen assailant, he was highly vulnerable with little time to react. Fortunately, he chose an appropriate tactic for dealing with the threat and could execute it quickly enough to avoid being hit with any more of Anderson's rounds. Most likely, his quick tactical response saved his life.

Citizens facing an MCI or other lethal attack can similarly escape danger by exiting the hot zone. This tactic's purpose is as obvious as it is simple—get out of the line of fire as fast as you can and then decide what to do next—but it isn't always as easy as it may seem. In Officer Conley's case, he was able to rapidly retreat to a relatively safe location before exiting and taking cover next to his car. But what if he had been on foot? Turning around and running down the block on foot would have exposed him to lethal fire for a precariously long time. In that case, it would have been safer to sprint to the closest house and take cover there. Likewise, someone indoors may find that it is quicker and safer to exit the hot zone by ducking through a nearby doorway instead of taking cover behind a flimsy display case or room divider.

Deciding the safest place to go in a crisis depends on the circumstances, and the decision-making process takes time, especially when caught off guard. Also, we humans naturally freeze for a moment when confronted with grave danger.[5] This temporary startle response is usually remarkably brief, but its duration depends on training, experience with similar dangers, level of mental preparation, and advanced warning of danger. A person who is caught by surprise has never been in lethal danger before or has never been trained in how to respond to a lethal attack will probably experience a significantly longer startle response or, in extreme cases, even freeze in place. Fortunately, however, there are some things we can do to dramatically reduce the duration of the startle response and thus shorten our reaction time:

1. Use the Safety-First Habit discussed in chapter 4 (pp. 55–56) to raise your awareness of your surroundings. By enabling you to spot possible danger sooner, this habit will help you avoid being caught by surprise while also buying you a little more time (even an extra

---

5. This is why police officers take the importance of remaining ever alert and ready for danger so seriously. Since danger can come at any time, and usually occurs without warning, they can't afford to let their guard down or trust that they will not be hurt by the people they encounter on the street.

millisecond can be a lifesaver) to decide your safest course of action. Police officers use this or similar mental tools to raise their awareness and prepare for the possibility of being attacked.

2. Plan ahead. Make a habit of scanning your surroundings at all times to pick out the nearby cover and escape routes. Police officers call this "cover awareness," and it is a habit that has proven effective in actual lethal confrontations. In these frightening days of an ever-increasing number of MCIs at schools and elsewhere, it is also a very good idea to teach your family this habit as well. Make a game of it by frequently asking them to identify nearby cover and escape routes and then rewarding them when they do well. Besides significantly speeding up their ability to exit the hot zone, cover awareness can lessen a child's fear of MCIs. This is because as our feelings of helplessness increase, so does our fear. Conversely, fear decreases when we understand that we have effective options for dealing with whatever it is that frightens us. By knowing they can vastly improve their safety by practicing cover awareness, children (and adults) feel more confident and considerably less vulnerable.

3. Understand the difference between concealment and cover. Cover is anything that will protect you from gunfire. It must be solid enough to stop bullets and large enough to protect at least your vital organs, and in most cases, it will also conceal you. On the other hand, concealment is simply any item or condition (e.g., shadows, bushes, running out of the assailant's view, etc.) that hides you from your assailant's view. Depending on its composition, it may or may not also serve as cover. Cover is preferable to concealment, but concealment alone is much better than remaining out in the open.

Firearms Proficiency and Training

It was fortunate for everyone involved, including the innocent citizens in the area, that Officer Koe was as proficient with firearms as he was. Remarkably, he hit his target with every round he fired, but perhaps even more important was the fact that he practiced exceptional firearms discipline by shooting only when he had a good visual on Anderson and could be reasonably certain it would not endanger anyone else.

A lot of the credit for Officer Koe's firearms proficiency and success in stopping Anderson's bloody rampage must go to his training. Besides giving him the well-honed firearms and tactical skills, he needed to do the job, his Marine, police, and SWAT training gave him confidence. The importance of the confidence that comes from good training cannot be overstated. This is because confidence creates a sense of control, a sense of control reduces stress and calms the mind, and a calm mind thinks more clearly, feels less fear, and makes better decisions. Thus, it was confidence in himself and his training that allowed Officer Koe to keep thinking on his feet, persist despite his wounds, and prevail.

It is well worth noting that most officers don't have the opportunity to be trained to the same level as Officer Koe. This is a shame because they need that level of training to meet the public's high expectations. The great majority of officers are highly dedicated and proud to serve their fellow citizens at risk to themselves. But they are also fallible human beings with normal human emotions and instincts, like fear, anger, and feelings of inadequacy. For the most part, they are fairly well trained in many of the skills they need to do the job, but it takes an enormous amount of high-quality training to perform flawlessly and keep one's emotions and instincts in check under stress. And it also requires a great deal of confidence that comes from good training, as discussed above. To be able to rely on officers to enter the scene of a mass casualty incident and then hunt down and neutralize the killer alone, like Officer Koe so courageously did, requires far more training than most officers will ever receive. Amazingly, most officers who respond to these tragedies do what is expected of them, despite inadequate training, and we need to appreciate why they do it. It certainly isn't because they are well trained for the task or because their bosses tell them to do it, but because they care about their fellow citizens and value human life enough to risk death to preserve it. Those who accuse our police officers of failing to respect the sanctity of life need to understand this, and all of us need to respect our officers for their dedication to protecting others.

Winning Mindset

Another key element in Officer Koe's success was his mental attitude. His extensive Marine and law enforcement training certainly had a great deal to do with this winning mindset, but he possessed other essential traits that contributed to it as well.

The first of these was his selfless dedication. He is a self-motivated individual with an unshakable outward focus on the needs of others. It was this selfless desire to serve others that gave him the courage to do what he did. It was behind his decision to put himself into the center of Anderson's firestorm so he could locate him, to withhold fire when others might be at risk, and if it came to it, to use his last few moments on earth to charge and eliminate his target. Confidence alone cannot inspire such selfless decisions. In Officer Koe's case, his motivation to risk his life for others came from the deep-seated belief that it was his duty to utilize his training to protect others. As he later put it: "To whom much is given, much is expected." Even at the cost of one's own life, if necessary, this kind of unselfish devotion to others is the essence of the warrior spirit.

It is interesting to note that Officer Koe is a man of deep faith, and, as is so often the case, this faith played a significant role in his success. People of faith tend to perform especially well in dangerous situations, and there are several reasons for this. The first is that a strong belief in the afterlife leads to less fear of death, making it easier to do one's duty despite the danger. Second, people of faith are generally taught to put others' needs before their own, which inspires the outward focus just discussed. Many officers—Officer Koe included—also believe that police officers are ordained by God to protect the innocent. This tends to inspire them to serve dutifully despite the risks involved.

Moreover, this belief makes it easier for many officers to cope with a deadly force incident's emotional aftermath. They believe that God deliberately placed them into a position to intervene in the incident for the specific purpose of stopping the perpetrator's violent actions. This, in turn, helps alleviate guilt and gives purpose to the event.

Officer Koe's attitude and actions provide an excellent example of what it takes to win. He stayed calm, kept thinking on his feet, took note of his wounds only in so far as they provided him with further motivation to win, kept going no matter what, and displayed selfless courage in the face of danger. These are the qualities that will often propel us to victory against all odds and the virtues that set warriors apart from those they so unselfishly serve.

CHAPTER 9

Never Say Die:
The Bryan Power Case

"Being a warrior is not about the act of fighting. It's about
being so prepared to face a challenge and believing so strongly
in the cause you are fighting for that you refuse to quit."
—RICHARD MACHOWICZ-FORMER NAVY SEAL,
UNLEASH THE WARRIOR WITHIN

DESCRIPTION OF INCIDENT

It was the first time Bryan Power had worked a day shift, which wasn't surprising since he had only been with the department for about four months. He was also unusually young for a cop. The minimum age requirement for police officers in his state was 18, and Power had started his career not long after his nineteenth birthday. With just six months of experience with another department before coming to work here, he was now barely 20. He was also working alone. Serving a town of fewer than 4,000 residents, the department had only seven officers, making it necessary to limit the number of officers on most days to just one. Backup was available from other agencies in the vicinity, but it was limited and often a long time coming. Fortunately, the crime rate was relatively low, with few violent crimes.

The shift, now nearing its end, had passed without serious incident. Power's most significant call had been a burglary, and he was just finishing the report when a middle-aged Hispanic woman, a teenage girl, and a younger boy came into the station. The woman was visibly upset and speaking excitedly in Spanish.

Power knew Spanish well, but the woman was speaking rapidly in a dialect he didn't understand. He could make out that she was upset about something her husband had done, but most of the rest was unintelligible.

It wasn't an insurmountable problem. Anita Reynolds, the municipal judge, spoke fluent Spanish in several dialects, and Power was sure she could help. He asked the woman to come with him and escorted her to the judge's office. After speaking with the woman for a short time, Judge Reynolds said the woman, a recent immigrant from El Salvador named Gloria Delgado, had been arguing with her husband, Carlos. Apparently, Carlos had ordered Gloria and her children to leave and refused to reconsider when Gloria tried to reason with him. The judge suggested that Power talk to Carlos to see if he could resolve the dispute.

Power would later learn that Mr. Delgado had a reputation as a law-abiding family man with no criminal record or prior incidents of violence but had recently been having trouble controlling his temper. On several occasions, he had suddenly erupted into a rage against his wife and children for no apparent reason. There had been no physical violence, but the intensity of his anger frightened his family. Earlier in the day, while Gloria was at work, he had verbally attacked his stepdaughter Leticia (the teenager who had accompanied Mrs. Delgado to the station) and kicked her out of the house. Leticia had gone to see her mother at work and told her about the confrontation. After returning home to talk to her husband, only to be ordered to take her children and leave, Mrs. Delgado had decided to ask the police for help.

Power didn't know all these details at the time, but he had heard enough to realize he would have to intervene. He wanted to help, but he didn't want to get involved without more information. With the judge translating for him, he asked Mrs. Delgado several questions, including if Carlos had been physically violent, whether he had been drinking or taking drugs, and if he owned any guns. She replied no to all three questions, and her answers to his other questions gave no hint that her husband might be dangerous.

Power thanked the judge for her help and told Mrs. Delgado he would follow her home. As he stepped outside, the scorching heat from the bright summer sun bore into his dark uniform shirt and wrapped itself around him. It was times like this that he became most aware of the thick ballistic vest encasing his upper torso. The thing wasn't much fun to wear, but Power understood the value of being prepared. Though he couldn't afford a new vest, he had borrowed enough money from his father to buy a used one just two weeks earlier. When asking his father for the loan, Power commented that body armor was the best life insurance money could buy. As he slipped behind the wheel of his sweltering patrol car and started following Mrs. Delgado home, he had no inkling how prophetic that statement would soon prove to be.

Within minutes, Mrs. Delgado's station wagon came to a stop in front of a rugged frame house set in the middle of a yard surrounded by a four-foot-high chain-link fence. As Power pulled up just a few feet behind the wagon, Mrs. Delgado and her children climbed out and headed for the side of the vehicle facing away from the house. The husband was nowhere to be seen, and the house was dark as night inside, making the windows shine like mirrors. Power walked over to where the family had gathered next to their car and again asked Mrs. Delgado if her husband had been drinking or had access to any guns. Again, she answered no, and he told her to stay behind while he talked to Carlos.

With his dark blue shirt still sopping up the hot sunlight, Power opened the front gate and moved up the sidewalk toward the front door. The solid door was open, but a dusty screen door stood between him and the pitch-black interior beyond. The darkness was so deep in contrast with the blazing sunlight that Power could see nothing beyond the screen door as he moved closer. Then, with a suddenness equaled only by its intensity, the young officer became aware of the utter silence! Power, a hunter since childhood, knew what silence meant. With his instincts crying out in alarm, he unconsciously slowed his pace. His every sense was fiercely alert to his surroundings, and he braced for the attack he knew was about to come.

Before he could pinpoint the source of the threat, the upper screen in the screen door blew apart, and something crashed into his chest like a wrecking ball. He heard no sound and felt no pain, but the blow instantly dropped him to one knee and started his ears ringing. Bright blood was pooling on the sidewalk below, and something warm was spilling from his mouth. Instinctively, he swiped one hand across his mouth, and it came away streaked with blood.

Without further hesitation, Power rose to his feet, drawing his six-inch Ruger .357 magnum as he moved, and started running to his left to get out of the line of fire. There was a large bush behind him and to his left, and he headed that way. The bush afforded no real cover, but at least it provided some concealment. Moreover, he could watch both the front and left side of the house from there, and he knew he had to keep Delgado inside. As he moved, he saw a hint of dim movement through one of the windows and fired two quick shots at it. He kept moving to his left, firing two more rounds through the next window in hopes of keeping his assailant's head down, and scurried the rest of the way to the bush. As he started to duck behind the bush, another shot slammed into his lower back, just to the right of the tailbone. It was a deer slug, fired from a 12gauge pump shotgun,[1] and it tore through his intestines and exited near his right-front pants pocket. Like the first shot, the blow caused no pain, but it knocked his right leg out from under him, and he crashed to the ground.

The first shot had also been a deer slug, and it had been fired at about five yards, the optimum range for maximum velocity. It had hit him in the left upper chest, clipping his badge and crashing into his newly purchased vest. Though not rated to stop 12-gauge slugs, the body armor had stopped the round. Nevertheless, the impact from the huge chunk of lead had driven the vest's front panel about three and a half inches into Power's chest, bruising his heart, collapsing his left lung, and causing considerable internal bleeding. It had also paralyzed his left arm. He was grievously wounded, deprived of the use of one arm and one leg, and battling an unseen barricaded madman from an exposed position. With only fourteen rounds of ammunition left, no backup en route, and no radio with which to call for help, his situation seemed hopeless. But he was not the kind of man to give up. He crawled behind the bush, where he proned out and watched for Delgado to appear.

More shots rang out from inside, and Power—his ears trained by years of hunting to recognize firearms from their report—didn't like what he heard. The shots cracked with the high pitch of a rifle, and such a weapon could do a lot more damage than the shotgun at this range. However, worse yet in Power's view was that the crazed gunman was now firing at his own family. Bullets were tearing into one side of the station wagon, and Delgado's wife and children were standing, frozen in terror, on the other side!

To Bryan Power—whose soul burned with the spirit of a warrior—this was intolerable. His safety was of little concern when the lives of others were at stake. He yelled at the family to get down and then fired his last two rounds through the screen door to draw Delgado's attention away from them. Reloading a revolver with just one hand is never easy, and Power was badly wounded and unable to rise to a position that would ease the effort. Still, he had been well trained for this task and was unwilling to give up. Using only his right hand, he

---

1. Whereas most shotgun fires numerous pellets from a single shell, a deer slug is a single projectile of the same diameter as the shotgun's barrel. Therefore, a deer slug fired from a 12 gauge shotgun is approximately 0.7 inches in diameter, and weighs 0.875 ounce. In contrast, a 9 mm projectile is about half the diameter of a 12 gauge deer slug (i.e., 0.355 inch) and one third is weight (i.e., 0.262 ounce). Needless to say, a 12 gauge deer slug causes far greater damage than a bullet fired from a handgun.

pushed the cylinder release, swung the cylinder out and, ejected the empties. After slipping the barrel of the gun behind his belt, making sure to keep the ejection rod on the outside, he reloaded with a speedloader.[2] That done, he drew the weapon, pushed its cylinder closed with his thumb, and trained it on the house again.

Delgado's family was still standing trancelike next to the station wagon, and Power still couldn't pinpoint the gunman's position inside the house. Somehow mustering the strength to do what he had to do, Power got to his feet, shuffled over to the four-foot fence while under fire, jumped over it, and made his way to Mrs. Delgado and her children. While pleading with them to get down, he grabbed each one, dragged them to the ground, and huddled them together behind the right-rear wheel of the station wagon (Figure 1).

After ordering everyone to stay put, he moved to the rear bumper and returned fire from there. Under a hail of gunfire from Delgado's rifle—a Winchester .3030 lever action—he crawled over to his patrol car, fired a couple more shots, took cover behind the right-front tire, and reloaded again.

The time to call for help was way overdue, but Power had no walkie-talkie, and this was the first time he had gotten into position to use the car radio. He would have to get into the car first, but all its doors were locked, and the engine had to be running before the radio would work. He reached for the keys on his belt, only to encounter another serious setback. The keys were missing, and they could have fallen anywhere in the battle zone he had just vacated. He moved back to the front of the patrol car to look for them, where he met with a stroke of good luck. The keys were lying on the ground just a few feet in front of the gate. Still drawing fire from Delgado but in desperate need of the keys, he crawled over to them, snatched them up, and returned to the relative safety of his patrol car. He scooted back to the front passenger door. While leaning back against the door, he reached up and tried the key in the lock but couldn't get it to work. Undaunted, he laid the muzzle of his .357 against the window and fired, shattering the glass. He reached inside, released the lock to open the door, and crawled into the front seat. Luckily, the key worked better in the ignition

---

2. A speedloader is a device that allows shooters to load revolvers much more quickly and easily by inserting all six rounds into the gun's cylinder at the same time. Before speedloaders were invented, the shooter would have to load by feeding just one round of ammunition into the cylinder at a time (skilled revolver shooters could feed two rounds into the cylinder simultaneously from ammunition loops, but few officers were issued or allowed to carry loops). Speedloaders were especially helpful when reloading with one hand.

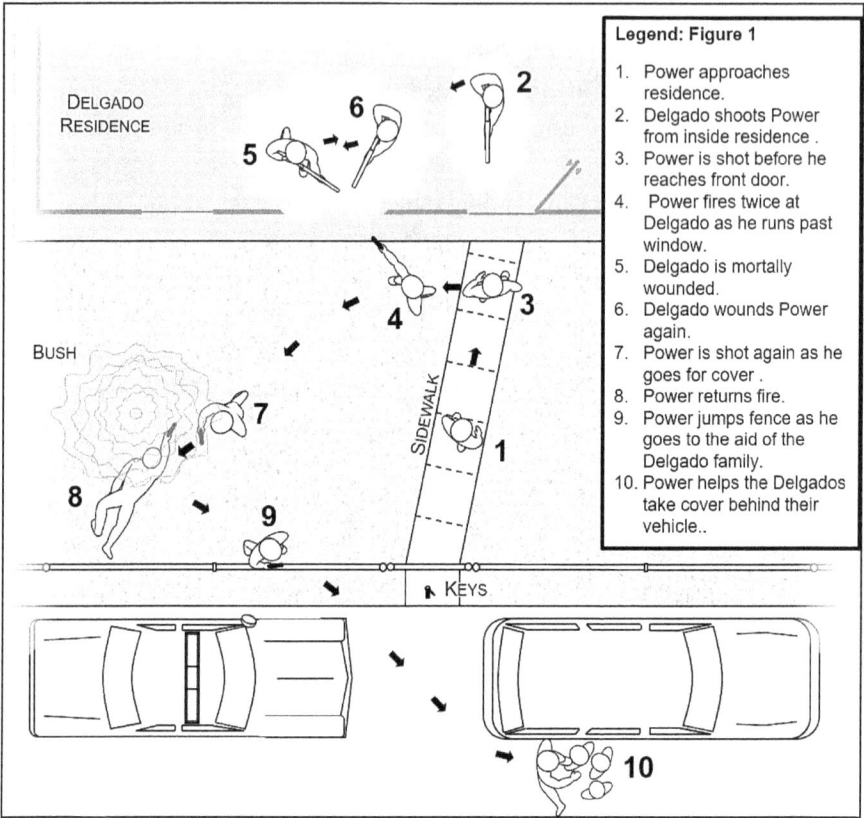

FIGURE 1: Power is severely wounded as he approaches the residence, returns fire, and helps the Delgado family take cover.

than it had in the door, and the engine started right up. He picked up the mic and called for assistance.

Just then, two young boys rode up on bicycles. The patrol car afforded them some protection from Delgado's gunfire, but they were still in grave danger. Power stopped transmitting long enough to shoo them away and then called in again to clarify his location. As he lowered himself back down into the seat, Power gave thought to his injuries. He knew he was grievously wounded and sincerely believed he would die but refused to dwell on it. There were more important things to worry about in his mind, like preventing Delgado from spreading his bloodshed to others. He quickly decided the only thing he could do was hold on and keep Delgado pinned down until help arrived. He crawled back to the front of his cruiser, where he split his attention between waiting to get a shot at Delgado and shouting at the spectators to stay back (Figure 2).

But he had already used his last speedloader and spent one of his remaining six rounds to break the car window. He was running dangerously low on ammunition and wanted to save his last two rounds in case Delgado rushed his position. Focusing on his goal of keeping Delgado contained inside the house, he used his ammunition sparingly, only firing when necessary.

Power had to wait another four long minutes before assistance arrived, but he managed to keep Delgado pinned down without anyone else getting hurt. Then, as two of his backup officers hustled him into a patrol car to take him to the hospital, Power noticed smoke seeping out of the home's windows. Within moments, it was engulfed in flames.

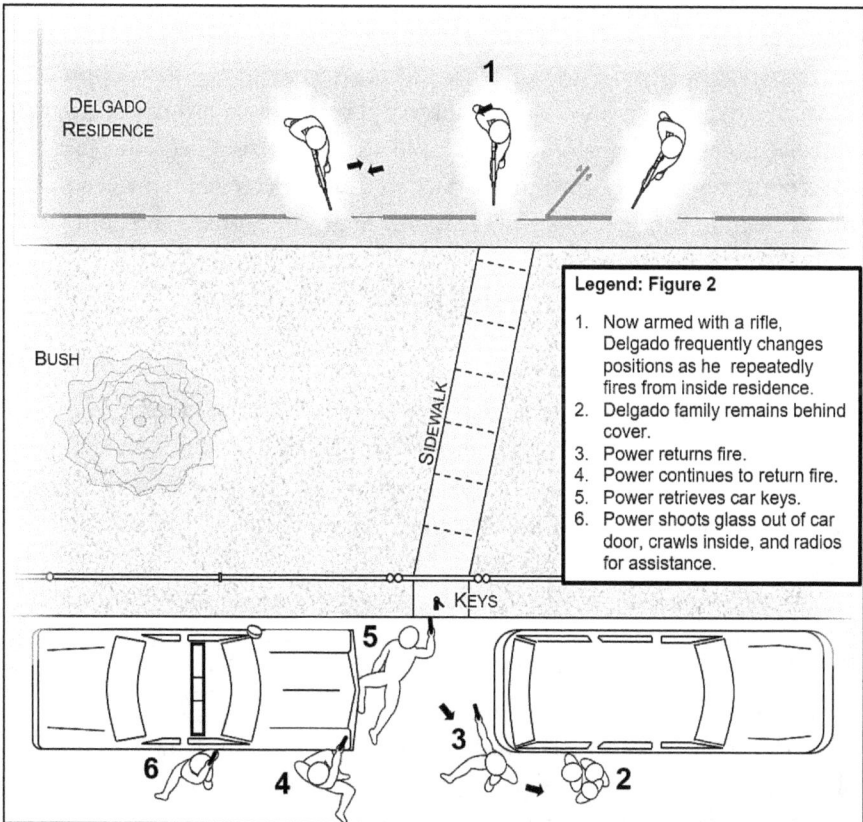

Legend: Figure 2

1. Now armed with a rifle, Delgado frequently changes positions as he repeatedly fires from inside residence.
2. Delgado family remains behind cover.
3. Power returns fire.
4. Power continues to return fire.
5. Power retrieves car keys.
6. Power shoots glass out of car door, crawls inside, and radios for assistance.

FIGURE 2: Delgado fires from several locations inside the residence. Power returns fire and radios for assistance.

THE AFTERMATH

Subsequent investigation disclosed that Delgado had fired 6870 rounds from his shotgun and rifle and had set fire to his house before succumbing to wounds from Power's magnum. It was never determined why Mrs. Delgado lied to Power about her husband's firearms, but investigators believed she was afraid because the police in her native country of El Salvador could not be trusted.

Power's first two shots had found their mark. The first one had hit Delgado squarely in the chest, pierced his left lung, and nicked his heart before lodging in his back. It had been a mortal wound, but the man had survived long enough to keep up the gunfire for another seven or eight minutes. Power's second round had struck Delgado in the lower right abdomen and lodged in his liver. Though not as critical as the first wound, it had caused extensive bleeding and would probably have proven fatal without immediate treatment. The reason for the sudden change in Delgado's behavior was never determined.

Remarkably, Bryan Power made a full recovery despite losing 33 pints of blood and dying four times during surgery. The paralysis in his left arm was short-lived, and he was able to regain full use of his right leg after just five weeks of therapy. He returned to full duty six months later and remained in law enforcement for another ten years. He is now in private business and doing well.

ANALYSIS

Danger Signs
Officer Power first realized something was wrong when he noticed the deep silence as he neared the front door. Since childhood, he had been an avid hunter, and hunters know that silence means a predator is nearby. And, although he wasn't consciously aware of it at the time, he later remembered that he had expected Delgado to show his anger by yelling, banging things around, or otherwise making a lot of noise, which made the silence even more ominous. Power didn't process this additional information at the conscious level, however. Instead, he only *felt* the danger, but that was enough to make him realize he was probably in serious trouble.

Similarly, he later realized that the behavior of Delgado's family was another subtle but significant danger sign. Rather than yelling at Delgado to come outside, attempting to run into the house to confront him, or otherwise showing their anger—as disputants often do when angry and emboldened by the presence of the police—they remained silent. Moreover, they stayed next to the station wagon with its body shielding them from the house. This indicated they were afraid of Delgado and perhaps even worried that he might shoot at them. Again, Power wasn't consciously aware of this fact at the time, but he probably perceived it subconsciously.

This is the way the mind works when danger is present. Since there is seldom time for the conscious mind to think through all the sensory input in its sluggish, rational manner, the subconscious mind does all the work. It detects danger signs, quickly analyzes them, and then communicates its conclusions to the conscious mind in the form of uneasiness, fear, or, when it believes danger is imminent, alarm. Consequently, it is essential to our safety to learn to trust our instincts. Rather than ignoring them or explaining them away, we must immediately recognize fear for what it is and then do something about it. This is not to say we should overreact when we feel the normal uneasiness that comes with potentially dangerous activities, but we must take action when our senses tell us there is cause for concern.

In Officer Power's case, he slowed down and began to take greater inventory of his surroundings. This is what we humans are hardwired to do because when danger is nearby in nature–where predators must make direct contact to kill their prey–we must move slowly while cautiously scanning for threats. However, even though it is still vital to be situationally aware in today's technologically advanced society, and even to slow down in many instances, slowing down can be dangerously counterproductive in others. This is because man's capacity to kill from a distance makes a slow-moving or stationary target vulnerable to attack from concealed or distant locations. Under such circumstances, it is best to immediately move to cover, or at least concealment, before pausing to scan for more danger signs. For example, in Officer Power's case, he might have been able to escape injury by immediately moving diagonally from the sidewalk to the home's closest corner. This unexpected movement would probably have surprised Delgado to the point that he would have missed Power's rapidly moving form as he ran for cover. Even moving forward to a position next to the front door would have been preferable to standing still, as it would have been an unexpected move that enabled him to move quickly out of Delgado's line of fire.

This brings up another key point regarding movement under fire: It is far safer to move laterally than to turn and run in a straight line away from one's assailant. This is because the assailant must keep his gun on target while moving it sideways to hit a laterally moving target. By contrast, he doesn't have to change his point of aim when the target runs straight away from him. So, even though our instincts tell us to spin around and run, it is much safer to quickly move to one side, even when there is no cover in that direction. Then keep going until you reach a safer place. In the event that you must turn and run directly away from your assailant, run in a zig-zag pattern to make you a harder target.

Nevertheless, Officer Power can hardly be faulted for not moving because he simply did what his instincts dictated. Unlike those who have the luxury of learning from his experience, he wasn't aware of this danger. However, if he had been preconditioned through forethought or training to move laterally when in an exposed position, he would have significantly reduced his chances of being shot. This is a primary reason why it is so vital for police officers to think ahead about possible dangers they may encounter, constantly maintain a high level of situational awareness, trust their instinctive warning system, and thoroughly train their minds and bodies in how to respond to various threats.

The same holds for armed citizens and others who want to respond properly to human threats. Besides learning to think ahead and maintain constant situational awareness, they must always be sensitive to their instincts and ready to act upon them in a manner appropriate to the situation. This requires forethought, training, and a commitment to developing a high proficiency level with firearms and unarmed self-defense. And for those who have dangerous jobs or who participate in extreme sports or other risky activities, it means carefully learning those activities' safety protocols and thorough training in the skills needed to apply them in the field.

Approaching Dangerous Persons and Circumstances
The four-foot fence surrounding the yard put Officer Power at a tactical disadvantage by prompting him to walk directly up to the front door in broad daylight. Hindsight suggests that he could have jumped the fence or quickly branched off to one side after entering the gate and then approached from a less vulnerable direction. However, an even better approach is one subsequently developed by Officer Power himself. When backup was scarce, as it often is in rural areas, he ordered the parties in domestic disputes to come outside. This tactic makes good use of a key officer safety principle–ordering individuals to come to the officer instead of going to them. This allows officers to stay behind cover while drawing the subject out into the open, where he can be observed for any signs of weapons or other danger signs. At the same time, the subject

is placed at a tactical disadvantage, and he knows it. In many cases, this will discourage potentially violent offenders from attacking, making the encounter significantly safer for both the offender and the officer.

The idea of being told to approach a police officer may seem unreasonably intrusive to some or even frightening or offensive, but such is not the intent. Rather, the officer's highest priority is to reduce the likelihood of violence by firmly establishing and maintaining control over every street encounter. This tactic is one of the safest and best ways to do that.

It is also worth noting that the core principle behind this tactic (i.e., maintain a safe distance from danger) is as good advice for any other citizen as it is for police officers. For example, when confronting an intruder in your home, it is much safer to keep your distance and stay behind cover, not only for you but for your loved ones as well. Consider the possible consequences to them if the intruder managed to incapacitate you when you exposed yourself by leaving cover. Violent criminals may not be particularly intelligent, but they often possess more than enough cunning to draw you into their kill zone. Similarly, it is best to let him go if he decides to run, especially if your state doesn't have a castle law[3] to protect you legally. Instead, stay with your family and call the police. That way, your loved ones and property stay safe while you avoid unnecessarily putting your life at risk by chasing the intruder. As every officer knows, foot chases are wrought with danger because they allow the offender to stop once he is out of view and then set an ambush for his pursuer.

Likewise, if you suspect that something is amiss when approaching a place you intend to enter, don't go in until you are sure it is safe. And don't rush ahead to investigate suspicious circumstances, satisfy your curiosity, record a potentially dangerous incident on your cell phone, or otherwise expose yourself to danger. Stay back, assess the situation further, and then decide what to do next. Depending upon the circumstances, you may decide to call 911, leave the area, cautiously approach the location to get a better look, etc., but don't rush into something that makes you feel unsafe.

And never do any more than necessary to keep yourself and your loved ones safe. When responding to one of the many prowler calls I handled over the years, I pulled up a short distance from the darkened home. It was set back from

---

3. Castle laws are laws that give citizens the legal right to use lethal force against persons unlawfully in their homes. In states without these laws, there is a much greater chance that someone who uses deadly force while defending his home will be charged with aggravated assault or murder. Regardless of the laws on use of force in defense of home, it is the author's opinion that deadly force should only be used when the resident has reasonable grounds to believe that it is necessary in defense of his life or the lives of others.

the street among several trees that only deepened the darkness. Before I could exit my car, a figure emerged from the shadows along one side of the house and strolled toward me. Fortunately, his body language gave no hint of danger, but I saw a shiny object in his right hand, resting casually along his right thigh. I looked closer. It was a gun, but again, there was something about his body language that told me he wasn't dangerous.

Nevertheless, any gun can hurt you, and I wasn't one to ignore the danger. I drew mine and pointed it at him. I don't know if he could see my gun, but I had barely completed the draw when he pocketed his and kept walking toward me. "Who are you," I asked, "What are you doing here?" He told me he was the homeowner and said he had called us and then come outside to look for the prowler. Who does that? It was just one of the many incredibly foolish things people do in the presence of police officers. Think before you act, and don't bite off more than you can chew.

Lighting Considerations

Delgado's attack was essentially an ambush, and the lighting conditions gave him a major advantage. It was a bright day, and the house's interior was dark, virtually turning all the windows into mirrors. To make matters worse, the dusty screen in the screen door blocked the outdoor light while also reflecting much of the sunlight like a dirty window. It was nearly impossible for Power to see inside and easy for Delgado to watch his approach in the bright sunshine.

This mirror effect can be used to your advantage in some situations. For example, by keeping the outside of your home well-lit at night, you can make it difficult for others to see inside as long as you keep your interior lights turned off, or at least as dim as possible.. Similarly, if you hear suspicious noises outside, turn off your interior lights before looking out to investigate. Depending upon the layout and lighting in your home, you may also be able to keep the room just inside your front door dark at night. This will allow you to approach your front door in darkness if someone unexpectedly knocks. And if your porch is kept well-lit, your door has a peephole, and you approach the door quietly, you can identify the person without being seen or heard.

If you suspect someone has unlawfully entered your home after you have gone to bed and decide to investigate instead of locking yourself in your room and calling 911 (usually your best option), it is best not to turn on any lights. Since your night vision will be at its best after being awakened from sleep, you can move freely about without the lights, which may give you some advantage over the intruder, especially if he is focused on negotiating through unfamiliar territory without making too much noise. Also, turning your lights on will alert him to your presence, which could make him panic and react aggressively against you. Conversely, if you approach quietly in the dark, you may be able to observe him without him seeing you, which will give you time to plan your next move before he sees you. Depending on the circumstances, you may want to watch him until he leaves, retreat, and call the police, shout out to him in the hope he will flee, or challenge him with a weapon. However, it is extremely dangerous to leave your room to look for an intruder after calling the police, especially if you are armed. Remember, the responding officers will be expecting an intruder, and they have no way of knowing you are the homeowner. There are few things more dangerous than surprising an armed police officer with a gun in your hand.

When to Call for Help

Officer Power delayed calling for assistance until he could get the Delgado family safely behind cover and then take cover himself. This was counter to our natural urge to summon help immediately when in grave danger, and his ability to do so was a testimony to his laser focus on fighting back and protecting others. It was also a wise choice because calling for help can be a time-consuming distraction that can divert us from doing other things that are more necessary to our safety. If trapped in a room during a fire, for example, calling 911 should be one of your top priorities, but even then, it would be better to drop to the floor to escape the smoke first. Likewise, even though it is important to call the police in a mass casualty incident, it is even more important to get you and your family behind cover or out of the hot zone altogether. Exactly when to call 911 depends upon the circumstances, but far more often than not, other things take precedence. Do what you have to do first, and then call 911 and go back to doing what you must do to survive.

Winning Mindset

By far, the most notable thing about Officer Power's awe-inspiring story is what it can teach us about the warrior spirit and winning mindset. Despite grave danger to himself, he never lost focus on his duty to protect others. Even though his desperate situation was largely due to Mrs. Delgado's lie about her husband not owning any guns, he was more concerned about her and her family's safety than with his own. Even as his life seemed to be ebbing away, he remained focused on keeping Delgado pinned down inside the house so he couldn't harm anyone else. This unselfish devotion to others when any less of a man would have been thinking only of his survival marks him as an inspiring example of a warrior of the highest caliber.

Unlike merciless killers who make war for selfish gain, oppress others, or force their beliefs on "infidels," true warriors fight because others depend on them. Like Power, they fight ferociously when necessary, not because they take pleasure in it but because it is the right thing to do. Motivated by a driving commitment to protect others, they stay focused on that commitment even when their own lives are on the line.

What makes some people true warriors? Like other human characteristics, the warrior spirit is innately stronger in some individuals than others. Still, it also appears to be a quality that can be developed and enhanced through proper motivation and training. Officer Power is a good example. From an early age, he had been taught to put others first. Raised by a devout family guided by principles like that expressed in the familiar Bible passage, "Greater love has no one than this, that he lay down his life for his friends" (John 15:13), he possessed a steadfast faith in God and strong devotion to others, traits the author has found to be common among officers who perform heroically when defending others. Moreover, many of his relatives and friends had served in combat while in the military, and everyone in his family held military service in high esteem. All this helped mold him into a person who honored warrior virtues, like the duty to protect others, regardless of the personal cost.

Officer Power's father had also taught him that many of the unfortunate things in life can't be prevented or controlled by us, but we can control how we respond to them. The key is to control oneself, assess the situation, decide, and then act. Power had been encouraged to think on his feet, act decisively, and have confidence in his decisions. He had learned that decisive action under stress virtually ensures good results, and this confidence helped him remain calm and mentally flexible under fire.

In a manner typical of winners, Officer Power also fought back despite the odds against him. Whether facing a violent opponent, a severe illness or injury, or any other grave challenge in life, the single most indispensable thing you can do is to keep fighting, no matter what. There is an enormously powerful connection between our mind and body, and with the right attitude, the human body can take a great deal more punishment than most would think. If we use our minds and spirits to inspire us to keep going, we can overcome just about anything. Officer Power demonstrated this in a dramatically courageous way.

But perhaps the most remarkable trait displayed by Officer Power was his ability to focus on his capabilities rather than the severity of the predicament confronting him. In reality, his situation was nearly hopeless. He was severely wounded, losing blood fast, dangerously exposed while fighting a well-concealed, heavily armed opponent, severely limited in his firepower, and compelled by his values to focus most of his attention on people who were making matters worse by their refusal to take cover. Nevertheless, he refused to dwell on the negatives. This was most evident in a comment he made later when talking about his thoughts while returning fire from behind the bush. Instead of focusing on the fact that he was paralyzed in one arm and one leg and down to only two live rounds in his gun, he confidently stated, "I knew I had two rounds left, one good leg and one hand."[iii] This is just the kind of attitude that turns the tide of battle in even the most hopeless situations.

In a follow-up statement to the one just quoted, Officer Power provides valuable insight into how such optimism can spring up in a warrior's mind in combat. He went on to say, "I was trying to figure out what I could do, and I knew I had to get those women (Delgado's wife and daughter) down."[iv] Driven by his duty to protect others, he made it his goal to get the women into a position of safety and concentrated on using the few assets at his disposal to achieve that goal. By setting worthy goals like this and forcing ourselves to focus on reaching them, we can crowd out any negative thoughts that might otherwise get in the way. When we learn to do this, we—like Officer Power—will be better prepared to overcome any obstacle, no matter how dangerous. By his courageous actions, Officer Power showed us the power of goal setting, a never-say-die attitude, and warrior-like optimism when facing any great trial in our lives.

CHAPTER 10

Tough Call, Tragic Ending:
The Nicholas Reed, J.T. Thomas,
Mitch Allen Case

Suicide by cop "involves a distraught and emotionally imbalanced individual using the officer to commit suicide. Thus, the officer is thrust into a situation in which he or she is the victim and essentially becomes victimized by the individual."

—DR. JOHN AZAR-DICKENS, CLINICAL PSYCHOLOGIST

"The only person who gets what he wants in a suicide by cop is the suicidal person. Nobody wins."

—ANONYMOUS POLICE OFFICER

THE INCIDENT

Officer Nicholas Reed, a 25-year-old rookie and former U.S. Marine with a bright mind, compassionate heart, and job he loved, heard the quiet radio come to life with his call sign. It had been a quiet, peaceful night so far, but something was about to happen that would change everything for the worst.

The call was for unknown trouble, possibly involving a domestic dispute, in a nearby residential neighborhood. And it didn't sound good. The dispatcher said a hysterical woman had pleaded for an officer to come to her home, hung up, and then failed to answer the dispatcher's return call. Officers generally dread domestics because tensions are high, anger is running wild, and things can go south instantly. And the fact that the woman had hung up suddenly and would not–or worse, possibly could not–answer the return call was especially concerning.

Reed flipped on his overheads and raced down dark streets toward the location, arriving there within about three minutes. Still not completely familiar with all the addresses in town, he shot past the house. Realizing his mistake, he stopped two doors away and started to back up. As he drew closer, he spotted a young man, later identified as 23-year-old Ronald Dale (J.T.) Thomas, Jr., standing next to a car in the street. He pulled up close to where Thomas stood and asked him if he knew the location of the address he was looking for.

"Right here," the young man replied, "What's up?"

Reed stepped from his cruiser into the warm spring night and approached the man. With only a few streetlights to pierce the darkness, it was hard to see. His eyes went to what he had been taught to focus on—the man's hands. Since hands hold guns and other weapons, every cop is trained to look at them first and keep them in view throughout every street contact. What he saw immediately raised a concern that needed to be addressed. Thomas's hands were behind his back.

"Show me your hands!" he demanded.

"No," Thomas replied, "I don't want to."

Reed wasn't yet alarmed, but Thomas's answer was cause for growing concern. Thomas might well be one of the disputants in this ominous-sounding call, which meant he might be wound tight, upset at seeing the police, and armed with anything from a small kitchen knife or screwdriver to a firearm. Worse, people who answer commands with a definitive "No" usually mean what they say. Reed repeated the command, this time with much greater authority and an expletive for added emphasis.

"Why you gotta cuss me?" Thomas asked.

Then he slowly moved his hands out from behind his back and held them at his side. In his right hand was a semiautomatic Smith & Wesson pistol. Almost without thinking, Reed drew his gun, pointed it at Thomas, and, while moving toward the parked car for cover, ordered him to put the weapon down.

"Can't do that," the man replied but kept the gun pointing down at his side.

The young officer sensed that this man was probably not a threat, but there was no way to know for sure. "I don't wanna shoot you, brother," he said and again ordered him to put the gun down.

"Just shoot me," Thomas pleaded in a voice filled with hopelessness as he started backing up the sidewalk toward the house. "Just shoot me!"

"Suicide by cop," Reed thought. With the uneasy feeling that it would be a useless plea, he repeated his command once again.

Meanwhile, Officers Lawrence Shaw and Mitch Allen had heard the call, and both had independently decided to assist. Like all officers responding to domestic violence calls, both had cut their lights and sirens as they drew closer to the scene.[1] Then they heard the dispatcher broadcast a warning to "Watch out for a weapon!"

Reed had also heard the warning. Now reminded that he should let his backup officers know what was happening, he radioed back, "Got a gun here."

Things had escalated to a whole new level. A rookie cop, alone on an already dangerous call, and now a gun. Fearful for Reed's wellbeing, adrenalin pumping, and coming in dark, Allen and Shaw nearly collided as they rolled up to the scene. Shaken but determined to help, they jumped from their cruisers and headed Reed's way with guns drawn.

Reed was grateful for the backup but sensed that their arrival might panic Thomas and escalate the crisis even further. Thomas was distraught, and two more armed police officers might inadvertently put him over the edge. Sadly, that is exactly what happened.

The young man started moving toward the driveway while again begging to be shot and then raised the gun. He pointed in Reed's general direction but well to his left. As all three officers repeatedly ordered him to drop his gun, Thomas advanced toward Shaw and Allen, his gun now raised to shoulder level and swinging back and forth from one officer to another.

Having no way of knowing what Reed had already ascertained, both Shaw and Allen credibly believed all of their lives were in danger. As Shaw again shouted a warning that he would shoot if Thomas didn't drop the gun, Allen opened fire.

He fired four shots, missing with three in the darkness, but hitting the suicidal young man in the head with his fourth, killing him instantly.

THE AFTERMATH

Later while the scene was being processed, it was discovered that J.T. Thomas's gun was unloaded. Though Officer Allen had no way of knowing it at the time, he had killed an essentially unarmed man.

Adding to the tragedy, the frantic caller (Thomas's ex-girlfriend and mother of his infant son) had told the dispatcher that Thomas had removed the magazine from his gun before going outside to confront the police. She then added

---

1. Officers do this on dangerous calls to make it harder for any violent offenders at the scene to see them coming and flee, prepare to resist with force, or even set an ambush.

that he had also said he intended to force the police to kill him. However, amidst all her fast-paced communications with the hysterical caller, aggravated by the need to warn the officers before it was too late, the dispatcher had failed to relay these two key pieces of information to them. It was an honest mistake under the circumstances, but one with disastrous consequences.

In a perplexing twist that added injustice to the tragic mix, Officer Reed was subsequently fired, ending his career with the department almost before it had started and made it considerably more difficult to find a police job anywhere else. The police chief could offer no reasonable explanation for dismissing the young officer, but in this author's opinion, the best, most logical explanation was that he did it to make Reed a scapegoat. Mr. Thomas's loved ones were devastated and understandably unable to grasp how an officer can justifiably shoot someone with an unloaded gun, and the police department had not trained its officers in how to handle suicide-by-cop incidents. Controversial police shootings are virtually guaranteed to lead to a civil suit, a severely tarnished image of the police department, and loss of public trust. There was no reason to expect this shooting would be any different, and firing Officer Reed was probably intended to add credibility to the department's assertion that the shooting was undeniably necessary. In essence, it appears that the department was saying, "It was so obvious that the officers' lives were at stake that only a coward would withhold fire." However, it didn't work out well for the department because Reed's dismissal only added to the controversy, did nothing to bring comfort to Mr. Thomas' loved ones, and culminated with the city having to pay $175,000 to settle a lawsuit by Reed for unlawfully terminating him.[v]

Officers Allen and Shaw are still with the same department, and Reed is currently working as a truck driver. It is unknown if he plans to return to police work.[vi] [2]

ANALYSIS

Differing Perspectives

This tragic incident provides several dramatic examples of how and why armed police encounters are so often misunderstood. The most significant of these can be seen in the stark contrast between Officer Reed's view of the encounter and that of Officers Allen and Shaw. In the short time before the other two

---

2. The incident recounted here is true, but the names were changed to ensure the privacy of those personally involved. Likewise, to preserve confidentiality and clarity, some facts have been altered, but the essential elements of the story remain unchanged.

officers arrived, Officer Reed had gathered enough information to correctly conclude that Thomas was bent on committing suicide and had no desire to harm anyone else. He had also had time to take cover, which gave him some safety if he was wrong, and with that safety came less stress and a calmer mind. Still, there was no way to know for sure what Thomas would do next, and it was clear that, since action is always faster than reaction, the man could easily get off the first shot. It took courage to withhold fire under the circumstances, but Reed had courage to spare, and his gut told him Thomas wasn't a threat (good police work often hinges on listening to one's instincts). Deciding it was worth the risk to withhold fire, he kept his gun trained on the man while trying to convince him to put the gun down. From Reed's perspective, he was doing the right thing. But then Officers Allen and Shaw showed up, and he immediately sensed the danger posed by their sudden, high-profile arrival. He would have liked to explain things to them, but things were happening too fast for that.

Meanwhile, Officer Allen knew that Reed–a rookie–was alone on the scene of a domestic dispute involving an armed disputant. The dispatcher hadn't mentioned that the gun might be unloaded, and even if she had, he could not be certain about the validity of her information. He rushed to the scene, adrenalin pumping and fearful for Reed's safety, and then almost collided with Officer Shaw's squad in the dark. Reed was standing there, holding an armed man at gunpoint. And even though the armed man was holding the gun down at his side, that soon changed. As he and Shaw approached, the gunman suddenly raised his pistol and pointed it at all three officers. People involved in domestic disputes are usually emotionally distraught and often see responding officers as authority figures who have no right to interfere in their personal lives. And when someone points a gun at an officer or anyone else, it is entirely reasonable to conclude that he means to use it. Allen had every right to defend himself, and he couldn't let the rookie or Shaw take a bullet either. From his perspective, he did the right thing.

Which of these two officers made the right decision? With the luxury of hindsight and all the additional facts that only came to light later, Officer Reed certainly did. Since Thomas's gun was, in fact, empty, withholding fire would have saved his life without endangering Reed or anyone else in the process. But Officer Allen acted from a different perspective–he had no way of knowing Thomas's gun was empty, and, unlike Reed, he didn't have the advantage of being able to assess Thomas's emotional condition. Moreover, time was not on his side. From all appearances, he and his fellow officers were facing an immediate threat that demanded immediate action. He had the right to defend himself and the obligation to defend his fellow officers by stopping Thomas's aggressive actions as quickly as possible. Therefore, the questions we should be asking ourselves is: "What if Allen had been correct in his assessment of the threat posed by Thomas and Reed had been wrong? What if the gun had, in fact, been loaded, and Thomas had been desperate enough to fire on the officers? How much of a threat would Thomas have been to other responding officers, other citizens who got in his way, or even his ex-girlfriend if he had shot the officers and fled the scene or barricaded himself inside the house?

Was the Dispatcher to Blame for Not Telling the Officers that Thomas' Gun Was Unloaded?

It would be easy to say "yes" to this question on the surface, but that is too simplistic. What if Thomas's girlfriend had been lying to protect him when she said the gun was unloaded, and he had decided to shoot the officers in his current irrational state of mind? Or more likely, what if she had been mistaken about the gun being empty? A gun is not fully unloaded just because the magazine is removed, as one round is still in the chamber, and, with rare exceptions, the gun can still be fired while it is removed. However, many people who are unfamiliar with firearms are not aware of this, leading them to believe the gun is safe. Considering these facts, would it be safe for an officer to assume a gun is entirely unloaded just because someone on the scene says so? Remember, police officers have a right to defend themselves and the duty to protect their fellow citizens and officers. People in emotional turmoil are unpredictable, and it would be irresponsible to assume that they would not harm others, including their loved ones. While it is enormously important to avoid hurting emotionally disturbed persons, we cannot allow them to hurt others. The burden of deciding where and when to use deadly force under such circumstances lies with the officers on the scene, and they have don't have the time or resources to make a fully informed, well-thought-out decision. And the decision isn't made any easier by hearing reports that the gun might be unloaded.

Lawful but Awful

This tragic encounter was what is often referred to as a "Lawful but Awful" shooting. While Officer Allen's decision to shoot was morally and legally justified, the consequences were tragic for everyone involved. Officer Reed was unfairly dismissed from a job he loved. Officer Allen had to live with the fact that he had killed an emotionally disturbed young man who–though he had no way of knowing it at the time–was not a serious threat to anyone. Thomas's ex-girlfriend and family lost a dearly loved one, and the police department's image was tarnished in the eyes of many. The only person who got what he wanted was Thomas, and he would probably act differently if he could do it all over again. Sadly, he was the only person at the scene who had much control over the outcome, and he made the wrong choice in response to Allen and Shaw's sudden arrival. No one wins in these tragedies, and finding someone to blame for the outcome does little to ease the pain of everyone involved.

Judging Police Shootings in Hindsight

Besides highlighting the utter heartbreak of lawful but awful shootings, another crucial point to emphasize here is that the only way to ensure proper justice in any police shooting—or any other self-defense shooting, for that matter—is to remove hindsight from the equation. Otherwise, we end up punishing people for the results rather than the correctness of their actions at the time of the shooting. To judge in hindsight is categorically unjust, especially in a criminal justice system where everyone—even a police officer—is innocent until proven guilty.

To better understand this issue from a lay person's perspective, let's say someone has just pushed your back door open in the middle of the night and is coming inside with what appears to be a handgun in his hand. You brought your gun with you when you went to investigate the sound of someone breaking in, and you raise it while repeatedly shouting at him to leave. But he keeps coming, yelling something you can't understand. Visibly oblivious to your commands, he points the gun at you. You pull the trigger, and he collapses to the floor as the gun falls from his hand and blood flows from his wound. You call 911 and ask for the police and an ambulance, but the man dies before they arrive. Later you learn that the gun had a broken firing pin,[3] and the intruder was a highly intoxicated but law-abiding neighbor you had never met but whose house is similar to yours. Most likely, he was confused and may have thought you were an intruder in his own home.

Since you just killed someone, your actions are ruled a homicide (a legal term meaning only that he died at the hand of another human being, either lawfully or unlawfully). Is this justified self-defense, manslaughter, or murder? Since the man's gun was harmless, and he was probably just confused and trying

---

3. A firearm with a broken firing pin is incapable of firing, even when the firearm is fully loaded. Firing pins rarely break, but when they do, there are no outward sign to indicate that the gun will not fire.

to get home, your actions would almost certainly be deemed unlawful *if judged in hindsight*. You would be charged with at least manslaughter, or more likely, murder. But fortunately, the courts don't look at it that way. They recognize that no one has a crystal ball. Human beings can only act on what they believe at the time, and as long as your belief was reasonable, you will be judged on that basis rather than hindsight. This common-law rule has long been basic to self-defense cases and is still in use today. It was terribly unfair for your neighbor to die for making a harmless drunken blunder, but it would only add a great injustice to the tragedy to punish you for doing what you honestly believed was necessary to protect you and your family.

The same holds for police officers. Lawful but awful shootings are indisputable tragedies because they ruin the lives of so many innocent people. Nevertheless, it would be wrong to judge them from the perspective of an unruffled judge sitting safely in a sterile courtroom, absent the stress, confusion, and rapidly changing circumstances that confronted those who were there. The courts wisely understand this when judging police officers as well as citizens, and they rule accordingly. But many activists, politicians, media personalities, and ordinary citizens do not.

Legal Principles Regarding Deadly Force

Many well-intentioned but uninformed people don't realize that the legal principles regarding deadly force are largely the same for police officers as they are for other citizens, with only two significant exceptions. The first is that police officers are permitted to use deadly force to stop fleeing felons. Many years ago, this held even for nonviolent felons, but since 1985 such force has been wisely restricted to persons who have threatened the officer with a weapon or incidents in which the officer has probable cause to believe the offender committed a dangerous felony or poses a lethal threat to the officer or others.[vii] Officers are given this authority because of their obligation to apprehend violent criminals for the public's protection, but they rarely use it except under the most extreme circumstances.

The second exception is that officers are not required to retreat when threatened or attacked, as is the case for ordinary citizens in some states. However, the laws in many states have long allowed, or have recently given, citizens the right to stand their ground when threatened. Moreover, we must not forget that officers would be virtually powerless to arrest hostile offenders if they were required to retreat in the face of threatened resistance. They would have to simply walk away and let the offender continue his criminal activities in the foolish hope that he would later have a change of heart and turn himself in. Even worse, officers would be required to back down if threatened while intervening in violent crimes in progress, including active shooter incidents. The bottom line is that the people you call when in danger—the police—have only slightly more of a right to defend themselves than you do. The idea that officers are somehow given unreasonably more latitude than other citizens in using deadly force is a fallacy.[4]

The "All Cops are Trigger-Happy" Myth

Another popular fallacy is the idea that police officers are trigger-happy brutes who prefer to shoot first and ask questions later or that such violence is encouraged in police training. While it is unfortunately true that police officers sometimes use excessive force, it is far less common than many critics claim. To suggest that police trainers and the officers themselves encourage the use of unjustified *deadly* force is absurd. It flies in the face of all logic to believe that any person, trainer, or organization with even minimal moral character would risk their integrity and legal wellbeing by encouraging the unlawful use of deadly force. Moreover, contrary to many, police officers are held accountable when they use excessive force, especially when lethal force is involved. They can and often are sued when they are negligent in their use of force and–on those rare occasions when their actions are done with criminal intent–even charged and convicted of crimes (the fate most officers fear most).

The assumption that cops are trigger happy is also inconsistent with all the training I attended during my 32-year police career, nor have I ever come across even a hint of it in my over 25 years as a police trainer. Even as far back as my academy days in the mid-1070s, we were inundated with horror stories about officers who were sued and imprisoned for unlawful use of deadly force. It was drilled into us that we could not, and should not, shoot unless the offender demonstrated the ability, opportunity, and intent to use deadly force against us or someone else. We were, of course, told that deadly force was authorized to

---

4. The opinions, comments and other ideas expressed in this section are, like the other comments in this book, based upon the author's training, research, and experience both as a police officer and as a police trainer. Though well-read in many aspects of the legal use of deadly force, he is not an attorney and his opinions should not be taken as legal advice. In addition, laws vary from state to state, and are often interpreted in different ways by the courts. Please consult with an attorney if you wish to know more about these legal issues or have any questions about use of force by citizens and law officers in your state.

stop fleeing felons, but it was discouraged, and few officers considered doing so unless necessary to protect themselves or others.

It appears that the myth that cops are taught to shoot first comes from the fact that they are told to be more decisive when applying force at all levels, including deadly force. There are two reasons for this. The first is that too little force can dramatically escalate violence by allowing the resisting offender to continue aggressive actions, thereby forcing the officer to apply ever-higher levels of force (more on this later). The other reason is because of the dangerous propensity among officers to delay using deadly force when their safety and the safety of others depends upon quick, decisive action. Unfortunately, as harsh as it may sound, we must also realize that there are times when the only way to save innocent lives is to use deadly force decisively (e.g., active shooter incidents, the infamous murders of Deputy Kyle Dinkheller and Officer Vetter,[5] etc.). Because of their reluctance to use such force, officers often ignore this harsh truth by putting themselves and sometimes others at great risk by repeatedly ordering armed offenders to surrender, drop their guns, etc.

Consequently, as regrettable as it may be, police trainers must take on the difficult task of thoroughly training their officers when to shoot as well as when to withhold fire. Many factors must be considered when making the shoot/don't shoot decision. This decision is made even more difficult because it must be made under highly stressful conditions and within severe time constraints. It is vital to public safety for every police officer to be properly trained for this most difficult task, but it isn't easy, and it takes a lot of time, resources, and money.

POLICE OFFICERS CAN GET BY WITH MURDER BY
CLAIMING THEY WERE AFRAID

This misconception is rooted in an alarmingly incomplete understanding of the law regarding self-defense as a justification for the use of force by police officers—or any other citizen for that matter. When critics assert that police officers can dodge prosecution for murder and other violent crimes by claiming they were afraid, they ignore that the law on self-defense is not that simple. The defendant can't get by simply saying he used deadly force because he was afraid. Rather, he must convince the court that a reasonable police officer under the same or similar set of circumstances would have believed his life

---

5. In separate shootings during two different traffic stops, both Deputy Dinkheller and Officer Vetter were killed after repeatedly ordering their killers to put their guns down. In both cases, the offenders ignored the officers' commands as they continued to aggressively carry out their planned attacks.

was in danger. If, for example, an officer was confronted by a man with a knife threatening him from the other side of a chain-link fence, would it be objectively reasonable for the officer to shoot him? Of course not, because there was an obstacle preventing the knife-wielding man from inflicting any serious harm on him. On the other hand, if there was no fence, and the man's actions were threatening enough to cause a reasonable officer to fear for his life, deadly force would be justified. Similarly, would it be objectively reasonable to shoot someone pointing a gun at you? Of course. But what if it turned out that the gun was a realistic toy, no longer functional, or—as in this case—unloaded? Since there was no way at the time for you to know the gun was incapable of harming you, deadly force would be objectively reasonable. In these cases, the matter in question is not whether the officer believed his life was in danger but whether a reasonable officer under the same set of circumstances would have been in fear for his life.

Though many police critics believe this gives police officers license to kill with impunity, it is significant to note that regular citizens are held to essentially the same standard as the police in cases of self-defense. Like police officers, their use of force is found to be justified as long as a reasonable citizen under the same or similar set of circumstances would have believed his life to be in danger. Note that citizens are not compared to police officers here but their fellow citizens. If this were not the case, it would be considerably more difficult for them to defend themselves because it would require them to be as knowledgeable about the laws related to the use of force as police officers, which is an unreasonably high expectation for regular citizens. To claim that police officers can beat a murder charge by simply claiming they were scared is absurd and only serves to stir up unwarranted anger toward the police and judicial system.

Nevertheless, some police critics are trying to change the law in at least two ways that unreasonably restrict police officers' rights to defend themselves. First, they are trying to allow officers to be judged in hindsight rather than on what they knew at the time (see the "Judging Police Shootings in Hindsight" section of this analysis). At first glance, this may appear to be a minor obstacle to justice, but it can have grave results for police officers when accused of murder or any other excessive use of force. The problem is that no human being can be expected to see into the future. This principle threatens to judge officers for what came to light after the fact, rather than what they knew at the time, thus creating a grave risk of unjustly convicting an innocent person.

Some police critics are also demanding that officers be held responsible for their assailants' death when they escalate dangerous confrontations by knowingly or unknowingly exposing themselves to danger. Apparently, they believe the officer should somehow be blamed for the death because his risky actions encouraged his assailant to attack him, thereby forcing him to use deadly force in self-defense. The problem here is that cops take risks all the time, especially when protecting others or apprehending dangerous offenders. For example, an officer can't respond to a domestic disturbance without exposing himself to danger as he approaches and enters the scene and to even greater danger as he attempts to deal with the disputants inside. Under this proposed change, he could be charged with murder if one of the disputants opened fire on him, thereby forcing him to return fire in self-defense. Whether this change would go to such an extreme as this is questionable, but the principle that officers should be held responsible for an offender's death simply because they put themselves at physical risk is absurd. Besides being morally wrong, it has the dangerous potential of creating confusion and hesitancy in officers' minds when handling already highly stressful situations. Since confusion and stress cloud thinking and lead to poor decision-making, the results could be disastrous for the offender and the police.

Should our officers, who put themselves in harm's way to protecting us from violent criminals, have less of a right to defend themselves than other citizens? How would that affect their willingness to take necessary risks to apprehend dangerous offenders? Would you blame them for walking away from any criminal who showed anger or an unwillingness to submit to arrest? Do any of us want such timid police officers protecting our lives and property?

The Qualified Immunity Defense Unfairly Protects Police Officer from Facing Justice When They Use Excessive Force

Before discussing the validity of this notion, we need to define qualified immunity: Qualified immunity is a legal defense that grants limited immunity to government officials, including police officers, in civil rights lawsuits. It grants police officers immunity from liability when they unknowingly violated a citizen's constitutional right that has not yet been clearly established in court. The standard for determining whether the citizen's constitutional right was clearly established depends on two questions 1) Has there been an earlier appellate court ruling on a case that is similar enough to the case in question to make a reasonable officer aware that such conduct is illegal, and 2) would it be obvious to a reasonable officer that such conduct was a violation of one's constitutional rights. If the answer to either of these questions is yes, qualified immunity will not be granted.

The purpose of qualified immunity is to free officers (and other government officials) from frivolous lawsuits when they unintentionally violate a citizen's rights in good faith. Whether it has been effective in achieving this purpose is a hotly contested debate in the legal community, as is the question of whether it is too lenient on officers. This is a much more complex legal issue than it may appear, with good arguments on both sides that require a great deal more legal knowledge to decipher than this author possesses.

However, I can say that qualified immunity is certainly not a free pass for police officers accused of using excessive force, as many police critics claim. Even if we concede that it is too lenient toward police officers, it is clear that it does not always protect them from losing a lawsuit. A recent *Reuters* article that severely criticizes qualified immunity[viii] cited a study of 252 excessive force cases in which the officers made a motion for qualified immunity and concluded that the officers won 50.5 percent of the time. Granted, 50.5 percent is a majority, but it certainly is not a large enough percentage to conclude that qualified immunity makes police officers virtually invulnerable to liability.

It is also worth noting that federal court rules give the citizen a great advantage over the officers when the court reviews qualified immunity requests. Rather than trying to determine who is telling the truth when there are conflicting statements about the material facts, judges must accept the citizen's version unless there is convincing evidence to the contrary. When one party must automatically be believed over the other, it is particularly difficult to ensure a fair and proper judgment.

Further, officers are also put at a disadvantage by the requirement that they will not be granted qualified immunity if there has been an earlier appellate court ruling against conduct similar to theirs. This means that even though this defense is supposed to prevent them from being successfully sued for unknowingly violating a citizen's rights, in practice, it is difficult for officers to stay abreast of recent court rulings. Most of them are not taught about the importance of staying updated on recent court decisions, let alone trained in how to access the necessary information to do so. Therefore, they may unwittingly violate a citizen's rights without even knowing that a recent court decision made their actions illegal. This ignorance may seem strange considering the dire need for police officers to know the law on constitutional rights thoroughly. Still, we must also consider that, although officers are relatively well trained in the major court decisions on civil rights violations, the law is ever-changing because of the findings of the United States Supreme Court, state supreme courts, and numerous appellant courts. These decisions usually pertain to small details that are not likely to be something officers will have to consider on the street, but the sheer volume of new decisions makes it very difficult to stay updated on them. My goal here is not to excuse such behaviors (ignorance of the law is no excuse), but only to point out that qualified immunity is far from being an easy way out for police officers accused of using excessive force.

However, the best argument against the claim that qualified immunity makes it virtually impossible to bring brutal police officers to justice is this— qualified immunity only applies to civil cases. Officers are still subject to dismissal or other sanctions if they violate their agency's use of force policy and to criminal prosecution if they commit a crime. To say that qualified immunity gives officers carte blanc in the use of force is absurd.

Rapidly Changing Violent Encounters
This case also highlights how quickly an armed encounter to go from bad to worse. Officer Reed believed he had the situation under control, at least to the point that Mr. Thomas was unlikely to attack him, and he was probably right. Then, Officers Allen and Shaw arrived on the scene in a perfectly understandable rush to help their fellow officer. This resulted in their near-collision, which only added stress to an already stressful situation. Meanwhile, Reed, who had been talking to Thomas long enough to tune in to the man's fragile state of mind, instinctively knew this sudden change could propel him into doing something rash. Sadly, he was right.

Armed encounters are fast-paced (most last about 3½ seconds, start to finish), rapidly changing, enormously stressful events that usually leave little or no time to make well-considered decisions. When, as in Mr. Thomas' case, one party is already in an emotional crisis, it is easy for that party to make irrational decisions. In the meantime, all three officers were also under a great deal of stress, hampered by a vital lack of information and viewing the crisis from different perspectives. It was a recipe for disaster that Officer Reed immediately recognized but didn't have time to stop.

Everything changed when Mr. Thomas pointed his gun at Officer Reed and then at the other two officers. From Officers Allen and Shaw's perspective, the incident had suddenly gone from an armed standoff to an active attack on them and Reed. There was no time for them to gather further information or determine if Thomas intended to shoot them. They tried to give him a chance to save himself by shouting warnings, but that failed to change his actions and ultimately led to his death. Thus, besides pointing out the tragedy of suicide-by-cop and other lawful but awful police shootings, this case provides a dramatic example of how little time officers have to respond to perceived threats and how difficult it is for them to make the absolute best choice every time without fail, especially when, as so often happens, critical information is lacking.

Training can help here, and many agencies are working hard at training officers to make better decisions under stress, but more is needed. We also have to recognize that no amount of training can change how human beings think to the point that they can perform flawlessly without exception. We can and should do our best to prepare our officers to the highest performance level possible, but we also have to accept that tragedies like this can never be eliminated.

The "Best Trained Officers in the World" Myth

None of the officers in Officer Reed's department had been trained in dealing with emotionally disturbed individuals. Reed was rather familiar with the suicide by cop phenomenon, but he had never been formally trained to deal properly with individuals attempting it. Perhaps he could have somehow done more to prevent the tragedy if he had been better trained, but, like most American police officers, his training was sorely lacking. Unfortunately, this lack exists concerning handling attempted suicides by cop and in just about every aspect of law enforcement that is vital to the safety of officers and those they are sworn to protect.

The comment above will probably come as a shock to most readers. This is due in large part to Hollywood's frequent depiction of cops as elite, supermen/women who can handle any crisis, easily take down hard-fighting opponents twice their size, never miss a shot, and fire magic bullets that send bad guys flying through plate glass windows. Our view of reality is influenced more by what we see on TV and in movies than we like to admit, and Hollywood's portrayal of police officers leads many to believe that cops are much better trained than they are.

To make matters worse, in the aftermath of questionable police shootings, we often hear police leaders commenting that America has the best trained police officers in the world. Some of them may truly believe this fallacy, but anyone familiar with American police training knows it is glaringly untrue. Such statements are particularly troubling because they erroneously shift the blame for the shooting away from the department's failure to provide adequate training to the officers involved.

The truth is that officers in many other countries receive far more training than ours. Since the quantity and quality of police training differ among states and even among the various political subdivisions and law enforcement agencies within each state, it is hard to say exactly how much our training differs from other countries. Nevertheless, police officers in many developed countries receive far more training than ours. For example, basic police training lasts one full year (2080 hours) in Japan,[ix] two and a half years in Germany, and two years (4160 hours) in France.[x] Basic training also lasts two years in the UK, and most of their officers don't carry guns,[xi] thereby relieving them of having to spend time on firearms training. In contrast, American police receive an average of only 843 hours of academy training and 521 hours of field training [6] (1,364 total hours). Worse yet, 19% of our police agencies do not provide any field training, which leaves their officers with an average of just 843 hours of academy training.[xii]

Of course, our officers also receive in-service training, but this varies considerably from state to state and from agency to agency, with the same variances in foreign countries. Detailed data on this subject is exceptionally hard to come by, if not nonexistent, but the wide disparity between basic police training in the U.S and the other abovementioned countries virtually guarantees that the vast majority of our officers receive significantly less in-service training.

Adding to this problem is that only a small portion of the things police officers learn in the academy are related to the use of force. Officers must be trained in a wide variety of subjects and skills, including report writing, various rules and operating procedures, investigations, first aid, constitutional law, and criminal law, to name just a few. These are important, but they leave less time for the seldom-used but enormously vital skills that affect police and public safety. The average amount of time recruits expend developing firearms skills is only 71 hours out of their total of 843. Seventy-one hours may seem to be a lot, especially for a seldom-used skill in the field, but not when we consider that there is absolutely no room for error when an officer discharges his firearm on the street. Unless he is fast, accurate, and justified, he or someone else is likely to suffer dire consequences.

Equally troubling is that the average amount of time spent in basic training on defensive tactics[7] is only 60 hours. This is especially problematic because

---

6. For readers who are not familiar with the term, field training refers to the training new recruits receive by riding with a specially trained officer who trains them in how to apply the things they learned at the academy on the street. It is a vital element in police training, especially with regard to officer safety and appropriate decision-making on the street.

7. For readers who are not familiar with the term, defensive tactics are defensive skills other than the use of firearms, including empty-handed fighting, control techniques, weapon retention, taser use, baton (i.e., nightstick) techniques, etc. Defensive tactics are also referred to as control tactics.

defensive tactics are considerably harder to learn and effectively apply in the real world than firearms skills. They also include a far wider variety of techniques, including use of the baton, pepper spray, Taser, and non-lethal weapons; take downs; weapon retention; empty-handed techniques; ground fighting; and more. Moreover, these skills are considerably more perishable than firearms skills, meaning they tend to quickly diminish to the point that they can no longer be properly executed on the street. This is a serious concern because many police agencies seldom conduct refresher classes or introduce new techniques in defensive tactics.

Worse yet, my many years of training police officers and analyzing violent police encounters have led me to conclude that a surprisingly large number of controversial police shootings–especially those involving unarmed citizens– have arisen from violent encounters that escalated to the lethal level due to the officer's inability to control the offender with defensive tactics. When an officer realizes his defensive tactics are not working as expected, he may react out of desperation by resorting to the one thing he knows is most likely to stop his assailant—his firearm. Or, in some cases, officers draw their guns in the hope of intimidating their attackers into surrendering. But some offenders are not that easily intimidated, either because they are too angry or desperate to care, are trying to commit suicide by cop, or don't believe the officer will pull the trigger. Others may decide to use the officer's mistake to attempt to disarm him. Whatever the reason, they don't stop, leaving the officer with the understandable belief that his only option is to shoot. Whether any given shooting of this nature is later found to be justified depends upon the totality of the circumstances, but no matter the findings, the fact remains that the tragic outcome was largely due to inadequate training.

The Dangers Associated with Misinformation about High Level of Police Training

Misinformation that leads people to believe police officers are far better trained than they are is dangerous and unfair to our officers. There are at least three reasons for this. First, it requires officers to do their dangerous work with too little training while also being second-guessed by people whose expectations go far beyond what their training has taught them. Also, since the public believes that officers don't need any more training, it is harder to get funding for necessary police training. Even worse, the highly trained police myth adds considerably to the false image of police officers as trigger-happy rogues who ignore their training for the sake of brutalizing their citizens. People begin to think, for example, that officers are trained to shoot well enough to hit their assailants in the leg, which can lead them to believe that the only reason an officer would aim for the chest is out of rage, racism, or for the thrill of it. This image of police officers only adds to the fear many people have of them, thus increasing the chances that future police encounters will turn violent. This is especially unfortunate because the assumption that the problem rests solely on innately brutal cops blinds us to the truth. In reality, the problem's primary cause is much easier to correct—a lack of police training.

Other Common Misconceptions about Police Training

Several other common misconceptions about police training contribute to the friction between the police and the public, with a corresponding increased likelihood of violence against and by the police. These include:

POLICE OFFICERS ARE TRAINED TO SHOOT TO KILL

Cops are not trained to shoot to kill. Rather, the purpose of deadly force is to stop the assailant from inflicting lethal violence on the officer or others. However, since the longer the assailant is allowed to continue his attack, the greater the chances that he will kill the officer or someone else, officers are trained to shoot to stop the threat as quickly as possible. If a device could be developed to do that more reliably and effectively than a firearm, police officers would rush to buy them, and guns would soon disappear from their duty belts. Tasers came closer to achieving this laudable goal than anything else, but they soon proved to be less effective than originally believed. If fired at the range in which most officers are murdered (1-5 feet), they may have little or no effect on the assailant, and their maximum range is only 21 feet. Their accuracy rapidly diminishes as the distance increases out to its maximum range,[8] and heavy clothing will often render them ineffective by preventing the barbs from penetrating through the fabric and striking the offender's skin. Also, both barbs must strike the offender to be effective, rendering the Taser useless if one barb misses or the fine wire

---

8. Tasers simultaneously fire two small barbs at the ends of fine wires, both of which must hit the target to close the circuit and have a chance of rendering the offender helpless. However, since the electric charge travels in a direct path from one barb to the other after striking the target, the area of the offender's body affected by the shock depends upon how close together they hit (i.e., the closer the spread, the smaller the area affected; and the wider the spread, the larger the area affected). Therefore, to help ensure that the offender will be disabled, the Taser is designed so the barbs are relatively close to one another when they first leave the device, but then spread farther apart as they travel toward the target. However, this also creates two problems. First, when fired at the range in which most officers are murdered (1-5 feet) they may hit too close together have much effect on the assailant. Second, by the time they travel to the farthest reaches of their wires (approximately 21 feet), the barbs have separated far enough to make it fairly likely that at least one will miss, rendering the device useless.

connecting one of them to the device breaks. Finally, Tasers must be reloaded—a rather awkward and time-consuming task—after just one shot (or two shots with some newer models), limiting their usefulness if the officer misses or is threatened by more than one assailant.

Unfortunately, firearms are the only defensive weapons with the range, "ammunition" capacity, and power to deal with the wide variety of lethal attacks police officers may confront on the street. Equally unfortunate, even firearms do not have the kind of instant "stopping power" that is commonly believed. Many of the chapters in this book tell of officers and their attackers who were able to keep fighting after suffering numerous severe gunshot wounds, some of which were head wounds. Moreover, officers are often attacked by violent individuals who are high on drugs or alcohol, suffering from mental illness, or in emotional crisis, any of which can increase one's ability to tolerate pain and severe injury.

Furthermore, handguns are not accurate as many tend to believe, and police gunfights occur under incredible stress, often in low light, and frequently against individuals on the move or shooting back. This makes it virtually impossible for even an excellent marksman to shoot accurately enough to hit smaller, often moving targets like arms or legs. Consequently, to reduce the chances of accidentally hitting a bystander if they miss, officers are taught to aim for the largest target, which regrettably happens to be the torso. Officers and their leaders would prefer to end the violence as quickly as possible by some other means. Still, sadly, gunshots to vital organs, and often multiple shots to those areas, are the only means currently available for doing that with any reasonable degree of reliability. While the goal is to stop, not to kill the offender, it is a dreadful fact of life that often ends that way.

POLICE OFFICERS NEED MORE TRAINING IN DE-ESCALATION TECHNIQUES, HANDLING PEOPLE IN CRISIS, IMPLICIT BIAS, HUMAN RELATIONS SKILLS, ETC.

It is certainly true that police officers need more training in these areas. Since police work is a people job that requires tact, a demonstrated concern for others, good listening skills, the ability to deal with others in every kind of mental and emotional state of mind, etc., these and other people skills are vital to their success, and sometimes to their safety and the safety of others as well. The vast majority of officers quickly learn these skills on the job and become remarkably adept at using them on the street. But there is always room for improvement, especially when it comes to handling people in crisis. No officer wants to make things worse during a crisis, especially when trying to help emotionally distraught, mentally ill, or suicidal individuals. They understand that such people are not criminals with evil intent but individuals who genuinely need help.

On the other hand, they cannot allow these unfortunate individuals to harm anyone. This puts them in a dangerous predicament when dealing with armed or otherwise dangerous disturbed individuals. To help alleviate this problem, many police agencies have CIT (Crisis Intervention Team) officers with specialized psychological training who are dispatched to all calls involving emotionally disturbed persons but more needs to be done.

However, we need to recognize that the police are usually called only after the situation has reached a crisis point and no one else has been able to handle it. To add to the problem, the scene may be chaotic or even unfriendly toward the police, and well-meaning but distraught family members may be present. Even highly educated psychologists who devote their careers to helping emotionally disturbed persons would find it difficult to work under such conditions. Yet, at best, a CIT officer with far less training and experience than any psychologist will respond to the scene. It will often be an average street cop who is even less trained to deal with such crises. Remarkably, however, officers usually manage to get by without using force by using common sense and their well-honed people skills. There are some tragic exceptions to this rule, of course, and it is those failures that make the headlines and forever haunt the officers involved.

The only way to reduce these tragedies is to give officers far more and better training. Fortunately, many police agencies have been addressing this problem with more training, either because of state mandates or because they recognize the need. This is long overdue, but it also comes at a price. With limited training budgets and the cost of such training, other essential training may have to be eliminated or reduced. As previously mentioned, training in many areas essential to the safety of our police officers and citizens is already dangerously inadequate, and cutting back in these areas will only aggravate the problem. Unless more money becomes available, we have to make some tough choices about spending our limited police training funds.

POLICE OFFICERS SHOULD BE THOROUGHLY TRAINED AND REQUIRED TO RESPECT THE SANCTITY OF LIFE

This misleading notion fails to recognize that officers have long operated under the core value that all life is of the highest importance. Even SWAT units, who regularly handle high-risk situations involving violent criminals, consider any mission a failure if anyone dies, even when that person is the offender. However, police officers work in a profession that sometimes demands tough decisions about whose life is more important. This may seem harsh, but we must sometimes prioritize lives in this often violent world of ours. The right to self-defense is the best example. Our legal system recognizes that the innocent victim of a lethal attack has the right to stop his assailant with deadly force if necessary, thus giving the innocent victim's life priority over the life of the person who chooses to attack him unlawfully. This principle is reflected in law enforcement's long-established priority of life, which prioritizes life from highest to lowest as follows:

1. Victims, or in the case of hostage situations, hostages. Besides being innocent targets of a violent crime, victims have done no wrong and have the least control over their fate.
2. Innocent bystanders. Bystanders are also innocent, but they have at least some control over their fate, as they usually have the option of leaving the danger zone or otherwise moving out of the line of fire.
3. Police officers. Police officers have chosen to accept the obligation of putting themselves at risk to save innocent lives, and they have some control over their fate. However, that control is minimal and largely dependent upon the actions taken by the offender. Also, they are not responsible for the criminal acts that require their intervention.
4. Offenders. The offender has chosen to commit a crime that puts the lives of others at risk and has the greatest control over the outcome, including his fate. He can either choose to stop his violent behavior and submit to arrest, or he can choose to risk death by continuing to put other lives in jeopardy. His life is still valuable, but it must not be elevated above the lives of those who he has knowingly put in danger.

An example of how this applies to law enforcement is the way officers respond to active killer attacks. The shooter's life is rightfully prioritized below the lives of his targeted victims, any bystanders, and the police officers who are there to stop him. Still, many police critics believe that police officers should put their lives on par with violent offenders' lives, or even below them. Unbelievably, one critic even went so far as to praise a group of Icelandic officers who allowed a gunman to fire multiple rounds at them, including one that hit an officer in his helmet (a round that would have caused a critical, if not fatal wound if it had not been for the helmet).[xiii] Though this dangerous attitude is currently far from the norm, it appears that it is gaining momentum in some circles.

Is that what we truly want? Is it reasonable to ask our officers to override their survival instinct by allowing armed criminals to take the first shot? Does our society even have the right to demand that officers put the safety of violent offenders on equal terms with their own, or worse, above it? Of course not! To expect our officers to subject themselves to unnecessary danger for the sake of dangerous criminals is both foolish and immoral for several reasons. It's foolish because it would encourage more lethal attacks on the police by making it far less dangerous for criminals to do so. Also, such rules would shatter many officers' confidence in their ability to defend themselves. Lack of confidence in one's ability to survive increases fear and stress, which clouds thinking and leads to rash decision-making. Thus, officers would be more reluctant to confront dangerous criminals, leading to much higher crime rates or more deadly mistakes by our officers. Finally, it would be morally corrupt to require officers to let criminals shoot first. Remember, an offender who initiates a lethal attack against a police officer has made a conscious decision to commit murder while the officer is rightfully attempting to protect himself and sometimes others from violence. It is tragic any time someone dies, but the life of a violent criminal's intended victim should never be of less importance than his assailant's. Also remember, when that victim is a police officer, his assailant will be free to attack other officers and even innocent citizens if he falls.

This is not to imply that police officers don't need better training in how to handle violent confrontations without resorting to deadly force, or that there are no bad apples in the group, but it is wrong to stereotype all, or even a large number of them, as bullies who lack proper respect for the sanctity of human life. They prove otherwise every day by willingly running to the sound of the guns to protect their citizens. And, with only the rarest exception, they do everything they can to avoid using deadly force.

POLICE OFFICERS ARE TRAINED TO TREAT ALL CITIZEN CONTACTS AS IF THEY PRESENT A LETHAL THREAT

Though technically correct in some ways, police critics often use this common misconception about police safety training to support their opinion that police officers are too aggressive. They perceive officers as unreasonably cautious to the point that they react violently without adequate provocation or use such "fear training" as an excuse to mistreat law-abiding citizens. What they don't understand is that this training doesn't encourage or even suggest that officers treat citizens as criminals; rather, officers are taught to be reasonably suspicious of everyone they encounter and to have a response plan if attacked. For example, they are trained to order citizens to show them their hands when they can't see them (as Officer Reed did in this case) while also mentally preparing themselves to respond with the legally appropriate level of force if the person refuses or pulls a weapon. Similarly, they often tell citizens to keep their hands on the steering wheel, stay in or exit their vehicles, stop moving around, etc. These practices sometimes offend citizens, but they are not meant to do so. Rather, they are meant to keep everyone safe. Critics of such practices often fail to realize that by taking firm control over citizen encounters, officers will often discourage violent individuals from attacking them, which reduces the chances of anyone getting hurt.

There are several other good reasons why officers are trained this way, none of which are motivated by a desire to offend or mistreat citizens. These include:

1. The most common killer of police officers during seemingly "low-risk" encounters is complacency. The best way to counter this problem is for officers to develop habits that help them remain ever vigilant and ready to defend themselves. In police work, no task is routine or completely without risk, as shown by the fact that officers are often killed when dealing with misdemeanor[9] incidents and even non-criminal matters. More officers are killed investigating suspicious persons and circumstances (13.4%) than any other single activity. Similarly, premeditated ambushes (11.6% of officers killed) and unprovoked attacks (8.8%) are the second and third biggest killers of police officers. Note that none of these three top killers are generally classified as criminal events unless violence occurs. The fourth most dangerous is vehicle stops for traffic violations, which are initially classified as misdemeanors. Almost half (44.3%) of the police officers murdered between 2007–2018[xiv, xv] were involved in activities that are not generally seen as high-risk until after the officer is attacked. These statistics unmistakably demonstrate that officers must be vigilant and

9. Misdemeanors are crimes punishable by no more than one year in prison. They seldom involve violence, with the only common exception being common assaults in which no one is seriously injured. Most often, they are minor property crimes.

in control of every encounter with the public because they can never know who will attack them or when.

2. Officers are often victims of their success. They regularly perform risky tasks (e.g., building searches, responding to holdups and other dangerous crimes in progress, etc.) without injury. Contrary to common opinion, they are rarely shot or otherwise subject to lethal attacks. Because of the way the human brain works, these repeated successes create unavoidable complacency, which, if allowed to grow, sets officers up to be caught off guard. Teaching officers to take reasonable precautions during every citizen contact is the best way to overcome this dangerous problem.

3. Gunfights are usually amazingly brief events and almost always catch officers off guard, thus putting police officers at a severe tactical disadvantage. The only effective way to lessen this danger is always to follow proper safety protocols that make it harder for potential adversaries to attack them effectively. A common maxim used in police work other dangerous occupations makes this point crystal clear: "Always hope for the best, but plan for the worst."

4. Maintaining control of citizen encounters can enable officers to spot danger early enough to bring the encounter under control before it escalates to the point that deadly force is needed.

5. Since most criminals are especially good at reading body language and often gauge an officer's level of preparedness before deciding whether to attack, they are less likely to attack officers who are vigilant, in control of the encounter, and ready to defend themselves. Thus, this kind of training makes police encounters with citizens safer for both the officer and the offender.

CHAPTER 11

God, the Gunman, and the Warrior Cop: The Jeanne Assam Case

"The wicked flee when no one pursues,
but the righteous are bold as a lion."
—Proverbs 28:1

INCIDENT DESCRIPTION

So many things had gone wrong in Jeanne Assam's life. Though raised by loving, successful parents, she had been sexually molested by several men and a few women during her childhood years. Like many molested children, she had kept the abuse secret from her parents and everyone else. Thus, she had carried the terrible memories into adulthood, which led to unhealthy personal relationships as she grew older. Later in life, she had also suffered multiple betrayals and was raped by a college professor who she had once respected and looked to as a father figure. But through it all, she had developed a strong work ethic and a powerful drive to protect others, which lead her to join a large urban police department that gave her plenty of opportunities to fulfill her passion. Not surprisingly, she did well and quickly fell in love with police work. But then, despite being an intelligent, resourceful, hardworking officer with a passion for defending the weak and a record number of letters of appreciation from citizens, the job ended badly after just five years. For some unspoken reason—probably a clash of personalities or jealousy—two supervisors disliked her, which eventually led to her dismissal from the department. Devastated by the inexplicably unfair loss of a job she dearly loved, faced with several other difficult personal issues—including the sudden loss of both parents—she worked at several security and law enforcement jobs to find peace and purpose.

Though she never wavered in her belief that her life's purpose was to protect others as a police officer, she eventually found some peace in her renewed faith. She had attended church during her childhood and teen years—her mother had seen to that—but, distracted by the turmoil of her past, she had pretty well forgotten about God and stopped attending church after leaving home. Then things gradually began to change. She moved to another state, where she found a kind, loving friend who took her to a nearby church, and she had begun watching a popular female television evangelist whose preaching was a great comfort to her. Over time, her faith grew.

Then, after inexplicably losing a parole officer job despite excellent performance reviews, she found a customer service position at a local ministry. She liked the staff there, but she still felt a burning desire to protect others. Fortunately, she had recently started attending a mega-church nearby with a sizeable security team, and she decided to volunteer to serve in that capacity. Because she was the only team member with police experience and an active police officer certification, she was accepted. These and other recent positive changes in her life led Assam into an otherwise tragic encounter that would give her life purpose and save many lives.

Meanwhile, a young man with a similarly difficult life was making decisions that would soon put him at the center of that same tragedy. Raised by loving, God-fearing parents and endowed with an intelligent mind, 24-year-old Matthew Murray had grown up as an obedient, kind-hearted boy. But he had Attention Deficit Hyperactivity Disorder, was socially awkward, and had trouble being accepted by other children. As he grew older, he suffered increasingly more rejection from his peers and became deeply engrossed in violent computer games.

After being laid off from a computer job he cherished, Murray became intensely depressed. Though he kept it from his parents, he started delving deeper into the occult, listening to black metal music[1] and viewing several thousand pornographic images on the internet. Also unknown to his parents, he bought an AR-15, a semiautomatic AK-47 rifle, a 9mm pistol, and over three thousand rounds of ammunition over several weeks; and stashed them in the trunk of his car. Then, on a cold Saturday evening in early December,

---

1. For those unfamiliar with the term, black metal music is music that contains antisocial, Satanic and anti-Christian lyrics.

he told his mother he was going out with friends to celebrate his recent 24th birthday and left the house with no hint that anything was wrong.

After eating alone at a nearby family restaurant, Murray made several phone calls to family members from various locations. Eventually, he drove to a nearby youth mission where he had been trained for missionary work a few years earlier. Apparently feeling rejected by some of the students and faculty there and believing they had treated him unfairly, he knocked on the door and asked 24-year-old employee Tiffany Johnson to come inside. Concerned about the bitterly cold weather, the young woman let him in. For reasons known only to him, he then asked Ms. Johnson if he could spend the night at the facility. When she told him there wasn't room, he asked if he could stay there a little longer while he arranged for a ride home. Ms. Johnson agreed, but after Murray had lingered on the phone for another half hour, she and the others grew increasingly uncomfortable with his untimely presence at midnight. Hesitantly, she ushered him to the front door and suggested that he wait for his ride at a nearby grocery store.

Seemingly pushed over the top by Ms. Johnson's "unfair" treatment, Murray whipped out his 9 mm and shot her twelve times at point-blank range. Others in the facility bravely came to her aid, but Murray wasn't finished yet. His semiautomatic continued its cruel work as he gunned down three of the valiant would-be rescuers. Philip Crouse, 21, was killed outright, Dan Griebenow was severely wounded in the neck, and Charlie Blanch was shot in the leg. Tragically, but not surprising considering the extent of her wounds, Tiffany Johnson died later at a hospital.

But then came a mysteriously fortunate twist to this otherwise dark incident. For some still-unexplained reason, Murray suddenly found himself locked outside as the front door—a security door of heavy metal construction—suddenly slammed shut in his face. This put a stop to a massacre that, considering the amount of ammunition Murray was carrying and the fact that no one inside was armed, could have cost the lives of all 45 people inside. Then, to add to this good fortune, several more of the center's residents arrived home from a social event while Murray was furiously pounding on the door. Instead of turning his wrath on this group, he scurried to his car and fled the gruesome scene.

As the police rushed to the mission center, Murray drove home and went to bed. He awoke at approximately 9:45 that same morning and went downstairs, fully dressed in black tactical pants, military boots, and a dark shirt and jacket. After exchanging a few words with his mother, he walked out the door. In keeping with his normal routine, he didn't mention where he was going.

Meanwhile, Assam had awakened early. She had been questioning whether she should continue to pursue a career in law enforcement or try something else and had asked for advice from a pastor husband/wife team she knew. They recommended a three-day fast as a good way to discern God's will. Taking their advice, she had started the fast two days earlier. She had later told the church's security team director about her fast, and he had suggested that she stay home and spend her Sunday morning asking God to reveal what He wanted her to do.

After spending a good portion of the early morning praying and reading the Bible, she decided to take a break by checking the news on the internet and reading her email. As soon as she turned on her computer, she spotted a small headline about a shooting just after midnight at a Christian organization about 75 miles away. The short article that followed indicated four people had been shot, two of them fatally, by an unknown gunman who was still at large. Instantly, every fiber of Assam's being told her the killer was on his way to her church to increase his body count. But she couldn't report an unsubstantiated gut feeling to the police, no matter how strong it happened to be. Instead, she called her security team supervisor, asked him if he had heard about the shooting at the mission, and told him she would be coming in after all.

While preparing to leave, Assam wondered if she would ever return home. She prayed about it, and now unafraid, finished getting ready. She habitually grabbed her 9mm Beretta, but—unlike when she had worked the streets as a cop—she had no spare ammo or body armor. As she drove the short mile to the church, she knew she would soon confront the gunman, but she also knew that she would succeed in stopping him with God at her side. Though she was also well aware that she might die in the process, she left that possibility in God's hands. Her only concern was to stop the killing, and she was ready and unafraid.

Assam had missed the start of the first worship service, but it was still in progress. She checked in and went about her duties on high alert. The remainder of the first service and entire second service were uneventful, but this was no time to let her guard down. The massive church was full of lingering worshippers. Since a popular guest speaker had spoken at the service, more visitors than usual were in attendance, and no one seemed in a hurry to leave.

In the meantime, Assam's deadly premonition was about to prove prophetic. Unknown to her or anyone else, Matthew Murray had been waiting outside in his car for at least an hour. Several uniformed off-duty police officers who had been providing extra security had just left, and it appears their departure was exactly what Murray had been waiting for. His first targets were the six members of the Works family—the father David, his wife Marie, their twin daughters, Laurie and Stephanie (18), Rachel (16), and Grace (11). Despite the large crowd in the parking lot around him, Murray calmly strolled up to their van as they climbed inside and opened fire with the semiautomatic AR-15 slung across his chest. As David Works shouted at his family to get down, Murray walked methodically around the van, sending a stream of bullets through its thin metal skin as the terrified family huddled inside. David was hit in the stomach and groin, and two of his four daughters were shot. David would survive, but Rachel, his 16-year-old middle daughter, was mortally wounded, and Stephanie, one of his 18-year-old twins, died in her twin sister's arms.

Murray had wreaked a heartbreaking nightmare on one loving family, but his bloodlust was not abated. He moved on to another family in a minivan—the Purcells. They were just starting to leave the parking lot to head home when Murray opened fire. As his bullets tore into the van, its otherwise reliable engine unexpectedly died, leaving the terrified family sitting ducks. The van rolled on, moving ever closer to Murray, and then coasted slowly past him as he fired two more shots into it. Then, as Mr. Purcell desperately tried to restart the motor while yelling at his family to get out of the van, Murray inexplicably lowered his rifle, turned, and headed for the church's east entrance. Moments later, the van started, and the Purcells headed for the hospital. Mrs. Purcell had been shot in the shoulder, but despite their desperate vulnerability during the attack, everyone else was unscathed.

Meanwhile, Assam had heard the faint "pop, pop, pop" of distant open-air gunfire coming from the far end of the church's east hallway. Then came the unmistakable sharp crack of rifle fire, the shots so loud that it sounded like the shooter was already inside. The immense hallway—over 100 yards long and ten yards wide—led to the nursery, youth rooms, special needs facilities, and classrooms and was crowded with parents and their children who had only recently been dismissed from their classes. With at least 500 adults and children crammed into the hallway, there was no worse place the gunman could be, and the screaming crowd rushing toward Assam blinded her from pinpointing his location. "Where is he?" she shouted.

"There he is," one of her security team members cried out, "He's coming through the doors right now!"

Assam looked toward the heavy glass doors at the far end of the hallway. Murray hadn't entered the building yet, but he was calmly shooting through the glass doors at the mass of men, women, and children inside. As Assam drew her Beretta 92 FS[2] and sprinted upstream through the throng of terrorized fleeing people, she prepared mentally for the upcoming gunfight. She was calm, unafraid, and confident in the knowledge that God was with her.

Remarkably, in the few seconds it had taken for Assam to run this far, the hallway had become devoid of all its panicky occupants. Only Assam and the gunman remained.

Murray, wearing all black, armed with the AR-15, and carrying multiple spare magazines on a load-bearing vest, had the coldblooded look of a single-minded killer. He had just pulled the second set of doors open and was now inside the massive, eerily abandoned hallway, firing at the terrified volunteers lying behind the counters in the church's main lobby. Several much smaller hallways were perpendicular to the main one, and Assam had just taken cover at the corner of the last of them (Figure 1). A distance of 63 feet now separated her from Murray. She was well aware that more than 60 feet is a fairly long shot with a handgun, especially under the stress of a gunfight, while it is hard to with a rifle miss at that range. Tactically, she was at a severe disadvantage.

---

2. The Beretta 92 FS is a high-quality Italian-made semiautomatic pistol with a magazine capacity of sixteen rounds. Though highly accurate and reliable, its smaller magazine capacity and limited range make it a poor match for the AR-15 rifle.

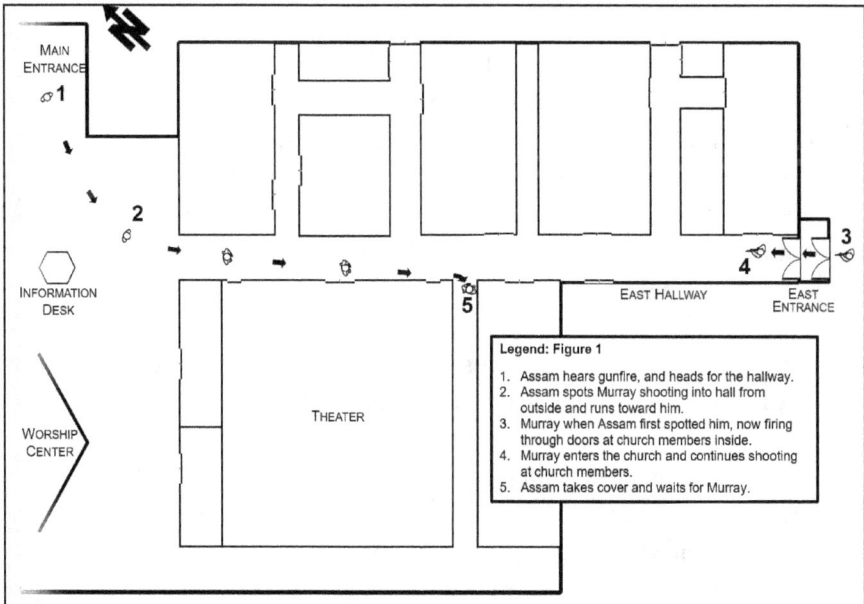

FIGURE 1: Assam hears gunfire, spots Murray, runs toward him, and takes cover.

Assam had just seconds to act. Having worked in one of the most dangerous districts in a large urban police department, she had faced armed offenders on numerous occasions before, but never like this. Nor had she ever received any active shooter training, much less training in how to respond alone against a single-minded, heavily armed rifleman in a building jam-packed with defenseless people. At this moment, God was her only resource. At first, she had planned to wait until Murray was parallel to her position before engaging him, but she now realized that she would have to scrap that plan. She had to engage him now.

Assam asked God to be with her one last time. Instantly, she felt His powerful presence surround her, a feeling she will never forget. She raised her gun, pointed it at Murray, and in accord with her police training, shouted, "Police officer. Drop your weapon!"

But Murray, still fixated on fulfilling his bloody mission, pointed the menacing rifle at her.

Assam opened fire, hitting him five times in rapid succession from a distance of over 60 feet. He went down, falling hard onto his back. But he was still moving and holding the deadly AR-15. Assam's Beretta, now down to only eleven rounds, was no match for the far more accurate rifle. She knew she would have to make every round count. Advancing toward her downed adversary with her gun trained on him, she gave him one last chance to live.

"Drop your weapon, or I will kill you!" she commanded.

Murray's answer to Assam's demand was to silently sit up, point the rifle at her, and fire again. She immediately returned fire, hitting him three more times, with one of the rounds striking him in the neck and severing his carotid artery. Still, he kept shooting, but not for long. He soon collapsed to the floor, rolled over onto his side, and crawled to one of the side hallways, where he rolled onto his back with his head propped against the wall.

Even with his life oozing away, the gunman was unwilling to give up. Assam had noticed grenades attached to his vest earlier, and now he was reaching for one of them.[3] She shot him twice more, finally putting a stop to his bloody rampage (Figure 2). As she watched him take his last breath, Assam felt no anger—only pity that this young man was so full of hate that he felt compelled to murder innocent strangers. For Assam, taking a person's life was nothing to rejoice about, and, like virtually every police officer in her position, it was a terrible memory she would never forget.

---

3. The grenades Murray was carrying were smoke grenades, but Jeanne didn't know that, and reasonably believed they were likely to be fragmentation, concussion or incendiary grenades.

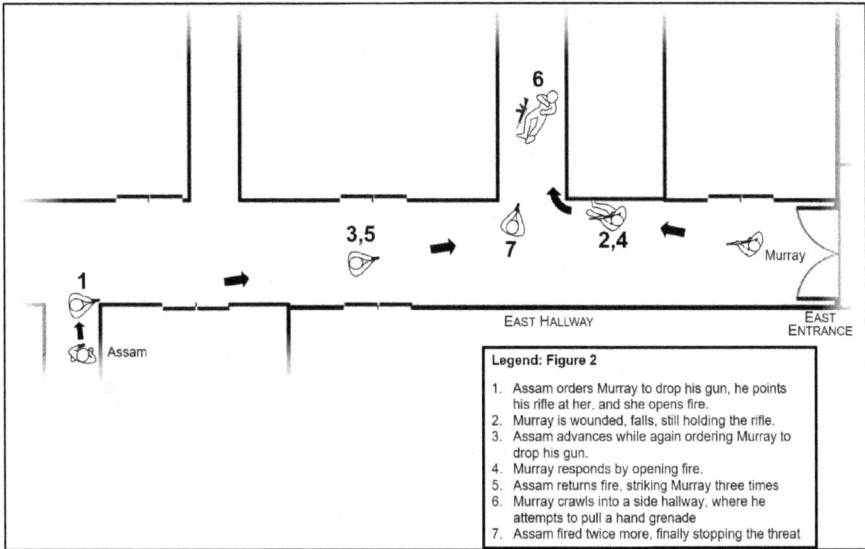

FIGURE 2: Assam engages Murray and stops the threat.

THE AFTERMATH

This tragedy was the culmination of a long series of complex, intertwined events and challenges in several people's lives. Many would call it a coincidence, but many others, including this writer, would call it a miracle. Regardless of what we chose to call it, this story didn't stop with the gunfight. Within weeks, Matthew Murray's parents, the surviving members of the Works family, and Jeanne Assam met to share their grief and comfort one another. There was no blame, anger, or hatred during the meeting—only genuine compassion and forgiveness. Such kindness is rare among people who had never met before, let alone a group of people who had every right to be hostile and unforgiving toward one another. But sharing a common faith that focuses on love and forgiveness, they could move past their anger and show uncommon love toward one another. The Murrays even went so far as to let Assam know they understood the necessity of her actions and respected her for her courage in confronting their son before he could do more harm.

Matthew Murray had killed four people and wounded five others, but it could have been much worse. He was armed with two pistols in addition to his rifle, carrying approximately 1700 rounds of ammunition, and determined to satisfy the hatred in his heart by taking as many innocent lives as possible. Equally, if not more ominous, the police later searched his car, where they found an AK-47 semiautomatic rifle, another 1,000 rounds of ammunition, and maps to other places he planned to attack. Fortunately, Assam was there to stop him. But is the word "fortunate" an adequate term to describe the way Matthew Murray's homicidal rampage ended? Assam would answer that question with a definite "no." She takes no pride in what she did and gives all the credit for ending the bloodshed to God. She firmly believes that—in light of all the challenges in her life and all the inexplicable things that happened to bring her to her confrontation with Murray—God used her as His instrument to save an untold number of lives. I agree.

ANALYSIS

Use of Cover

Like many other officers, Office Assam left cover and advanced on her assailant during the gunfight despite being trained to use cover. The reasons why officers so commonly do this are not fully understood, but it probably has a lot to do with human instincts and the large amount of training it takes to overcome them. In many ways, we human beings are hardwired to behave much in the same way as animals when it comes to self-defense. For instance, animals don't like to be cornered when in danger, apparently because they instinctively recognize that it limits their ability to maneuver. Like them, we humans don't like to be confined when our lives are threatened. Even barricades like the corner of a wall or an open car door can trigger this instinctive aversion to being confined. Also, our view of our environment is partially blocked when behind a corner or similar large barricade, thus limiting our ability to see and respond to the threat. When combined with the fact that all officers are acutely aware that their accuracy markedly improves as they move closer to their target, many officers intuitively move closer to their assailants when engaging them, often without any conscious thought as to why they are doing it.

The only way to correct this problem is with enough training to override the instincts behind it, including frequent recurring exercises to reinforce what was learned. Since few police agencies can afford extensive training in the proper use of cover and other tactical uses of firearms, it is up to the government and, ultimately, taxpayers to provide the necessary funds.

Verbal Warnings

It is exceedingly dangerous to issue verbal warnings when confronting armed attackers, especially when they have obvious murderous intend. This is because action is always faster than reaction, which virtually guarantees that the first person to decide to fire will also be the first to discharge his firearm. The first one to discharge his firearm usually wins. The science behind this action v reaction principle in a gunfight is that the person responding to the threat cannot start his response until he realizes that he is in danger. And then his mind must still send the message to his brain to pull the trigger, and the appropriate muscles must then make that happen. This happens almost instantly, but not quick enough to stop the bullets coming at him.

Also, the law does not require officers, or anyone else for that matter, to issue a verbal warning before shooting someone who is about to shoot them or others. There are times when it is the right thing to do morally, legally, or even tactically, but not when confronting an obvious active shooter.

Nevertheless, Officer Assam ordered Murray to drop his gun at great risk to herself. But why? This was partly due to her training and experience. Police training strongly emphasizes verbal warnings when feasible. This emphasis is reinforced by officers' past experiences during armed confrontations and often by what they see on television and in the movies. However, like other officers, she also issued the warnings because she didn't relish the idea of shooting another human being, no matter how necessary it happened to be. Unlike the gun-happy cops on TV, and unlike the way officers are portrayed by some critics and activists, police officers are–like most other people–very reluctant to take a human life. Moreover, like Officer Assam, they are decent, service-oriented people dedicated to protecting others, even if it means putting their own lives at risk.

Equipment

Although not a factor in this incident's outcome, it is well worth mentioning that Officer Assam, like many police officers when off-duty or otherwise out of uniform, didn't carry any spare ammunition. This practice is not surprising when we consider how seldom officers are involved in armed confrontations under those circumstances. However, given today's ever-increasing number of mass killings and the continuing threat of terrorist attacks, police officers should be well equipped to respond to any emergency that may require the expenditure of large amounts of ammunition. Modern semiautomatic pistols have rather large magazine capacities, but it is surprising how quickly they can run dry in a large-scale shooting. Furthermore, an extra magazine may also be needed if the gun jams. With most malfunctions, the jam can be cleared without changing magazines, but not always.

In some cases, the old magazine must be stripped from the gun and then reinserted, or preferably, replaced with a different one. Also, many officers are trained to reload their guns before the magazine is empty, in which case the partially empty one is dropped—either intentionally or unintentionally—to the ground, where there may not be time to recover it until after the gunfight is finished.[4] Finally, since worn or damaged magazines are often the culprit when semiautomatic pistols malfunction, officers may need to replace a damaged one before they can return fire. They are trained to check their guns and magazines frequently to alleviate these problems, but mistakes can still occur, and spare magazines are vital when that happens.

Fortunately, due to Officer Assam's superior marksmanship skills, outstanding focus on protecting the innocent, and properly functioning firearm, the fact that she didn't have a spare magazine didn't negatively impact the outcome of the gunfight. But for other officers or armed citizens under different circumstances, the result could be tragic. Every police officer should carry at least one spare magazine when off-duty, and armed citizens who carry firearms to protect others, as well as themselves, should do the same. And make sure to keep your firearm and magazines clean and in good working order because you can't afford to leave anything to chance in the unlikely but tragic event that you need them.

We also need to recognize that helping others in a mass shooting, terrorist attack, or other catastrophe may require more than a firearm. In most cases, it will probably be necessary to provide emergency first aid to you or other victims, in which case you will need the proper equipment. A tourniquet and trauma dressing are the bare minimum, and these can usually be carried on your person, or at least in your car, without too much inconvenience. See the "Aiding a Wounded Person" in chapter 4 (pp 57–59) for more information on providing emergency first aid to others.

Likewise, it is important to be properly equipped to deal with other emergencies besides mass violence and make sure the necessary equipment is well

---

4. This is because it is takes time to recover a dropped magazine, and there isn't that much time to waste when all the officer's focus needs to be directed at stopping the assailant as soon as possible. Also, the officer will have to take his eyes off his assailant to recover the dropped magazine.

maintained. For example, make sure your vehicles are well maintained, especially before going on a long trip. And always wear your seatbelt. Keep at least one fire extinguisher in your home (the room where one is most often needed is the kitchen), ensure that you have enough smoke and carbon monoxide detectors and that their batteries are changed as required, repair anything in your home that creates a safety hazard, install good outdoor lighting and a peephole in your front door, etc. Keep a good supply of water, nonperishable foods, blankets, flashlights, first aid supplies, and other essentials. in your home in case of a natural disaster, etc. If you participate in extreme sports or other hazardous recreational activities, make sure all your equipment is in good working order, don't skimp on the quality of any equipment essential to your safety, etc. The list goes on, but the key thing to remember is that it is essential to your safety to have the right equipment when needed. Make your safety and the safety of your loved ones a top priority, and do your best to obtain and properly maintain the best equipment you can afford for that purpose.

Winning Mindset
Officer Assam loved police work. Like every other cop, she thrived on the excitement, but it wasn't just the thrill of the job that made her passionate about law enforcement. Rather, it was the fact that it made it her duty to fulfill her lifelong desire to help others, especially when defending the innocent against vicious predators. With the only exception being military service, no other occupation does that. When people in their communities who are unable or unwilling to protect themselves are threatened with violence, they call the police and no one else. No doubt, police work is exciting, but in the end, the thing that gives it real meaning is the fact that their citizens look to them to keep them safe. Officer Assam was well aware of that fact, and it fueled her passion for the job.

Her drive to protect others despite all personal risk was, of course, what compelled Officer Assam to engage Murray, and it was also what gave her the focus so crucial to winning. When forced to defend oneself or others against violence, there is no room for distractions. Since the mind can only focus on one thing at a time, the sole focus should be on stopping the violence as quickly as possible. Fear, worry, even concern for one's wounds or the wounds of others must be pushed aside until the threat is stopped. Officer Assam's ability to focus solely on stopping the bloodshed—spurred on by her concern for others—was crucial to her ability to win against Murray's superior firepower.

However, even more crucial was her faith. Imbued with unwavering faith in God, she feared death far less than most and was able to accept the dreadful possibility of dying. That acceptance, when coupled with her natural protective instinct and the selfless devotion to others that often comes with deep religious conviction, enabled her to look beyond fear to her God-given duty to act. Like many devout Christians who find themselves thrust into situations in which they must use righteous violence in defense of others, she firmly believed that God put her in that exact time and place for that specific purpose. While the intent here is not to preach, it would be a disservice to ignore the vital role that strong faith plays in enabling officers to perform courageously in the face of danger, especially when innocent lives are at stake. Selfless courage is not exclusive to officers of faith, of course, but it is certainly displayed by them often enough to make it well worth emphasizing here. Faith is a key component of our lives, and it can also be valuable when facing danger and other tough challenges.

Though no longer an active police officer, Jeanne Assam exemplified law enforcement at its best. It is one thing to defend one's own life with violence, but it takes far more courage and immeasurable selflessness to risk death in defense of others, especially when they are people we don't know. Cops are called upon to do that as part of their job, and with rare exceptions, they do it bravely. It is what makes law enforcement a supremely noble profession, and it is also what earned Officer Assam the right to stand with the best of her fellow officers.

Author's Note: For several reasons, this chapter is unique to this book and to everything else I have written. First, Jeanne Assam was not an active police officer at the time of the shooting. Nevertheless, I included her story because she was still a certified police officer at that time and, without a doubt, still possessed the heart of a true cop. Also, she possessed many of the other attributes of police officers who perform well—often even sacrificially—to protect the innocent, which makes her a perfect fit among the other hero cops in this book. Finally, Jeanne's story provided me with a way to focus on my Christian faith, not only as a valuable element in winning mindset and warrior spirit but also as something I want to share with others. I tried to tell her story in a non-preachy manner, in a way that wouldn't come across as pushy, condescending, or holier than thou. I sincerely hope I was successful because my only goal was to simply tell this remarkable story and leave you, the reader, to decide what it means to you.

CHAPTER 12

Selfless Focus:
The Brian Murphy Case

"The true soldier fights not because he hates what is in front
of him, but because he loves what is behind him."
—G.K. CHESTERTON

DESCRIPTION OF INCIDENT

Life is unpredictable, especially for cops.

Lieutenant Brian Murphy—a 51-year-old former US Marine with 22 years
in the department—had awakened to a beautiful spring morning, and it was
Sunday, a day of rest for most people. But like other police officers, this was
another workday for Murphy. He had originally been scheduled to be off today,
but he had volunteered to take a shift for a sergeant who wanted to attend his
son's graduation from boot camp. The fact that he was just filling in, coupled
with the soothing spring weather and bright sunshine, imbued the morning
with a feeling of tranquility as he cruised down the lightly traveled street. But
then the unthinkable happened.

The radio abruptly came to life: "I'm taking a report of an altercation. Sikh
Temple, 532 East Market. There's a lot of noise. I'm not able to get much info,
but there's a fight, and now it's . . ."

Not good. A fight at a house of worship never is, especially on a Sunday
morning when the building is crowded with worshippers. Then things got a
whole lot worse. After a brief pause, the dispatcher added, "A bald male with
glasses may have shot someone."

The temple was only about twelve blocks away, and Murphy knew he would be first on the scene as soon as he heard the shift's other seven officers call out their locations. But he also knew his officers. They wouldn't lose any time getting there and would know what to do when they arrived.

A long driveway led to the temple's parking lot, sloping lazily upward to a slight crest before reaching the lot, and a hill to its right blocked Murphy's view of the property even more as he turned into the driveway. He couldn't see much until he reached the crest of the driveway, and when the lot finally came into view, it was eerily quiet and void of activity. Meanwhile, the dispatcher had advised that more shots were being fired, adding that the shooter was wearing a white shirt with black pants.

As Murphy pulled onto the lot, he saw two men lying motionless near a car parked along its left edge. He stopped his cruiser, called out, and headed for the two men to see what he could do for them. Both had bullet wounds; one was dead, and the other was probably dead as well. As he headed back toward his cruiser to retrieve his AR-15, he caught movement out of the corner of his eye and turned to see more. A bald man in a white shirt and black pants ran from the temple toward the other side of the parking lot with something that looked suspiciously like an empty holster riding on his right hip.

But Murphy couldn't see if the man was holding a gun. Things were happening so fast; he barely had time to think. He drew his gun and started to go after the man, walking rapidly away from his cruiser and out into the open as he moved. Still unable to tell if the man was armed, Murphy raised his gun into firing position. He aimed but didn't pull the trigger. The man met the shooter's description, wasn't wearing a turban as one would expect at a Sikh temple, and otherwise looked out of place. The protrusion on the man's hip looked a lot like a holster, but it could also be a cell phone holder. And if he was the shooter, why couldn't he see the gun? All this information raced through Murphy's mind so fast he was scarcely aware of it, but he was convinced that he shouldn't shoot unless he saw a gun.

"Police! Stop!" he shouted.

The words were barely out of his mouth when the man, an angry 40-year-old white supremacist named Wade Michael Page, suddenly turned and opened fire. Murphy saw the gun and pulled his trigger at almost the same instant, but Page got lucky, and Murphy did not. Page's 9mm round screamed across the 30 yards between them and crashed into Murphy's chin, but Murphy's bullet missed.

Murphy was lucky in one respect, however. After blasting through his chin, the bullet deflected downward, ripped through his larynx, mercifully ricocheted off his spinal column, and lodged in his neck. It was a devastating wound, but it didn't enter his brain or sever his spinal cord, nor did it disable him. Staggered by the hammer-like blow but not down, Murphy dove alongside one of the cars parked nearby and squatted down for cover.

Still stunned, Murphy stayed low for the moment while his head cleared and then tried to ascertain his adversary's exact location. He could hear Page shooting at him, but the sound of the gunfire was echoing all around, making it impossible to determine where it was coming from. Since Page had been running from Murphy's left to his right, Murphy logically assumed he had kept going in that same direction and taken cover behind a nearby parked car or was coming straight at him. But where exactly was he? Then, before he could give any more thought to the question, his gut told him he had kept his head down too long. He stood and started looking for Page.

Wham! Murphy's left thumb erupted into a shower of red. "Ooh, that's gonna leave a mark," he thought. Then, another round and yet another smashed into his upper arm and thigh. He could see Page coming up behind him, blasting furiously away as he moved. Worse, his gun had been knocked out of his hand, sending it skidding across the pavement and out of sight. He was now unarmed, and the crazed gunman was still coming!

More rounds were tearing into his upper arms. "Better get small," he thought and dove under the car (Figure 1). Rolling over on his side so his armored back would help shield him from Page's gunfire, he curled up into the fetal position as silence descended over the scene (Page had paused to reload). Inexplicably, the brief silence enveloped Murphy in a feeling of cozy warmth, and his mind drifted off into thoughts of his wife, Ann. They had only been married for a little over a year and hadn't been able to take their honeymoon yet, but they had purchased tickets for a trip to the Florida Keys. "Boy, Ann's gonna be pissed," he thought.

The thought brought him back to reality. "I'm not goin' out on this parking lot," he thought, "Not like this! I'm not gonna let my wife and kids down."

His duty gun was nowhere to be seen, but his shotgun and patrol rifle were in his squad car. If he could just get back to it, he would at least have a fighting chance. He crawled out from under the car, looked up at Page standing just ten feet away, and saw nothing in the gunman's eyes. No bloodlust, no hatred, no

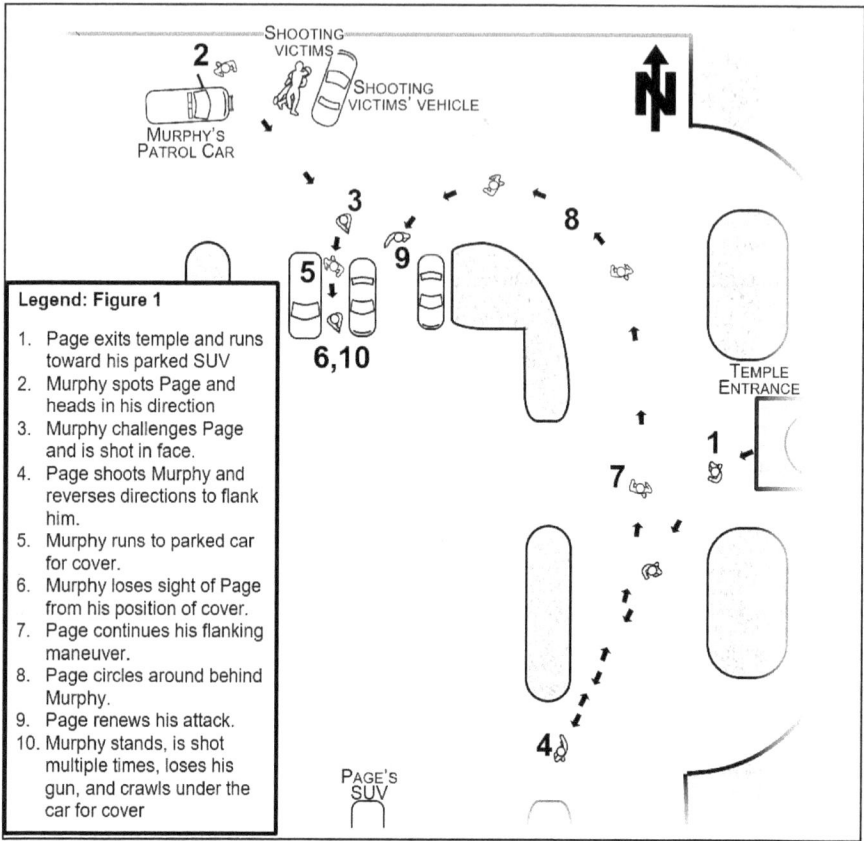

FIGURE 1: Murphy spots Page, shouts a warning, is wounded, and then flanked and shot again by Page.

excitement. Just cold, businesslike emptiness as if he was comfortable in what he was doing.

Murphy started to crawl toward the cruiser. It was no more than ten yards away, but that's a long crawl, and Page was just ten feet behind him, now reloaded and firing away. Murphy kept crawling through the barrage as more bullets tore into the backs of his biceps and thighs. Then came the most brutal of them all—a bullet to the back of the head! Luckily, the bullet had hit his body armor first, high up on his right shoulder, and deflected upward between the first and second layers of the vest. After exiting the vest, it had smashed into Murphy's skull just behind his right ear. It was a terrible wound that felt like someone had stomped on his head, but he would survive.

"When is enough, enough?" Murphy thought. "Are you ever gonna run out of bullets?"

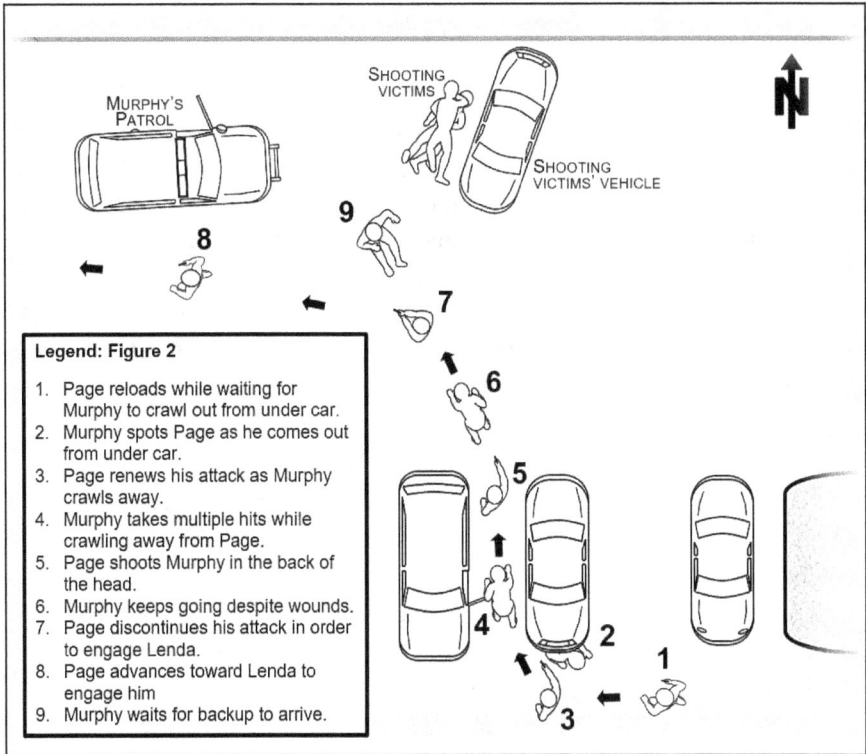

Legend: Figure 2

1. Page reloads while waiting for Murphy to crawl out from under car.
2. Murphy spots Page as he comes out from under car.
3. Page renews his attack as Murphy crawls away.
4. Murphy takes multiple hits while crawling away from Page.
5. Page shoots Murphy in the back of the head.
6. Murphy keeps going despite wounds.
7. Page discontinues his attack in order to engage Lenda.
8. Page advances toward Lenda to engage him
9. Murphy waits for backup to arrive.

FIGURE 2: Murphy rolls under the car, crawls out to retrieve a long gun from his cruiser, and crawls away from Page as Page continues to attack him.

His wounds hurt like hell, but he refused to give Page the satisfaction of hearing him cry out in pain. Ignoring the agony, he never let out so much as a groan.

As he crawled away, Murphy remembered the knife in his pocket. He would use it to kill the son of a bitch, that bloodthirsty less-than-human piece of shit if he got the chance. But it never came. Page kept his distance as the grievously wounded lieutenant rolled over and tried to push himself up on one elbow. By then, screaming police sirens, barely audible just moments before, could be heard closing in fast, and Page stopped shooting. Instead, he turned and moved off to his left toward the driveway (Figure 2). Then came voices on Murphy's radio, shouted commands from the direction of the driveway, and finally the distinctive sound of AR-15 rifle fire.

Officer Sam Lenda, a streetwise 55-year-old, a 33-year veteran of the department, had arrived first. With no better view of the temple parking lot than Murphy, Lenda had been unable to see anything until he reached the crest of the driveway, and even then, he couldn't see his lieutenant. But he caught a glimpse of white that instantly captured his attention. It was a man wearing a white t-shirt walking directly toward him. Realizing he might need his patrol rifle at this range, Lenda backed his cruiser up a short distance so he would be below the crest of the hill while accessing his AR (the release operated slower than most). He removed the rifle from its rack and drove forward again.

Then he heard the dim pop of open-air handgun fire from Page's direction. He stopped his cruiser at the crest of the driveway again and got out while calling in "shots fired." Page was still coming toward him, but now Lenda could see the silhouette of a pistol in front of his white shirt. Ominously, Page was marching steadily forward as if on a mission while casually slipping a fresh magazine into the weapon.

Raising the AR into firing position, Lenda ordered Page to drop the gun, but Page ignored him and kept coming. Lenda repeated the command, and again Page ignored him and kept marching forward.

"Drop the gun!" Lenda repeated once more.

This time Page answered with more gunfire. His first round crashed through Lenda's windshield just above the steering wheel, sending fragments of glass into Lenda's face, and struck the driver's headrest where Lenda had been sitting just seconds before. The unexpected sting from the broken glass distracted Lenda, but only for an instant. He returned fire at his adversary, who was now walking rapidly to the right at a distance of about 60 yards, firing as he moved.

Both men kept up their fire, but Page's luck had run out. He kept missing, while Lenda, a tactical team member, was too good with a rifle to miss. With lives on the line and Murphy's condition unknown, Lenda knew he couldn't let Page leave the parking lot, or worse yet, get back inside the temple. He tracked his moving target, stayed calm, and struck home with his third or fourth round. Page stumbled forward with a bullet to the abdomen, fell face down onto the pavement, and crawled out of sight (Figure 3).

As Lenda held his position, waiting to see if Page reappeared, he heard another gunshot but couldn't tell where it had come from. It was a bad omen with Murphy nowhere to be seen and no way of knowing what was happening inside the temple. Fortunately, Lenda, now assisted by several other officers who had arrived on the scene, quickly located Page and discovered that he was dead from a head wound. Lenda kicked the 9mm away from the body, left a couple of officers there to watch it, and sprinted over to Murphy's squad car in search of his lieutenant.

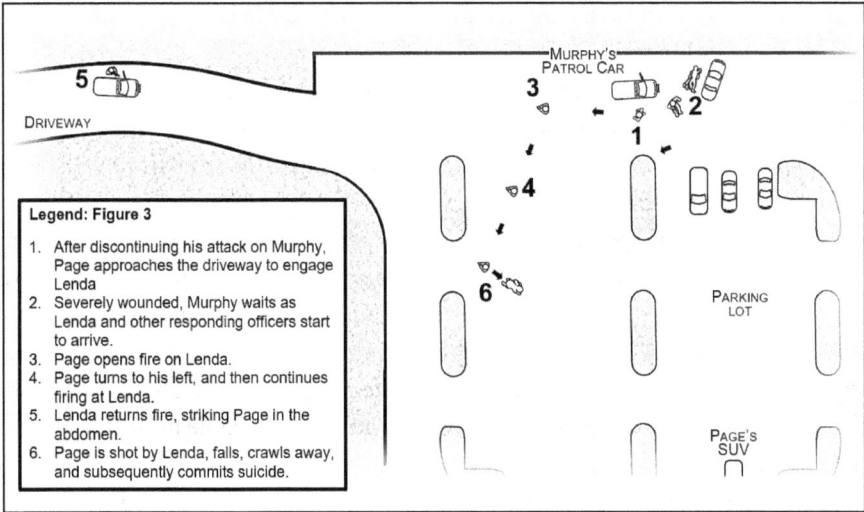

FIGURE 3: Officer Lenda wounds Page, who then commits suicide.

It didn't take long. Murphy was lying close by, riddled with gunshot wounds. Lenda held back the rising fear in his stomach, trying hard not to show his alarm, and went to Murphy's aid. He wanted to say something to encourage him, to inspire him to believe he would be alright, but Murphy spoke first. Raising a torn and bloody hand to wave Lenda off and speaking in a raspy voice through the blood pouring from his chin, he said, "Don't worry about me, Sam. Go check on those people in the temple!"

THE AFTERMATH

Lt. Murphy had taken 15 hits. His body armor had stopped three rounds, but two had hit him in the head: one in the chin and then down through his larynx, and the other behind his right ear. Four others had struck him in the upper arms, three in his left and the fourth in his right. His hands had taken three more hits, one in his right and two, including one that nearly severed the thumb, in his left. Lastly, he had received one wound to his right thigh and two more to his left.

Remarkably, Murphy spent only three days in intensive care and four weeks recovering at the hospital. But after months of therapy and despite his best efforts to return to work, his wounds forced him into retirement ten months later. Nevertheless, he is grateful for all he has, has no regrets, and sees his sacrifice as a price worth paying for the lives he saved. He is currently in private business and doing well.

Tragically, the two men killed in the parking lot were not Page's only victims. He had managed to shoot five other people before Lt. Murphy's arrival interrupted his bloodbath, killing two and wounding three others, one of whom died from complications seven years later.

The one bright spot in the tragedy was that none of the several children inside were injured or killed. Just moments before Murphy pulled onto the lot, Page had opened fire on three people who had escaped his gunfire by running into a nearby pantry. Still hellbent on continuing the carnage, Page had started to follow them into the room when he suddenly spotted Murphy outside and decided to flee instead. Several children were among 15 people huddling in fear just inside the closed door.

The motives for Page's actions remain unknown, but since he was a white supremacist, racism probably had a lot to do with it.

Subsequent investigation revealed that the bullet wound to Page's stomach was the only one caused by Officer Lenda—his head wound was self-inflicted. After wreaking untold grief on so many, he had taken the coward's way out.

ANALYSIS

Verbal Warnings

If Lt. Murphy had shot Page without warning, there is a good chance he would have been able to stop him without suffering any injury to himself. He knew the risks involved, of course, but he believed a warning was required under the circumstances. This begs the question: Was he correct in this belief? Most probably, he was. When officers act in self-defense or the defense of others, the law prudently allows them to use deadly force if they *reasonably believe* it is necessary to protect them or others from death or serious bodily harm[xvi] (essentially the same standard frequently applied to ordinary citizens in cases of self-defense). However, when the offender is fleeing, officers may not use deadly force unless he threatens them with a weapon, or they have a high level of certainty that he has committed a crime involving the infliction or threatened infliction of serious physical harm . . . , and if, *where feasible, some warning has been given.*"[xvii] (emphasis added).

Even under these more restrictive rules for fleeing offenders, Lt. Murphy may have been able to justify shooting Page without warning, but three factors make this unlikely: 1) It is questionable whether Lt. Murphy had adequate cause to believe that Page had shot the two men in the parking lot or anyone else for that matter. 2) Page didn't point his gun at him; in fact, he couldn't even be sure Page was armed. 3) From all appearances, it was highly unlikely that Page could accurately shoot at him while so far away and running, which increased the feasibility of issuing a verbal warning before using deadly force. Without having seen the gun, Page's attacks on his victims, or other more solid evidence of Page's guilt, it would have been difficult for Murphy to justify shooting him, especially without warning him first.

If this all seems confusing, imagine having to weigh all these factors with too little information to go on, under severe time constraints, and with your life and possibly the lives of others on the line. Officers have to make these kinds of difficult use-of-force decisions far more often than most of us realize. Lt. Murphy's was probably among the most difficult, but he was far from alone. During this author's police career, for example, I was twice put into situations in which I came perilously close to shooting one of my fellow officers in the mistaken belief that he was an armed criminal threatening the lives of others. Fortunately, in both cases, I saw my mistake soon enough to withhold fire, but it was only by the grace of God that I was able to do so. I also came close to making several other grievous errors, and so have many of my fellow officers, as is evident from several of the other cases in this book. And even when it is obvious that deadly force is needed, the shoot/don't shoot decision is a weighty one with no margin for error.

No other profession requires as difficult life-and-death decisions as police work. Even though police officers must make lethal decisions far less often than doctors, EMTs, etc., when thrust into crises that require them to do so, they must decide in milliseconds, with their careers, financial well-being, and very lives on the line. They don't have time to consult with any of their colleagues or even pause to weigh their options before making the most crucial decision of their lives. Moreover, unlike physicians, they don't have the luxury of years of high-quality education (including an internship and residency) or any other way to gain practical experience in applying their most crucial knowledge and skills under the tutelage of a seasoned practitioner. This is most evident when it comes to their most critical skillset —firearms skills. They can't learn how to gunfight or make life-or-death decisions by engaging in real-life gunfights under the guidance of their trainers. They can train with simulated combat, which comes as close as possible, but it still isn't the same.

Furthermore, simulated firearms training is too expensive and time-consuming for many agencies, and to make matters worse, it must be repeated frequently. Contrary to common opinion, many officers seldom receive such training, and some never do. It is not uncommon for officers to receive no more firearms training than one or two firearms qualifications[1] per year. Some officers receive better training than others, of course, but none are well enough trained to flawlessly make the right choice under enormous pressure, every time, in every situation.

While on the subject of deadly-force decisions, we need to consider the awesome responsibility that every armed citizen must bear. Any citizen who wants to exercise his right to bear arms must fully accept that with every right comes the duty to use it responsibly. There is no calling back a bullet once the trigger is pulled, and many deeply regretful citizens have gone to prison or been forced to live with the guilt of having killed an innocent stranger—or even a loved one—because of their ignorance of the law, carelessness, or rash actions with a firearm. Every gun owner, especially those who carry firearms in public, owe it to themselves, their families, and their fellow citizens to thoroughly learn and fully understand all gun safety rules and laws regarding the use of deadly force. Learn and study the statutes in your state regarding self-defense and the justifiable use of deadly and nondeadly force. And then spend time thinking deeply about situations in which you would use various degrees of force, especially deadly force. Also, give the same serious thought and consideration when you would not elect to use force and various alternatives you could employ instead.

MULTIPLE WARNINGS

Like Lt. Murphy, Officer Lenda issued a verbal warning before using deadly force, apparently for much the same reason. Lacking sufficient information about the circumstances at the scene, he couldn't be sure Page was the shooter. However, unlike Lt. Murphy, he could see Page's gun and continued to shout verbal commands until Page opened fire. Considering the sizeable risks involved

---

1. A firearms qualification is a course of fire in which officers must meet a minimal score to keep their certification as police officers. Depending upon state standards and the agency's requirements, the minimum score is usually no more than 70–80 percent, within relatively liberal time limits, on a standardized range, and with targets set at standardized distances, the greatest of which is usually no more than 25 yards. Ordinarily, there are no moving targets, no tactical movements on the part of the participants, no nighttime or low-light conditions, no shoot/don't shoot decision-making, and no stress other than the need to pass the course. Firearms qualifications are simply tests to verify that officers meet minimum standards, not training for the realities of using a firearm in self-defense or defense of others.

in issuing even one warning when confronting an armed offender[2] and the fact that warnings are usually not required unless the gunman is fleeing, it is easy to wonder why an officer would issue several. Yet, many do, as can be seen in many dash and body camera recordings of officers confronting armed offenders.

There are various reasons why even seasoned veterans like Officer Lenda issue multiple warnings so often, despite the considerable risks involved and their legal authority to shoot without warning. First is their fear of making even a minor mistake that can cost them their jobs, lead to a lawsuit, or even send them to prison. This can make them so cautious that they are unwilling to shoot until the danger becomes so severe that their instinct for survival demands their immediate application of deadly force. Doubts about unclear elements of the law regarding the use of deadly force, or the uncertainty and confusion that so often accompanies lethal encounters, can also cause officers to keep issuing commands long after it is obvious they are not working, sometimes even to the point that it costs them their lives. Fatigue (a common ailment among police officers), lack of confidence in their training, and other factors can also play a part in this phenomenon.

However, probably the greatest reason for their reluctance is human nature. Normal human beings have a strong aversion to taking the lives of their fellow humans in any except the most extreme circumstances. Moreover, contrary to the image of police officers often portrayed by their critics, all but a minuscule few rogue officers have immense regard for human life, as is evident by their willingness to risk their own lives when their fellow citizens are in need. To stereotype all cops as heartless brutes who devalue human life is inaccurate, morally wrong, and an insult to every officer who has, or ever will risk his life for others, including those who despise him for the uniform he wears.

Cop Killer Mindset

The cold-blooded aggressiveness of Page's attack was characteristic of cop killers. By flanking Lt. Murphy and then relentlessly continuing to pump round after round into him, he demonstrated more than a willingness to kill. In a warrior, willingness to kill is rooted in selfless dedication to serving their country and protecting the innocent, but in a violent criminal, it is fueled by burning

---

2. This is because after issuing a warning, the officer must then wait to see if the gunman complies, which gives the gunman the vital tactical advantage of being able to fire the first shot, and the person who shoots first usually wins.

anger, hatred, or some other perverted emotion. Page was so full of bloodlust that nothing short of executing Murphy would do.

Fortunately, Lt. Murphy was a warrior equal to the challenge. Though effectively unarmed, grievously wounded, and taking one hit after another, he kept going and persevered. Predators like Page are a fact of life in a police officer's world. For warrior cops like Lt. Murphy, this fact doesn't frighten or discourage them; rather, it increases their resolve to work hard, train hard, and otherwise prepare themselves to win against all odds.

Resistance to Gunshot Wounds and Other Severe Injuries

This case provides an inspiring example of how tough the human body can be against gunshot wounds and other trauma. Real-world experience has made it clear that people can often withstand incredible damage, but Murphy's ability to keep going after absorbing round after round—including two to the head–was exceptional. Moreover, his amazing toughness clearly shows us that there is no reason to assume a head wound or other grievous injury will render you incapable of defending yourself.

It is also worth noting that Lt. Murphy credits deep breathing with helping him survive his wounds. It is beyond the scope of this analysis to explain why deep breathing lessens the negative impact of trauma on our bodies, but Murphy's story, and the stories of countless others like him, prove that it does. Moreover, deep breathing is also a vital skill for calming our nerves, clearing our thinking, and otherwise helping us perform at a high level under the stress of mortal danger. As such, it is well worth the relatively small amount of time and effort it takes to learn it.

The Role of Faith

Like many officers who display courage and perform well when the lives of others are on the line, Lt. Murphy is a man of faith. While not universally the case, it appears that people of faith tend to be more focused on others' safety than those without it for at least three reasons. First, they usually fear death less than most. Like others, they may be afraid to die, but their confidence in a joyous, unending afterlife makes death much less frightening. Second, they generally have a robust outward focus on the needs of others. The result is selfless courage that drives them forward in a quest to save lives even at grave risk to their own. This is not to imply that people without faith lack courage or will not sacrifice for others, but faiths that emphasize self-sacrifice help motivate their believers to act courageously. Lastly, officers with strong faith often see themselves as God's servants who are placed into a particular situation for the divine purpose of stopping violence. Lt. Murphy doesn't hesitate to express his belief that God put him in Page's path and for a good reason. He recognizes that his arrival at the temple brought him immense pain and cost him his career, but he is convinced that it was God's will to put him at that precise time and place to save lives. It's hard to argue with this assessment because, as mentioned earlier, his timely arrival had convinced Page to flee the scene rather than attack a large group of innocent victims, including several children. Tellingly, when asked later if he thought it was worth it, Murphy humbly replied that he wouldn't have it any other way.

Winning Mindset
Lt. Murphy gives a lot of credit for his mental toughness to his time in the Marine Corps. Marine Corps training and esprit de corps drive marines to stay focused on the mission and keep fighting no matter what. This never-say-die mindset, bolstered further by a family history of perseverance and a personal habit of always pushing himself beyond his comfort zone, enabled Murphy to persist against all odds. Despite being hopelessly unarmed—every cop's worst nightmare—and suffering multiple grievous wounds in a seemingly unending close-range attack, he never even considered giving up. He did what he could to defend himself, and when it became obvious that it wasn't working, he decided to reenter the hot zone and head for the long guns in his patrol car. It was a decision that could have gotten him killed, but he refused to lie there and let Page finish him off. This acceptance of one's circumstances, combined with a determination to do whatever it takes to win, is one of the most admirable traits that separates true warriors from all others.

Lt. Murphy also ignored his wounds and pain as he focused on doing what he could do to win the fight. This is crucial when wounded. Worrying about wounds will only raise your blood pressure, causing you to bleed out faster, and may lead to panic or even surrender in the false hope of receiving mercy. More importantly, it's distracting, which can create an opportunity for your assailant to close in for the kill. By contrast, focusing on winning will allow you to channel any fear or stress you may feel into powerful motivation to win. Lt. Murphy didn't win the gunfight in the conventional sense of the term, but he kept going despite everything Page threw at him and kept Page busy until Officer Lenda arrived to finish the fight. In that sense, he was a true winner.

In all these ways, Lt. Murphy proved himself to be a courageous, tough-minded warrior, but that was only the tip of the iceberg. The true depth of his courage came through in how he responded to Officer Lenda's concern over his wounds. The purest, most noble form of courage is selfless courage that utterly subordinates one's safety to the needs of others. Lt. Murphy displayed such courage when he told Lenda to ignore his wounds and check on the people inside the temple instead. That selfless act marked him forever as a warrior and set an inspiring example for all of us to follow.

Conclusion

It is my sincere hope that I have succeeded in my goal of showing the commitment, courage, and, in many cases, selflessness of the fine officers whose stories are told in this book. They are some of the best–but certainly not the only–heroic servant-warriors in blue who serve on the front line against crime and violence in this country. I also hope that I have shown that our police officers deserve our respect. Cops don't need or even want sympathy or praise from those they serve, but they do need our respect.

They also need the cooperation of the public to fight crime effectively. Unfortunately, cooperation is virtually impossible without trust, and there is growing mistrust of the police in our society today. Moreover, as this mistrust continues unabated and criticism of their every move grows, our police officers are becoming ever more uncertain and insecure, which can and does lead to de-policing. A lot of this mistrust and criticism is due to misunderstandings about the police, their training, their character, and why they conduct themselves in the way they do. One of my other goals in writing this book was to correct many of the damaging misconceptions about the police, and I hope I have done that as well.

However, my chief goal was to honor the officers herein by telling their stories and inspiring others to learn from them. These officers, and how they handled themselves in the face of adversity, can teach us a lot about what we can do to stay safe, keep our loved ones safe, and overcome the many challenges in our lives. To that end, the following is a short review of what I consider to be the most crucial things we can learn from these officers:

Planning: Any hazard is easier to handle if you have planned and otherwise prepared yourself to deal with it. A simple example of this concept is developing the habit of using your seatbelt. You probably won't need it, but it is vital to your safety if you are involved in an accident. Other planning is much more complex, of course, like securing your home from intruders, carefully checking your equipment before engaging in a risky sport and knowing what to do if something goes wrong, conducting fire and active shooter drills, and–like police officers and military personnel–using mental imagery[1] to prepare for the possibility of a lethal encounter.

Trust your instincts: Instincts are an essential part of our natural defense system. They warn us of danger via the emotions of uneasiness, fear, and even alarm, and we cannot afford to ignore them.

Respond appropriately to danger signs: However, it is also important not to overreact when our instincts warn us of a possible threat, especially when it involves a fellow human being. For example, we certainly don't want to use deadly force–or any other level of physical force for that matter–unless it is justified under the circumstances. Often, we can deal with potential human threats by simply slowing down, scanning for more information, and planning how we will respond if our suspicions prove warranted. At other times, we can back off, change our route to circumvent the problem, detour to a safer place, call the police, etc. Depending upon the circumstances, more overt actions may also be necessary for some situations, but the key is to execute a measured response.

Practice the Safety-First Habit:[2] Make a point of continually asking yourself, "In what way am I vulnerable right now, and what can I do about it" everywhere you go, no matter how familiar you may be with the location. Through repetition, this will eventually become a habit that helps you stay alert, continually scan and plan for danger, and more quickly adapt to changing circumstances.

Focus: The effectiveness of how we respond to any threat or challenge depends greatly upon our focus. Do we worry about our injuries when under attack or trapped in a fire, for example? Certainly, we may have to

---

1. Mental imagery is a mental exercise that enables you to use your imagination to practice how to respond to various situations without having to actually experience them firsthand. It is regularly used by special forces and SWAT members to practice skills when away from the gym or range, and more importantly, to mentally prepare for various challenges they may face in the field. See chapter 2, pp. 34–35 and chapter 6, p. 95 for further information on this mental skill.

2. See chapter 4, pp. 55–56, for a discussion on how to develop and use this essential mental skill.

focus briefly on applying a tourniquet if we are bleeding profusely, but even that action would have to be delayed when under attack from an assailant who is still trying to kill us. If attacked, winning the fight is usually our highest priority. When the challenge is related to our physical health, personal relationships, emotional problems, financial issues, etc., we may not have a human adversary to defeat, but focusing on winning is still the goal. We need to determine what is most essential to reaching our ultimate goal and then stay focused on that to the exclusion of any unhelpful distractions. It is also important to note that police officers often focus temporarily on their loved ones when under attack. They don't linger on the thought but use it instead to inspire them to keep fighting, no matter what. Of course, this is not exclusive to police officers or even to violent encounters. It is vital to winning, regardless of the challenge.

Warrior Optimism: Optimism in the face of danger is a common trait among those who excel in a crisis. They choose not to focus on their injuries, the apparent hopelessness of their situation, or any other negative thoughts, focusing instead on how to best use their existing resources, no matter how limited they may be, to win.

Perseverance: Often, officers who show great perseverance in the face of serious injuries or other grave challenges, are also individuals who persevere in many other areas of their lives. This is because persistence is a habit, and, like any other habit, it can be developed through repetition over time. By forcing ourselves to persist in everything we do, no matter how unpleasant it may be, we can eventually become habitually persistent, which can pay big dividends in a crisis.

Mental flexibility: Probably the most valuable yet difficult to develop the mental skill to possess in a crisis is mental flexibility. Most crises are rapidly changing events, and it is crucial to adapt our response accordingly. Though difficult to develop, mental imagery and the Safety-First Habit are excellent tools for this purpose. So is reading this book as suggested on page 4 of its introduction.

Training: Training is essential in preparing for any kind of danger. It is one of the major reasons why our brave military personnel do such an outstanding job of battling our enemies overseas and why police SWAT personnel are better prepared to handle dangerous situations than patrol officers. If you do a hazardous job, participate in hazardous sports or other activities, or are otherwise regularly exposed to any particular danger, you cannot afford to take your training lightly. Take advantage of as much high-quality training as possible, even if it requires finding outside resources and paying for the training out of your own pocket. And take all training seriously as something that may well save your life someday. Train hard, and train often.

One final remark about training: Our police officers need a great deal more of it. Cops are only human. They do a job that sometimes requires near super-human decision-making under incredible stress, usually with too little information to go on and too little time to think. And many, if not most of them, also lack other skills essential to the safety of others as well as themselves. In fact, as someone who did the job for almost 33 years and has trained officers for almost that long, I can unequivocally say that it often amazes me that–considering the amount and quality of the training our officers receive–they don't make far more mistakes than they do.

Because of the power our police officers hold over us, we citizens have every right to be free of police brutality, and our police have the duty to make sure it doesn't happen. However, is it reasonable to expect perfection from our officers? We can come closer, of course, but it won't be easy or cheap. Good training is costly, and it will require a lot of time and effort to convince our politicians to spend the money–money that will have to come from us taxpayers. Are we willing to pay that cost? Considering its importance to officer and citizen safety, I believe we should be. But there is one more brutal reality that we should not ignore–no matter how good the training, no matter how good the people we have wearing a badge, no matter how harsh the punishment for those who shame the badge, mistakes will still be made. Like I said earlier, cops are only human.

Stay safe, be strong, and God bless you and yours.

ADDENDUM

Racism in Policing and the Aftermath of George Floyd's Death

I had hoped to avoid addressing racial issues in this book because it is such a complex problem that I felt it was beyond the book's scope to address it properly. However, in the wake of George Floyd's tragic death at the hands of the police (which occurred just days before this book was accepted for publication), and the ever-growing belief since then that all police officers are brutal racists, I can no longer remain silent. For the sake of brevity, I will not attempt to cover every aspect of the problem in great detail. Instead, I will only address what I consider to be the salient points as concisely as possible. Along the way, I will also address other key issues related to Mr. Floyd's death that I believe will be informative or useful to you.

Racist Cops

First, I will not insult anyone's intelligence by claiming there are no racist police officers in America. Like all human beings, they are not flawless and are thus vulnerable to all the evil thoughts and actions common to humankind. However, my experience as a police officer and trainer has shown me that racist cops are extremely scarce today. They are screened for racist beliefs, rejected if identified as a racist, monitored for any hint of racism, and made well aware of racist behavior's severe consequences. This may not have been the case in days gone by, but law enforcement has been steadily improving in many ways, especially concerning racism, for decades, and it is continuing to move in that direction. This doesn't mean we can't do better, but anger, divisiveness, and misunderstanding will only make things worse. Instead, we need to acknowledge how far we have come, strive to listen to and understand one another, and commit to working together to resolve our differences.

We must also consider that police officers are only human, and all human beings have biases and prejudices. Biases and prejudices are a vital part of how our minds work. This is because it would be impossible to navigate efficiently through our lives if we had to pause long enough to form a judgment about every person, every living thing, every aspect of our environment to determine if it is friendly or unfriendly, helpful or harmful, etc. Our minds' solution to this problem is to categorize things with common characteristics into groups. It instinctively forms opinions about the people and things we encounter based on our past experiences and what others have taught us about them. For example, we don't have to get to know our loved ones all over again every time we encounter them because experience has taught us that they love us and can be trusted. Likewise, we don't have to carefully examine a shark every time we encounter one to recognize that it may be dangerous because we have been taught that they are. Taking this analogy a step further, even though there are only a minute number of species of man-eating sharks, we tend to group all species into a single group because we don't know any better, making for an unfair but understandable bias against all sharks.

Such prejudices are part of human nature, and fortunately, most are either helpful or at least not harmful enough to cause significant conflict, hostility, or other serious social problems. But racial prejudice is an entirely different matter. Like any other prejudice that categorizes any group of people as inferior or evil, it causes divisiveness, lack of empathy for others, inequality, anger, and many other wrongs. Racism is so sinister that I fear that even the perception of it—whether accurate or not—has the potential to tear our country apart.

My hope here is to help correct the misunderstanding that most if not all police officers are brutal racists, not only because it troubles me to see our dedicated police officers demonized in such a vicious way, but even more, because it threatens to have such a devastating effect on our citizens, police officers, public safety, and even our society at large. This false image is especially harmful because it creates undue fear and hatred of the police that can easily lead to more, not less, violence when officers attempt to enforce the law. But even worse, it creates wary, stressed-out cops who are afraid to put their careers, reputations, financial wellbeing, and even their freedom on the line by doing their job. Besides leading to de-policing, the added stress generated by such fear can leave officers poorly equipped to make good decisions on the street.

Most of us believe that police officers are experts at handling stress, but we tend to forget that they are only human. Putting on a badge and even the supposedly outstanding training officers receive does not transform them into supermen. They are already under considerable stress from their frequent exposure to death and other tragedies in other people's lives, shift work, pressures at home and work, and even the inescapable necessity of remaining ever vigilant against the ever-present threat of a sudden physical attack. Under the circumstances, more stress is the last thing they need in their lives. Some of us can take more stress than others, but we all have our limits, and the more stress we have, the greater the likelihood that we will make a mistake, especially during stressful events. In just about every other occupation, mistakes can be corrected or at least mitigated later, but there is no calling a bullet back once the trigger is pulled. Few jobs demand perfect decisions under the stress of mortal danger, often with insufficient information to weigh options or accurately assess the threat.

Do we want stressed-out cops making such decisions on the street? Is it even reasonable to expect such superhuman perfection from mere human beings? As discussed earlier in this book, more and better training can go a long way to alleviate this predicament, but it will be prohibitively expensive for all except the wealthiest police departments, and even the best training in the world cannot produce perfect decisions every time under all circumstances. This is not to imply that police officers should not be held responsible when they do wrong—accountability from our police is essential to our freedoms—but when judging their actions, we need to consider the pressure under which they must operate and the limitations placed on them by their humanness. And we must also take great care to avoid falling into the trap of stereotyping every officer for the mistakes made by a few. To do otherwise would be not only unjust but counterproductive to their willingness and ability to enforce the law.

The false narrative about "racist" police officers can also have the adverse effect of making our citizens unduly afraid of them. After being inundated with repeated videos of every police encounter that even hints at police brutality before all the facts are in, comments from politicians and anti-police activists in support of that narrative, other news coverage that paints officers as racists, and more, it is no wonder that many people of all races believe it. The constant exposure to negative images of police is especially problematic. What if, instead of images of police brutality, the media showed equally graphic videos of police officers being killed by people of color? No legitimate newsperson would dare even attempt to do so because it would immediately create a false but powerful, highly racist image of that race as vicious cop killers. Every decent person knows better than to believe such garbage, but violent images generate powerful emotions that cloud thinking and make such events appear to be far more prevalent than they are. This is not to say that such videos should be kept from the public.

On the contrary, the public has a right to know, and the press has an obligation to keep them informed. However, it is unwise to overdo it, not only because it unduly escalates anger and misunderstanding but also because it adds tension to an already volatile situation that can lead to more, not less violence. It is far better to de-escalate the tension so we can start working together toward a greater understanding of one another's views and concerns and initiate fair and effective change.

Police Officers Disproportionately Kill African Americans
This observation is true. The *Mapping Police Violence* database is probably the most extensive database on killings by police officers in America. It clearly shows that during the seven years from 2013 to 2019,[3] 28 percent of the people killed by the police were African Americans.[xviii] Since African Americans only comprise 13.4 percent of the U.S. population, there can be no doubt that police officers disproportionately kill them at a rate 2.1 times their proportion in the population. However, this can be perilously misleading when presented without considering other critical facts from other reliable sources.

The FBI has been collecting detailed statistics on police officers' deaths for decades. These statistics show some revealing correlations when contrasted with the statistics on the victims of police violence. For example, while almost half of our population (49.2%) are males, the FBI data shows that 97.3 percent of the individuals who killed police officers from 2013-2019 were men.[xix] From this data, it would be logical to conclude that since men kill police officers far more often than women, they are also killed by the police far more often than women. Not surprisingly, this commonsense prediction is verified by the *Mapping Police Violence* database, which reveals that 94.8 percent of the people killed by the police during the same reporting period were, in fact, men.[xx] It would be illogical to assume that this is because cops are prejudiced against males. Rather, the only reasonable explanation for this statistic is that men commit the vast majority of violent crimes, including attempts to kill or seriously injure police officers, thereby prompting the officers to defend themselves with deadly force?

---

3. Since the statistics used here were taken from two different sources that spanned two different periods of time, the only way to fairly compare and contrast the statistics was to limit the data to the period of time where both sources overlapped (i.e., January 1, 2013 – December 31, 2019).

Similarly, the data shows that police officers kill citizens of different age groups in just about equal proportion to the rate that those age groups attack them. Of special note here, officers kill 18 to 40-year-olds far more often than those in all the other age groups combined[xxi] (63.6 percent versus 36.4), but almost three-quarters (74.7 percent) of the offenders who kill police officers[xxii] are in that same age group. It doesn't make sense to automatically assume from this data that cops are prejudiced toward younger adults; rather, it is far more logical to conclude that, since that group uses deadly force against police officers more often than other age groups, police officers more often use deadly force against them.

This begs the question: Does the same hold true regarding African Americans? Though it may not be politically correct to say so, the answer is yes. Even though police officers disproportionately kill black citizens at a rate 2.1 times their proportion of the population, 36.1 percent of the people who kill police officers are African Americans,[xxiii] which is 2.7 times the percentage of our African American population. This contrast between the percentage of black citizens who kill police officers and the percentage of those killed by the police offers a well-grounded argument that police officers are less, not more inclined to use deadly force against African Americans. The reason for this is not clear, but I would not be surprised to learn that it is because police officers are acutely aware of the fact that the likelihood of being disciplined, unfairly labeled as a racist, sued, crucified in the press, or even imprisoned is significantly greater when the offender is black.

The point here is not to imply that our officers never commit unjustified killing or other acts of police brutality against black citizens. Tragically, it does happen, but at a much lower rate than police critics, many in the media, and a growing number of politicians claim. Rather, it is to present conclusive statistical evidence that debunks the dangerous false narrative that American policing is steeped in racism or that such racism is so pervasive and extreme that it leads officers to disproportionately kill African Americans. In support of these statistics, I can also say without a doubt that my many interviews with police officers who have survived lethal encounters have made it clear to me that there isn't time to think about anything except how to survive when someone is trying to kill you. Their race, age, gender, or any other personal characteristics mean nothing at a time like that. This research, along with the statistics presented above, convincingly support what our police officers and their defenders already knew—that, with rare exception, our officers are color blind when it comes to self-defense and the defense of others.

Police Officers Kill Too Many Unarmed Citizens

Sadly, this is true. The *Mapping Police Violence* database supports this notion with the troubling statistic that 13.4 percent[xxiv] of the people killed by the police during the reporting period were "unarmed."[xxv] However, like so many other elements of violent encounters between human beings, things are never as simple as they seem. The first complication comes from the complexity of trying to determine how to define unarmed. For example, while it is technically correct to say that someone who points a replica or unloaded gun at an officer is unarmed, no human being can be expected to know the difference, especially when we consider that there isn't time to examine the item when it is pointed at you. Such shootings are tragedies to the extreme, but not murders.

Further, we have to account for the fact that many items that are not considered to be weapons can be used to inflict lethal injuries. Depending on the circumstance and part of the body targeted, even a pen can cause death or permanent injury if used to stab someone in the eye or neck; a belt, tie, or scarf can be used to strangle someone; a short-bladed pocketknife can be used to slash a carotid artery or wrist, etc. Also, unarmed people are sometimes accidentally killed with nonlethal weapons (i.e., devices designed to incapacitate, not kill). Though incredibly rare, someone can die from being sprayed with OC spray, especially if he has an unknown serious medical condition. Though far less frequent than claimed, Tasers can cause, or more likely, contribute to unwanted deaths. In such cases, even though the officer is not trying to kill him, his death will still be categorized as the police killing of an unarmed citizen. Finally, many murders perpetrated against citizens are committed by unarmed assailants (8.7% between 2015-2019),[xxvi] and police officers are equally, if not more, vulnerable to such attacks than other citizens. This is because, as the time-honored police adage wisely warns, "There is always at least one gun in every fight—yours!" Despite their best efforts to protect their sidearms, police can sometimes be disarmed by otherwise unarmed attackers, and when that happens, there is a good chance the officer will not survive. For a good reason, officers are taught that any attempt to disarm them is a lethal threat that justifies using deadly force, if necessary, to prevent it. When that happens, the attacker will likely be categorized as unarmed.

As should be evident from the foregoing discussion, an officer's use of deadly force against an unarmed citizen should not automatically be judged as unjustified. Nevertheless, killing an unarmed citizen happens way too often and is, therefore, something we cannot ignore. First and foremost, as mentioned in

Chapter 10, we need to do a much better job of training our officers in control tactics. Violence is highly volatile by nature. Anything can happen at any time, including an instantaneous jump from a minor struggle to mortal combat. Therefore, for the safety of all involved, it is vital for police officers to bring violent encounters—no matter how seemingly minor they may be—under control as quickly and effectively as possible. This is made much more difficult when officers are not adequately trained. Also, when officers lack the skills they need to control combative offenders properly, loss of confidence follows, leading to increased fear and stress, loss of mental flexibility, and poor decision-making. Imagine, for example, that you are a police officer engaged in what started as a relatively minor fight, but you have so far been unable to gain control of your opponent, and he is becoming increasingly more violent. Nothing you try is working. You are now on the verge of passing out, thereby making you even more vulnerable to being disarmed, losing confidence in yourself and your ability to end the threat, and starting to genuinely fear for your life. But the one thing you can count on is your firearm. So, in desperation, you draw it, hoping that it will convince him to stop his attack. If that doesn't work, you pull the trigger. Right or wrong, you did what you felt you had to do to survive, and now you have to live with the fact that you just used deadly force against an unarmed citizen. Skill training that develops confidence based upon true competence is our best hope for avoiding such tragedies.

Other training that can go a long way in reducing police use of force against unarmed citizens includes significantly more and better training in legal issues related to police use of force, decision-making under stress, rapid recognition of danger signs, realistic de-escalation skills, and other human relations skills that can help officers avoid violent encounters altogether. If done correctly, this kind of training is expensive, but we owe it to both our officers and the citizens they serve to find ways to get it done.

No-Knock Warrants

There has been a great deal of attention focused on using no-knock search warrants, especially in the aftermath of Breonna Taylor's death. These warrants prevent drug dealers from disposing of their product between the time when the officers announce their presence and when they enter the building. This can also make the task safer for the officers by enabling them to enter before the alleged offender can plan and execute violent resistance. And, since such quick and decisive police action can often discourage violent resistance or enable the officers to gain control of the situation before it can escalate, it can be safer for the building's occupants as well.

On the other hand, since no-knock warrants can also have the opposite effect on officer and occupant safety, it may be worthwhile to ban them or limit their use. But, like so many other controversial issues, we should not rush to make changes until we have carefully considered the consequences. For example, we must consider that, while banning them may make things safer for everyone involved in some situations, it may increase the risks in others. Thus, if we ban them altogether without developing any mechanisms for permitting them when the risks of not using them outweigh the benefits, we eliminate a valuable safety option for our officers and citizens alike. It is also important to bear in mind that any restrictions on the use of no-knock warrants will unquestionably lead to a reduction in the number of high-risk warrants our police officers serve, with a corresponding reduction in arrests of dangerous drug dealers.

Chokeholds

One of the major consequences of George Floyd's death is the growing movement to ban police "chokeholds." Before delving further into this subject, it will be helpful to note that the term "chokeholds" can be confusing. A true chokehold is a technique that applies pressure to the windpipe or throat in a way that hinders the victim's ability to breath, while a carotid restraint (which is often erroneously referred to as a chokehold) is a restraint that temporarily restricts blood flow to the brain. Many police departments have long banned chokeholds because they have significant potential of causing death. But since carotid holds are much safer, they are not banned as often. Any nonlethal use of force, no matter how safe, can cause death under the wrong circumstances. For example, even struggling to subdue an arrestee can unwittingly cause his death if he has severe heart disease or other serious medical issues. Since there are risks in everything a police officer does, the only way to guarantee that no citizen will ever die from an otherwise nonlethal use of force is to ban police officers from making arrests, with the obvious result of preventing them from enforcing the law.

The best option for dealing with the chokehold controversy is to allow carotid restraints, but with carefully constructed policies limiting their use and adequate training to support those policies. This is because, though not free of all danger, these restraints give officers a valuable option for restraining highly combative offenders in a way that creates a very low risk of death or serious injury while also enabling them to control the encounter before it can escalate. Every police encounter is different, with its own unique set of concerns and challenges that require various options for dealing with it. When we unnecessarily limit those options, we deprive officers of essential tools for gaining control with minimal use of force.

On the other hand, chokeholds do not fall into the same category. The risks they create are serious enough to exclude them from the nonlethal options available to police officers. However, it would be dangerously unwise to ban them from use when the life of an officer or other innocent person is in danger. For example, an officer attempting to rescue his partner from an attacker trying to disarm him would be justified in shooting the offender. But that option would create a serious risk of missing the offender and hitting the officer's partner or someone else. Under such circumstances, it would be much safer for the rescuing officer to place the offender in a chokehold while pulling him off his partner. Moreover, since chokeholds are far less likely to kill or seriously injure someone than a bullet, this option would be safer for the offender as well as everyone else within range of the gunshot. Knee-jerk reactions to controversial police uses of force can lead to unforeseen negative consequences and should only be implemented after careful consideration of all their possible pros and cons.

It is also important to note that the restraint suffered by Mr. Floyd was neither a chokehold nor a carotid restraint. Without all the facts, it is not proper to make assumptions about why former Officer Chauvin applied such a hold or why he let it go on for so long, but the video shows him kneeling on the side of Mr. Floyd's neck. He did not appear to be choking off Mr. Floyd's windpipe or throat, as would be the case with a chokehold, and it is obvious that the technique was not a carotid restraint, as such restraints require the officer to be behind the arrestee with his arm held in a V shape. When done properly, the officer presses his upper arm against one side of the arrestee's neck and his forearm against the other side, with his elbow held far enough away from the arrestee's windpipe to keep from cutting off the airflow to his lungs. No doubt, Mr. Floyd's death was a tragedy, and Chauvin's actions were unconscionable, but it is clear that he wasn't killed by any accepted police "chokehold" technique.

Unfortunately, however, it may be that a rather common myth within the police community contributed significantly to Mr. Floyd's death. Many officers believe the false notion that if one can speak, he can breathe. While it may be true that an arrestee who complains that he can't breathe is not literally suffocating, this doesn't mean he is not in danger. Rather than assuming that he is merely stressed, exaggerating, or even lying to escape restraint (a rather common ploy by individuals who are resisting arrest), officers need to understand that "I can't breathe" may well mean, "I'm having trouble breathing!" Since difficulty breathing is a common symptom of heart attacks and other serious medical conditions, it is imperative for them to take such complaints seriously. Therefore, police agencies must develop policies that clearly state the importance of taking arrestees' breathing complaints seriously and then back up their policies with appropriate training. Such training must include practical alternatives to restraining arrestees by kneeling on their back or neck, followed by realistic, high-stress exercises that reinforce these new techniques.

The Duty to Intervene

Even the most tragic events can yield some positive results. One such silver lining from George Floyd's death is that it has opened the eyes of police officers everywhere to the importance of intervening when another officer appears to be using excessive force. The harsh truth is that, despite the many successes in law enforcement's efforts to put an end to excessive force, it still happens, and until now, many cops were reluctant to intervene. But Mr. Floyd's death has shown them the consequences of failing to do so in an alarming way that is impossible to ignore. It has shown officers that they must override their reluctance to intervene by focusing on the fact that everyone suffers when they allow a colleague to do the wrong thing. In Mr. Floyd's death, for example, the assisting officers' failure to stop Chauvin not only led to the unjustified death of a citizen but also to grief for Mr. Floyd's family and friends, Chauvin's arrest, their arrests, and a loss of trust in law enforcement that will take years, if not decades, to repair. I suspect that none of these officers, including Chauvin, expected Mr. Floyd to die, but—as can so easily happen in a violent encounter—things went wrong, and all the officers involved must now pay the price.

This tragedy will undoubtedly lead to more interventions by assisting officers and, consequently, fewer excessive force incidents. However, this is not enough. Police departments must establish no-nonsense policies requiring officers to intervene and reinforce them with classroom and reality-based training that teaches officers how to apply the policy on the street. For example, one Midwest police department trains its officers to move up close to the offending officer, touch him on the shoulder, and tell him, "I'll take it from here." This simple action achieves two purposes. First, it establishes a code phrase that every officer understands to mean that he is getting out of control and in danger of making a big mistake. Second, it gives officers a method for intervening in a low-profile manner that encourages the offending officer to calm down, objectively rethink what he is doing, and consider the possible consequences of his actions. Finally, when reinforced with proper reality-based training, it reminds officers of the importance of intervening for the good of all and helps cement the intervention policy into the department's culture.

Defunding the Police
The concept of defunding the police comes in three forms: 1) eliminating the police altogether, 2) shifting police funds to other services, or 3) reducing the police budget by eliminating positions, training, etc. The first form of defunding is too irresponsible and extreme even to be considered by any reasonable person and is therefore not likely to come about. Consequently, there is no need to discuss it further here.

However, the second form, though unreasonable, is not so extreme as to be of no concern. It has the appearance of a fair degree of reasonableness, and in some of its elements, it seems to be a good enough idea to be seriously considered. It is also gaining traction in some places, making it more dangerous than the utterly radical idea of total defunding.

First, I must say that the idea of shifting funding to other services is rather attractive. Depending upon what services are handed over to these unarmed service workers, such defunding would alleviate a lot of the drudgery and vital concerns of the officers who remain on the job. For most officers, handling domestic disputes, neighborhood disputes, ordinance violations, etc., are frustrating, time-consuming disruptions from fighting crime. Similarly, many officers consider issuing traffic tickets to be a rather boring task that leads to a lot of unwanted court time and minor complaints from citizens claiming they were treated unfairly. Moreover, many of these tasks are especially dangerous (e.g., domestic disputes and traffic stops, both of which are near the top of the list of dangerous police activities), which, by shifting them to someone else, improves not only officer safety but also reduces their risk of becoming involved in questionable use of force that threatens their career, livelihood, and freedom. Lastly, shifting work to others would relieve officers from some of their stressful responsibilities, thus providing them with a welcome relief from some of the stress that comes from such a high-pressure job.

While this defunding would make the job easier and less dangerous for the officers still on the street, it would undoubtedly have grave unintended consequences for others. The most obvious and tragic would be the unnecessary deaths of the poor unarmed souls who must now take on a dangerous job they are not trained or equipped to handle. Interestingly, this problem could be alleviated by arming and training these new service workers, but that would make them just as vulnerable as police officers to the consequences of a questionable police shooting, especially if the training were not up to the standards of police officers. And if they were training like cops in armed and unarmed self-defense, decision making under combat stress, the legal issues related to the use of force, etc., it would only shift the cost of training to the service workers instead of the police, with no actual savings to the budget. Furthermore, it would probably cause the public to view them as armed authority figures that would hardly be distinguishable from police officers. I doubt that this would be what the politicians intended. In the end, this new breed of public servant would be left unarmed and vulnerable.

Another likely unintended consequence of putting these service workers on the street is that, since their safety depends on using police officers as backup on dangerous calls, it would do little to reduce police officers' presence in volatile situations that may lead to deadly force. Likewise, police officers would still have to be dispatched to crimes in progress, shots fired calls, alarms, fights, and other calls too dangerous for the service workers to handle, again placing them into situations in which they are more likely to become involved in questionable uses of force. Ironically, if, as appears to be the case, the goal of this scheme is to reduce the number of police shootings, implementing it will do little or nothing to reach it.

The third form of defunding is to simply reduce funding by reducing positions or training. It has long been known that reducing the number of police officers increases the crime rate, which puts our citizens and their property in danger. And it has also long been known that the best way for patrol officers to reduce crime is to make a lot of car stops and pedestrian checks, thereby letting offenders know that they are likely to be stopped and arrested if they commit crimes. In short, fewer cops means increased crime rates and increasingly more dangerous streets.

When the budget cuts include reductions in police training, which is often the first thing to go during trying economic times, the police lose the one thing they need most to serve the public better—training. As stated repeatedly throughout this book, many of the problems between the police and those they serve can be solved with more and better training. Training may not be a panacea, but our best hope is to advance cooperation between the police and their citizens, renew our trust in our police officers, and build safer communities. The question we need to ask ourselves is this: Why should our citizens be made to suffer for our politician's ill-advised attempts to reform the police by defunding them?

CONCLUSION

If the false narrative and other fallout from George Floyd's death and similar tragic cases over the past decade only affected the public's image of the police, it would be regrettable but not especially dangerous. But this is not the case. When citizens view their officers as bigoted bullies who frequently kill citizens without just cause, the consequences can threaten the safety of both the police and the citizens. People are far more likely to make irrational decisions when angry or fearful, and this view of police officers breeds that kind of fear and anger. Such powerful emotions only increase the likelihood that individuals will attack the officer or do something else, either consciously or subconsciously, to escalate the situation. Simultaneously, many cops feel hated, increasingly more vulnerable, unjustly second-guessed, unsupported by their leadership, and unsure of themselves. This can lead to a growing unwillingness among our officers to risk the possible negative consequences of proactive policing. Since proactive law enforcement is the most effective way for patrol officers to reduce crime, our communities may well suffer from drastically higher crime rates.

Another unfortunate result of the current anti-police environment is that officers who are angry or fearful are also more likely to either overreact or underreact to apparent threats. The results of overreacting with excessive force are obvious, but the results of underreacting are far less apparent. When an officer fails to use enough force to overcome a lesser threat, he vastly increases the likelihood that the incident will escalate. This is because too little force is likely to do nothing more than anger the offender, and anger tends to increase one's tolerance to pain significantly. The result is an even angrier assailant who is virtually oblivious to pain, which in turn means more force will be needed to subdue him. Unfortunately, such failures to control combative offenders can quickly escalate to the point that an officer's life is threatened, which may well compel him to use deadly force in self-defense. When that happens, we all lose.

As long as these kinds of misunderstandings are allowed to persist, it will be virtually impossible to close the rift between citizens and the police. This is not to imply that our police don't have to do their part by increasing their understanding of the needs and concerns of the citizens in their communities. They have an obligation to do so, and even though many departments are currently working hard at it, there is still a lot more they need to do. But we also need to recognize that failure to understand the police officer's perspective can lead to more fear and anger on both sides, threatening to increase violence between citizens and the police. Something needs to be done, and it starts with understanding.

Endnotes

[i] Blum, L.N, and Ph.D. (2000) *Force Under Pressure: How Cops Live and Why They Die.* Lantern Books, NY, NY. p. 68.

[ii] Hammersfahr, R., MD. and McBryde, D. *First Aid for Gunshot Wounds* Pocket Guide, 1st edition. Stanley Marie, LLC. 2017, pp. 5-53 – 5-55.

[iii] CBS Television (May 1993). *Top Cops; Bryan Power.* NY, NY, CBS Television.

[iv] Ibid.

[v] Wand, A.B. and Phillips, K. S. (2018). "'Just shoot me,' an armed man told a cop. The officer didn't—and was fired, his lawsuit claimed." *Washington Post.* Accessed July 1, 2019, https://www.washingtonpost.com/news/post-nation/wp/2018/02/12/an-officer-who-was-fired-after-refusing-to-shoot-an-armed-man-just-won-175000-in-a-settlement/?noredirect=on&utm_term=.6dfddf8f844a.

[vi] Sexton, J. "'I Don't Want to Shoot You, Brother' A shocking story of police and lethal force. Just not the one you might expect." *ProPublica.* Accessed July 1, 2019, https://features.propublica.org/weirton/police-shooting-lethal-force-cop-fired-west-virginia/.

[vii] *Tennessee v. Garner,* 471 U.S. 1 (1985).

[viii] Chung A. "For cops who kill, special Supreme Court protection." Reuters.com. May 8, 2020. Accessed August 28, 2020, https://www.reuters.com/investigates/special-report/usa-police-immunity-scotus/.

[ix] *The World Factbook-Japan.* Central Intelligence Agency. (2009). Accessed July 2, 2019, https://www.cia.gov/library/publications/the-world-factbook/geos/ja.html.

[x] Bolosier, V. "Requirements to Become a Police Officer in France" (October 2017). Accessed July 2, 2019, https://classroom.synonym.com/requirements-to-become-a-police-officer-in-france-13583787.html.

[xi] *Law Enforcement in the United Kingdom Revised History* (2019) Wikipedia. Accessed July 2, 2019, https://en.wikipedia.org/w/index.php?title=Law_enforcement_in_the_United_Kingdom&action=history.

[xii] *State and Local Law Enforcement Training Academies 2013.* US Department of Justice, Bureau of Justice Statistics, table 5 (July 2016). Accessed June 18, 2019, https://www.bjs.gov/content/pub/pdf/slleta13.pdf.

[xiii] Danby, N. (March 2017). "Lessons from Inspector Clouseau: What America's Police Can Learn from Europe." *Harvard Political Review.* Accessed July 19, 2019, http://harvardpolitics.com/online/lessons-inspector-clouseau-americas-police-can-learn-european-nations/.

[xiv] F.B.I. (2016). *Law Enforcement Officers Killed and Assaulted 2016.* Washington, D.C., U.S. Department of Justice, table 23. Accessed June 22, 2019, https://ucr.fbi.gov/leoka/2016/officers-feloniously-killed/tables/table-23.xls.

xv   F.B.I. (2018). *Law Enforcement Officers Killed and Assaulted 2018.* Washington, D.C., U.S. Department of Justice, table 24. Accessed June 22, 2019, https://ucr.fbi.gov/leoka/2018/topic-pages/tables/table-24.xls

xvi   Ibid.

xvii   *Tennessee v. Garner,* 471 US 1 (1985). Accessed January 8, 2016, https://supreme.justia.com/cases/federal/us/471/1/case.html.

xviii   "Mapping Police Violence." (n.d.) mappingpoliceviolence.org. Accessed October 14, 2020, https://mappingpoliceviolence.org/.

xix   F.B.I. (2019). *Law Enforcement Officers Killed and Assaulted 2019.* Washington, D.C., U.S. Department of Justice, table 42. Accessed October 22, 2020, https://ucr.fbi.gov/leoka/2019-spring/tables/table-42.xls.

xx   "Mapping Police Violence," accessed 2 October 2020.

xxi   "Fatal Force." (n.d.) washingtonpost.com, accessed October 14, 2020, https://www.washingtonpost.com/graphics/investigations/police-shootings-database/.

xxii   F.B.I. (2019). *Law Enforcement Officers Killed and Assaulted 2019.* Washington, D.C., U.S. Department of Justice, table 40. Accessed July 4, 2008, https://ucr.fbi.gov/leoka/2019/topic-pages/tables/table-40.xls.

xxiii   F.B.I. (2019). *Law Enforcement Officers Killed and Assaulted 2019.* Washington, D.C., U.S. Department of Justice, table 42. Accessed October 22, 2020, https://ucr.fbi.gov/leoka/2019-spring/tables/table-42.xls.

xxiv   "Mapping Police Violence," accessed October 2, 2020.

xxv   Ibid., accessed November 6, 2020.

xxvi   F.B.I. (2019). *Crime in the United States 2019.* Washington, D.C., U.S. Department of Justice, table 8. Accessed October 26, 2020, https://ucr.fbi.gov/crime-in-the-u.s/2019/crime-in-the-u.s.-2019/tables/expanded-homicide-data-table-8.xls.

Index

About the Author

BRIAN MCKENNA is a 33-year police veteran, now retired from the Hazelwood (MO) Police Department, where he served as a patrol lieutenant, lead firearms instructor, in-service training instructor, and crime prevention officer. When serving in crime prevention, he researched and presented numerous classes on personal safety, home security, and other safety subjects to various citizen groups. He is also a state certified police instructor, former police academy instructor, and active shooter response instructor, and holds a master's degree in human resource development from National Lewis University.

Brian has written extensively on officer safety topics, and for 23 years authored the "Officer Down" column for *Police Marksman Magazine*, a regular feature that analyzed officer involved shootings for key learning points. Brian's extensive research for his column led him to become a leading expert on the dynamics of armed encounters, how officers think and behave under stress, and the most effective ways to prepare for dangerous encounters. Besides his extensive writing background, Brian provides police training through his company, *Winning Edge Training*.

Brian is also involved in his church, where he has served on several boards and currently teaches a semiweekly adult Bible study class. His priorities in life are his Christian faith, the safety of our country's police officers and the citizens they serve, and his family. He has little time for hobbies, but enjoys studying American history and spending time with his beloved wife Lynn, three lovely daughters, Elizabeth, Rebecca, and Katherine, and two wonderful grandchildren, Ellis and Mae.